THIRD EDITION

Fundamentals of Music

Earl Henry

Webster University

Prentice Hall

PRENTICE HALL, Upper Saddle River, New Jersey 07458

Library of Congress Cataloging-in-Publication Data

HENRY, EARL.
   Fundamentals of music / Earl Henry.—3rd ed.
     p. cm.
   Includes index.
   ISBN 0-13-917121-5 (pbk.)
    1. Music—Theory, Elementary. 2. Musical notation. I. Title.
  MT7.H49 1999 <Phon Case>
  781—dc21   98-23418
                                                   CIP
                                                   MN

Editorial director: *Charlyce Jones Owen*
Publisher: *Norwell F. Therien*
Project manager: *Carole R. Crouse*
Prepress and manufacturing buyer: *Bob Anderson*
Copy editor: *Carole R. Crouse*
Marketing manager: *Sheryl Adams*

This book was set in 10.5/12 New Baskerville by Stratford Publishing Services, Inc.,
and was printed and bound by Hamilton Printing Company.
The music was set by MPT Music Engraving.
The cover was printed by Phoenix Color Corp.

 © 1999, 1993, 1988 by Prentice-Hall, Inc.
Pearson Education
Upper Saddle River, New Jersey 07458

10 9 8

0-13-917121-5

PRENTICE-HALL INTERNATIONAL (UK) LIMITED, *London*
PRENTICE-HALL OF AUSTRALIA PTY. LIMITED, *Sydney*
PRENTICE-HALL CANADA INC., *Toronto*
PRENTICE-HALL HISPANOAMERICANA, S.A., *Mexico*
PRENTICE-HALL OF INDIA PRIVATE LIMITED, *New Delhi*
PRENTICE-HALL OF JAPAN, INC., *Tokyo*
PRENTICE-HALL ASIA PTE. LTD., *Singapore*
EDITORA PRENTICE-HALL DO BRASIL, LTDA., *Rio de Janeiro*

In Memory of
Robert E. Orner
Professor of Music
East Tennessee State University

Contents

Preface

Scholars speculate that sometime before the year 1000 C.E., an anonymous monk, hand-copying a music manuscript on dried parchment, decided to scratch a horizontal line across the page in an effort to represent pitches more precisely. Before that historic development, music was notated (written down) primarily as a memory aid. Notes were copied relatively higher or lower on the page, but only in an *approximate* sense; performers still had to learn the music "by heart" and try to remember hundreds of compositions with only the most elementary of visual guidelines.

From those humble beginnings, Western composers and performers gradually developed the staff, various clefs, and other components of a language of pitch notation that we continue to employ today with only minor improvements. In addition, by about 1300, composers had devised an effective means of portraying time values so that virtually any one tone could be represented in virtually any length. With the development of musical notation, Western composers no longer needed to rely on the performer's memory; the basic sounds and time values of a composition could be illustrated graphically with a set of symbols. Those who knew this language of music—the *fundamentals*—might study, perform, arrange, or teach a piece of music as if they, themselves, had written it.

Today, most of us can sing, whistle, hum, or pick out a tune on the piano or the guitar, but only those who can read and write the language of Western music are able to share their accomplishments effectively with an audience of potential performers. In each era since our Medieval monk's experiment, musical style and vocabulary have continued to evolve. Along with each stylistic change, the musical language of notation has accommodated innovative sounds with new symbols to represent them on paper. At the same time, however, precise notation has had its price. Succeeding generations of music professionals, fluent in the language of traditional music, have consistently rejected new instruments, combinations of tones, and innovative styles if their notation would require wholesale changes in the system. In short, since about 1550 when the language of traditional Western notation began its final stage of evolution, the fundamentals of music have changed very little.

Fundamentals of Music familiarizes you with the notation and performance of Western music. Whether you are preparing for a career in music or desire simply to develop an appreciation of the musician's language, you will learn the terms, symbols, practices, and conventions that make our music sound the way it does. For some, performance as well as theoretical knowledge will be a course goal. To that end, in addition to fundamental musical materials in theory, you will find numerous musical excerpts (many recorded on the companion compact disc), performance exercises, and creative activities that will address those needs.

USING THE TEXT

The third edition of *Fundamentals of Music* is especially easy to use. In addition to prose text and examples from traditional "classical" music, you will find exercises and examples that center on musical theater, jazz, and rock styles. Alongside the traditional excerpts by male composers of yesterday and today, there is music by women composers of various historical eras. Boxed text in most chapters gives you an additional perspective, offers a method of study, or provides a shortcut.

Each chapter centers on four areas: text, skill exercises, a self-test with answers, and supplementary studies. Begin each chapter with a look at the "Essential Terms," which are listed alphabetically. You will need to know these terms and their definitions to master the chapter material, and more likely than not, they will be essential in later studies as well. The *Skill Exercises* throughout each chapter vary from simple objective questions to performance activities and elementary keyboard studies. Some instructors will ask students to tear out the exercise pages and submit them for correction; others will employ the drills to facilitate class discussion. If you remove pages from the book, be sure to keep them in a ring binder for later reference.

Once you have completed the chapter, take the *Self-Test* in a timed situation. Although the later tests are naturally more involved than those in the first few chapters, all of them are designed to be completed in fifteen or twenty minutes. The answers to self-tests appear in this text as Appendix E. Compare your responses with those given in the appendix and note any errors or misunderstandings.

Finally, your instructor may ask you to complete one or more of the *Supplementary Studies* that conclude each chapter. These are divided into "Drill Exercises," which parallel skills-oriented activities in the chapter text, and "Fundamental Skills in Practice," which suggest ways of using your new knowledge about music more creatively.

THE COMPACT DISC

The CD that accompanies *Fundamentals of Music* has been revised and re-recorded for the third edition. Using the recorded examples as you study, you will more effectively correlate the sounds of traditional music with their notated symbols. In addition, a number of types of aural skills exercises are recorded and available for your use in class or at home. As we will discuss more fully in the text, the ear-training, sight-singing, and keyboard drills are provided primarily as an introduction to the full range of professional music study. They are not intended to facilitate your mastery of a given topic.

ACKNOWLEDGMENTS

As *Fundamentals of Music* reaches its third edition and ends a decade on the market, I am naturally grateful to the students and instructors who have used the text since it appeared in 1988. I am especially indebted to several Webster University colleagues who kindly cataloged the book's strengths and weaknesses so that in the current edition, I believe I have been able to provide a more accurate and useful teaching supplement. Webster professors Kendall Stallings, Glen Bauer, Wesley Lowe, and Karen Trinkle all supported my work in this edition and provided many helpful suggestions. Bob Waggoner helped me choose and obtain permission to use many of the pop music examples. For their help with the compact disc that accompanies the text, I am indebted to Chris Miller, who recorded and edited the music, and to Jim Wayne, of Silverdisc Productions, who produced the CD for Prentice Hall. Finally, as she did for the second edition in 1993, Carole Crouse ably designed, edited, and supervised the production of the present book. Her attention to detail, accuracy, and consistency were remarkable and are much appreciated.

Earl Henry

CHAPTER 1

The Notation of Rhythm

ESSENTIAL TERMS

- beam
- beat
- dot
- flag
- measure
- notation
- note
- rest
- rhythm
- stem
- tie

MUSIC is sound in time. When we speak of "music" today, we usually mean *Western music* or music with roots in the "European tradition." This text is intended to help you identify and master the elements of a musical system common to Western composers since about 1600.

NOTATION

Throughout the history of Western music, composers and performers have been driven to represent sounds with symbols—a process we call NOTATION. Western musical notation, in fact, is a written language. In most other cultures, memorization and improvisation are central tools of the musician, but in the West, musical training begins with a flexible but rather complex system of precise notation. Our insistence upon exact notation explains, at least in part, why our music sounds the way it does. Some sounds can be represented with our traditional symbols; others cannot. Historically, when we in the West encounter sounds that cannot be notated exactly, we tend to avoid them.

THE NOTATION OF RHYTHM

RHYTHM is the element of time in music. In traditional Western music, rhythm is measured in *beats* or their fractional parts. One of the duties of a modern conductor is to outline those beats so that the ensemble members can perform their parts at exactly the right time. A BEAT is a regular pulse, like the heartbeat or the ticking of a clock.

Note Values

The NOTE is the basic symbol for sound and can be altered in a variety of ways to indicate differences in duration. The largest single traditional value is the WHOLE NOTE (**o**); other notes have fractional relationships to the whole note and receive one-half its value, one-quarter its value, and so on. Observe the names, the values, and a graphic comparison of the three notes shown below.

Note Name	*Note Symbol*	*Value*	*Comparison of Note Length*
WHOLE NOTE	o	Maximum[1]	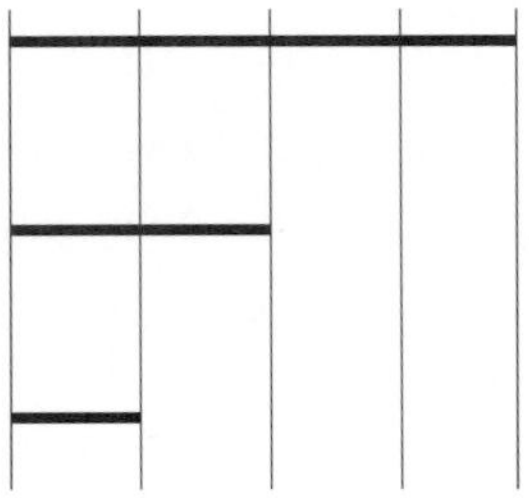
HALF NOTE		½ value of whole note	
QUARTER NOTE		¼ value of whole note	

The half note includes a STEM; the quarter note has both a stem and a solid notehead. Stems extend down from the left side of the notehead or up from the right side. Guidelines for placing stems either up or down will be discussed in Chapter 2.

stem → ← notehead   notehead → ← stem

The value of rhythmic symbols is set in beats. Any rhythmic symbol can have the value of one beat, but once that designation is made, other symbols relate to it as multiples or fractions of the beat unit. With the quarter, half, and whole notes, respectively, as the beat in the three following lines, the performances would be identical.

---

[1] Although the whole note is the maximum value used commonly, greater values are encountered occasionally (see "The Breve" on page 14).

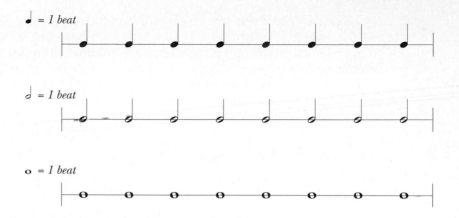

The quarter note is often assigned the value of one beat. In that case, the whole note has the value of four beats; the half note, two beats.

If the whole note receives four beats, two half notes or four quarter notes are required to fill the time occupied by a single whole note (four beats).

Given the half note as the beat, the fractional relationships among the notes are the same: The whole note receives twice the value of the half note; the quarter note, one-half the value of the half note. Notice that in this instance, the quarter note receives *less* than one beat; two quarter notes are required to total one beat in time.

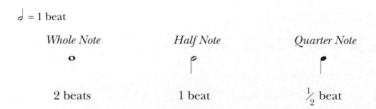

Regardless of the value of the whole note, the half and quarter notes stand in the same relationships to it. Two half notes have the same value as a single whole; four quarter notes represent a combined duration equivalent to the whole note.

2 beats   2 beats   2 beats

Measures

Groups of notes that comprise a like number of beats (two beats, three beats, and so on) are called MEASURES. Each new measure begins with a vertical mark termed a BARLINE. The particular values in a measure may be the same or varied as long as they add up to the number of beats specified. In later chapters, we will discuss time signatures. These are the traditional symbols that convey to the performer information about the note designated as receiving one beat, the number of beats in a measure, and, perhaps most important, the pattern of strong and weak accents.

Measure Icon.   For the present, we will indicate the beat unit and the number of beats in a measure with an icon such as ♩♩ or ♩♩. The numeral gives the number of beats in a measure; the note symbol represents one beat. The measure icon provides necessary information for our current studies without implying a particular accent pattern. Observe the following examples.

2 Two beats in a measure
♩ Quarter-note beat

3 Three beats in a measure
♩ Half-note beat

4 Four beats in a measure
♩ Quarter-note beat

The lines below are complete rhythmic phrases with two, three, and four beats per measure. The end of a composition or major division is marked with a DOUBLE BARLINE.

(Measures with two beats)

(Measures with three beats)

(Measures with four beats)

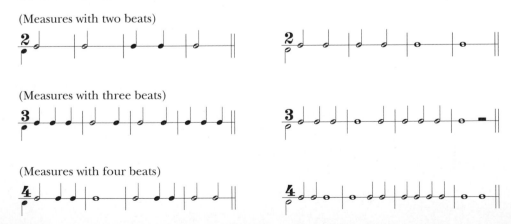

EXERCISE 1-1

Fundamental Skills

Notating Whole Notes, Half Notes,
and Quarter Notes

Follow the model and complete each line with notes of the same value. Make the noteheads oval, and extend the stems down from the left side or up from the right as shown.

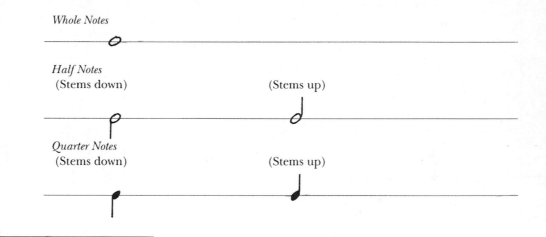

Whole Notes

Half Notes
(Stems down)   (Stems up)

Quarter Notes
(Stems down)   (Stems up)

EXERCISE 1-2

Fundamental Skills

Larger Note Values

A. Given the quarter note as the beat unit, compute the value of each note shown.

♩ = 1 beat

   1. o _____   **3.** ♩ _____

   2. ♩ _____

Given the half note as the beat unit, write the total value of each note shown.

♩ = 1 beat

   1. ♩ _____   **3.** o _____

   2. ♩ _____

B. With the quarter receiving one beat, give the cumulative value of all notes shown in each line.

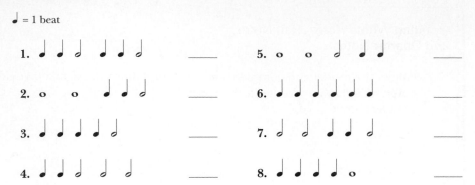

Given the half note as the beat, write the cumulative values of the notes in each line.

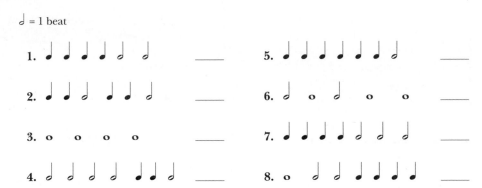

C. Incomplete Measures. In several chapters of this text, you will be asked to locate and complete any measures in a passage that do not contain the specified number of beats. In the lines below, study the measure icon to determine the number of beats per measure and the note receiving one beat. Next, total the number of beats in each measure. If a measure is incomplete, choose and provide **one note** that will complete it. Use only whole notes, half notes, and quarter notes in this exercise. More than one answer will be correct in some cases.

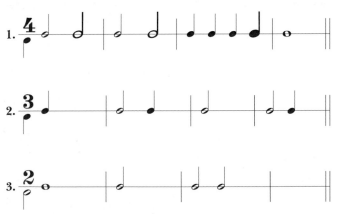

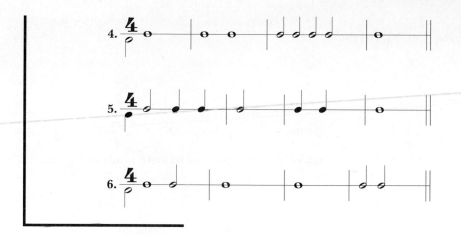

Lesser Rhythmic Values

For time values smaller than the quarter note, other symbols are available that follow the familiar pattern of relationships.

Note Name	Note Symbol	Value
EIGHTH NOTE	♪	$\frac{1}{8}$ value of whole note
SIXTEENTH NOTE	♬	$\frac{1}{16}$ value of whole note
THIRTY- SECOND NOTE		$\frac{1}{32}$ value of whole note
SIXTY- FOURTH NOTE		$\frac{1}{64}$ value of whole note

Flags. A FLAG is a curved line affixed to a note stem to indicate lesser value. Notes smaller than the quarter note include one or more *flags,* which are affixed to the right side of the stem. Each flag diminishes the value of the note by one-half.

	Eighth Note	*Sixteenth Note*	*Thirty- second Note*	*Sixty- fourth Note*
Flags	♪ ♪	♬ ♬		

If the quarter note receives one beat, lesser note values have fractional relationships to the quarter.

Quarter	*Eighth*	*Sixteenth*	*Thirty- second*	*Sixty- fourth*
1 beat	$\frac{1}{2}$ beat	$\frac{1}{4}$ beat	$\frac{1}{8}$ beat	$\frac{1}{16}$ beat

Observe the values of the most common note symbols in relation to the whole note.

Note Name	*Note Symbol*	*Value*
WHOLE NOTE	o	Maximum
HALF NOTE		$\frac{1}{2}$ value of whole note
QUARTER NOTE		$\frac{1}{4}$ value of whole note
EIGHTH NOTE		$\frac{1}{8}$ value of whole note
SIXTEENTH NOTE		$\frac{1}{16}$ value of whole note
THIRTY- SECOND NOTE		$\frac{1}{32}$ value of whole note
SIXTY- FOURTH NOTE		$\frac{1}{64}$ value of whole note

EXERCISE 1-3

Fundamental Skills

Notating Lesser Values

Follow the model and complete each line with notes of the same value. Make the noteheads oval, and extend the stems down from the side or up from the right side as shown. The flags should extend from the right side of the stem.

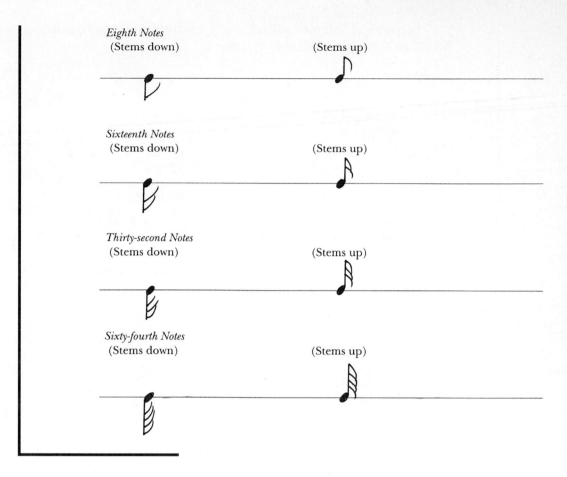

Eighth Notes
(Stems down)   (Stems up)

Sixteenth Notes
(Stems down)   (Stems up)

Thirty-second Notes
(Stems down)   (Stems up)

Sixty-fourth Notes
(Stems down)   (Stems up)

EXERCISE 1-4

Fundamental Skills

Reading Lesser Note Values

A. Given the quarter note as the beat unit, compute the value of each note shown.

♩ = 1 beat

1. ♪ _____   4. ♪ _____

2. ♩ _____   5. ♪ _____

3. o _____   6. ♪ _____

With the quarter still valued at one beat, compute the cumulative value of the series of notes shown in each line.

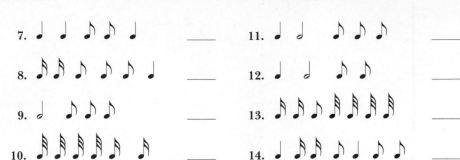

B. If the half note is the beat unit, compute the value of each note shown.

C. Incomplete Measures. As you did in Exercise 1-2, study the measure icon to discern the beat unit and the number of beats in a measure. Complete any partial measures by adding **one note.** If a measure is entirely blank, again use **one note** to fill it. Several possibilities exist for many measures.

Rests

Silence in music can be as important as the sounds themselves. The symbols for silence are called RESTS and correspond to the values of note symbols. The WHOLE REST falls below a line (▬); the HALF REST lies on a line (▬). Observe too that the number of rest "flags" duplicates that for the notes.

Note Symbol	Name	Rest Symbol
o	WHOLE	▬
𝅗𝅥	HALF	▬
𝅘𝅥	QUARTER	𝄽
𝅘𝅥𝅮	EIGHTH	𝄾
𝅘𝅥𝅯	SIXTEENTH	𝄿
𝅘𝅥𝅰	THIRTY- SECOND	𝅀
𝅘𝅥𝅱	SIXTY- FOURTH	𝅁

EXERCISE 1-5

Fundamental Skills

Notating Rests

Follow the model and complete the lines with rests of the same value. Quarter rests are made like an angular number *3* or the letter *M* on its side.

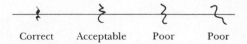

Correct   Acceptable   Poor   Poor

Flags for eighth, sixteenth, and thirty-second rests should extend from the right side as shown. The stems themselves angle from left to right. Make sure that the flags actually meet the stem.

Correct   Flags fail to   Improper
                 meet stem   angle

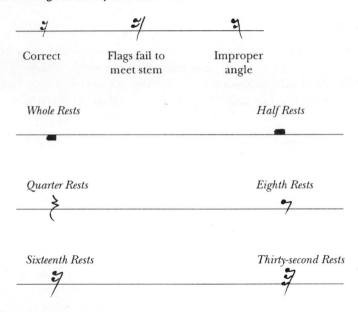

Whole Rests   *Half Rests*

Quarter Rests   *Eighth Rests*

Sixteenth Rests   *Thirty-second Rests*

EXERCISE 1-6

Fundamental Skills

Note and Rest Values

A. Given the value of the quarter note (and rest) as one beat, compute the value of each rest shown.

♩ = 1 beat

1. 𝄽   _____   2. ▬   _____

3. ▬ _____   5. ⅞ _____

4. ⅞ _____   6. ⅞ _____

With the quarter note still the beat unit, compute the total value of the series of notes and rests shown in each line.

♩ = 1 beat

7. ♩ ♩ ♩̆ ♩ ♩̆ _____   11. ▬ ♪♪♪♪ ⅞ ♪ _____

8. ♩̆ ⅞ ♪ ♩ ▬ _____   12. ♪♪♪♪⅞ ♪♪♪⅞ _____

9. ♪ ♪ ♩̆ ♪ ♪ ♩̆ _____   13. ♩ ♩̆ ⅞ ♪ ♪ ♪ _____

10. ♩ ♪♪ ⅞ ♩̆ _____   14. ♩ ♩ ♩ ⅞ ♪ ♩ _____

B. Given the value of the *eighth note* as one beat, compute the value of each rest shown.

♪ = 1 beat

1. ⅞ _____   4. ⅞ _____

2. ▬ _____   5. ⅞ _____

3. ♩̆ _____   6. ▬ _____

C. Incomplete Measures. Study the measure icon to learn the beat unit and the number of beats in a measure. Complete any partial measures by adding **one rest**. If a measure is entirely blank, again use **one rest** to fill it. Several possibilities exist for many measures.

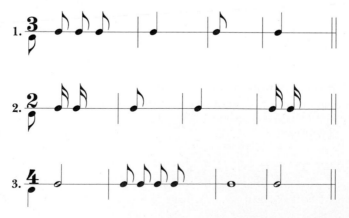

The Breve

An older note value found occasionally in modern scores is the BREVE (⊐), which has double the value of a whole note. The corresponding rest has the same value.

⊐ = o ‿ o

▮ = ▬ ▬

The Dot

The DOT (·) is employed to extend the value of a note or a rest by one-half its original value. If the half note, for example, receives two beats, the *dotted half note* has the value of three beats.

♩ = 1 beat

♩ . ♩.

2 beats + 1 beat = 3 beats

If the half note receives one beat, the *dotted half note* receives one and one-half beats—an increase of one-half the original value.

♩ = 1 beat

♩ . ♩.

1 beat + ½ beat = 1½ beats

Whereas the quarter note divides into two eighth notes, the dotted quarter note comprises *three* eighth notes. A DOTTED NOTE is one that includes a dot; notes without dots are classified as SIMPLE. As we will discuss more fully in a later chapter, the use of a dotted note as the unit of beat permits the composer to divide the beat into three rather than two smaller parts.

Simple Note   Dotted Note

The principle of the dot applies to rests as well. If the quarter note and the quarter rest each receive one beat, the dotted quarter rest has the value of one and one-half beats.

♩ = 1 beat

1 beat + ½ beat   =   1½ beats

If the whole rest has the value of four beats, the dotted whole rest receives six beats.

♩ = 1 beat

4 beats + 2 beats   =   6 beats

The Tie

Whereas the dot increases the value of a single note or rest, the TIE (⌢ or ⌣) combines the values of two or more notes of the same pitch (see Chapter 2). If the half note receives two beats, a half note tied to a quarter note has a combined value of three beats.

♩ = 1 beat

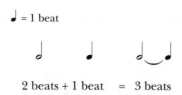

2 beats + 1 beat   =   3 beats

If the quarter note receives one beat, an eighth note tied to a quarter receives a beat and a half.

♩ = 1 beat

♪   ♩   ♪‿♩

½ beat + 1 beat   =   1½ beats

EXERCISE 1-7

Fundamental Skills

Reading Dotted and Tied Notes

A. Follow the model and rewrite the tied notes given as *one* simple or dotted note of the same duration. The quarter note is the beat in lines 1–4; the eighth note is the beat in lines 5–8.

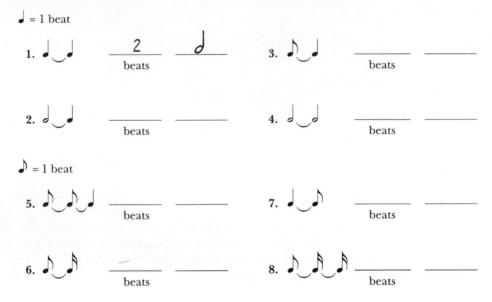

♩ = 1 beat

1. ♩‿♩   2 _____ 𝅗𝅥 _____
              beats

2. 𝅗𝅥‿♩   _____ _____
              beats

3. ♪‿♩   _____ _____
              beats

4. 𝅗𝅥‿𝅗𝅥   _____ _____
              beats

♪ = 1 beat

5. ♪‿♪‿♩   _____ _____
                beats

6. ♪‿♪   _____ _____
              beats

7. ♩‿♪   _____ _____
              beats

8. ♪‿♪‿♪   _____ _____
                beats

B. Compute the cumulative value of the notes and rests shown in each line. The quarter note is the beat.

♩ = 1 beat

1. ♩‿♩ ♪ ♩ 𝄾   ____   4. 𝄾 ♪‿♩ 𝄾 ♪   ____

2. 𝅗𝅥· ♩ – ♩   ____   5. ♪ ♪ ♪ ♪ ♩ 𝄾   ____

3. ♩ ♪ ♪ 𝄾 ♩   ____   6. 𝄾 𝄾 𝄾 ♪ ♪   ____

Compute the combined values of the notes and rests shown in each line. In lines 1–4, the eighth note receives the beat. The half note is the beat in lines 5–8.

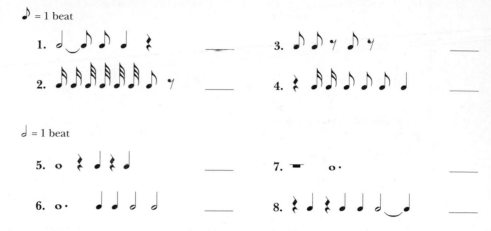

C. Incomplete Measures. As you have done previously, study the measure icon, then complete measures as necessary by adding notes or rests. Where notes or rests are given, add **one note** or **one rest** (as specified) to complete the measure. Your added symbol may be simple or dotted. If the entire measure is blank, choose **one rest** to fill it.

Add one rest if the measure is incomplete.

Add one note if the measure is incomplete.

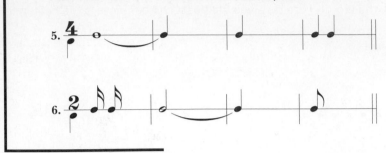

Beams and Flags

In addition to flags, which you encountered earlier in this chapter, composers often show relative note values with beams. Beams are thick, horizontal bars that connect two or more note stems. Flags and beams are equivalent in value; eighth notes have one flag or one beam, sixteenth notes have two flags or two beams, and so on.

The purpose of beams varies according to whether the music is vocal or instrumental. In vocal music, flagged notes appear with single syllables of text; beams, on the other hand, show that two or more notes are performed on the *same* syllable (the five-lined staff, as well as other symbols in the following passage, will be discussed in the next chapter).

Henry Purcell, *Tyrannic Love*

In instrumental music (without text), beams identify groups of notes that have the combined value of one or more beats. Notice how the preceding passage would be written for flute or violin.

Flute/Violin

Beamed Note Groups

Beaming clarifies beat units in instrumental music. The first passage below is notated with flags and would be confusing to an instrumentalist. The same music is much clearer with beams.*

Flags   *Beams*

The second example above is clear because beats are beamed together. As shown in the next passage, however, incorrectly beamed notes can be more confusing than flags.

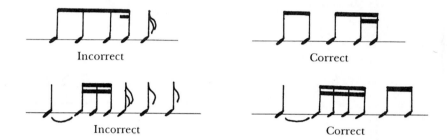

Incorrect   Correct

Incorrect   Correct

In your own notation, be careful to observe the conventions of beaming beat groups. Whereas flags are used for any number of consecutive single syllables in vocal music, flagged notes are reserved in instrumental music for single notes.

*The complexities of beaming in vocal music lie outside the scope of this text. Unless otherwise specified, all music in this text is to be considered *instrumental*.

EXERCISE 1-8

Fundamental Skills

Beaming

Replace flagged notes in the following passage with beams. Align your notation directly under the given music. There are no single flagged notes in this exercise.

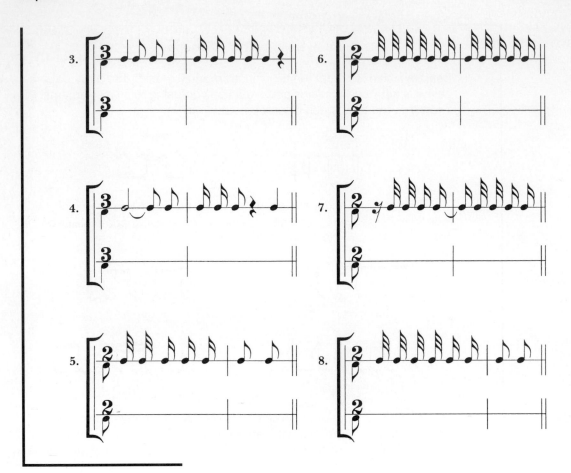

SELF-TEST

1. (30 points) The following passage is a rhythmic reduction of a composition by Florence Price. Where letters appear above symbols, identify those symbols in the blanks below the music.

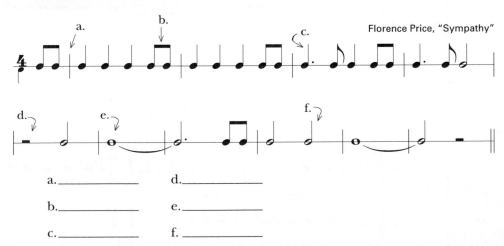

Florence Price, "Sympathy"

a._____   d._____

b._____   e._____

c._____   f._____

2. (20 points) If the quarter note has the value of one beat, compute the values of the notes and rests shown.

♩ = 1 beat

𝄽 _____   𝅗𝅥 _____   𝅗𝅥. _____   ▬ _____   ♪ _____

3. (20 points) With the *half note* having the value of one beat, supply one *rest* (it may be simple or dotted) that has the value indicated.

𝅗𝅥 = 1 beat

_____ 2 beats   _____ 1½ beats   _____ 3 beats

_____ ½ beat   _____ ¼ beat

4. (10 points) Rewrite the dotted notes as tied notes.

　　a. 𝅗𝅥. _____   b. ♪ _____

5. (20 points) Rewrite the following passages in an instrumental style. Use beams to connect groups of notes that have the value of one beat.

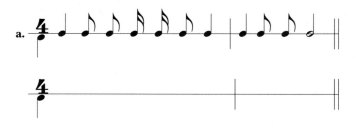

SUPPLEMENTARY STUDIES

Drill Exercises

1. In earlier exercises, you completed a given measure by adding one or more notes or rests to those notated. In this exercise, fill any incomplete measures by adding *one* note or rest (**as** directed) to those given. Compute the total beats in any incomplete measure, then choose one note or rest to complete it. Remember that some measures are complete as given.

   a. Add a note if necessary.

   b. Add a rest if necessary.

   c. Add a note if necessary.

2. Provide the values of the notes and rests shown below.

a. ♪ = 1 beat

b. ♩ = 1 beat

c. ♩ = 1 beat

Fundamental Skills in Practice

3. The following lines are rhythmic reductions of compositions by well-known composers. In the space provided, TRANSCRIBE each passage by halving or doubling values as specified. Where a quarter note appears in the original, for example, you will *double* the value with a half note in the transcription. Likewise, reduce values by half by replacing quarter notes with eighth notes, half rests with quarter rests, and so on.

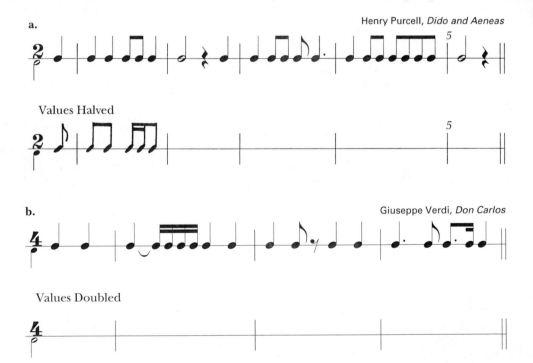

a.   Henry Purcell, *Dido and Aeneas*

Values Halved

b.   Giuseppe Verdi, *Don Carlos*

Values Doubled

NAME _____

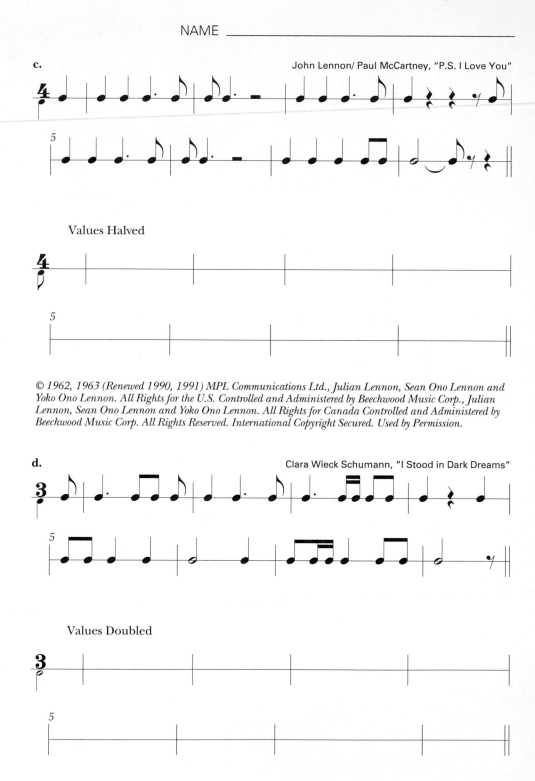

c.

John Lennon/ Paul McCartney, "P.S. I Love You"

Values Halved

d.

Clara Wieck Schumann, "I Stood in Dark Dreams"

Values Doubled

CHAPTER **2**

The Notation of Pitch

ESSENTIAL TERMS

- bassa
- *bass clef*
- *grand staff*
- *interval*
- *ledger lines*
- loco

- *octave*
- *octave sign*
- *pitch*
- *staff*
- *treble clef*

For about a thousand years, traditional Western music has been based on the symbols we now call NOTES. As we discussed earlier, the shape of a note designates its relative duration. Notes also represent PITCH—the psychological perception that sounds are relatively higher or lower. Like the practices associated with rhythm, the notation of pitch in Western music evolved over many centuries. Although some early systems of pitch notation employed letters of the alphabet as note symbols, today we represent pitch simply by placing notes higher or lower on the printed page. The first three notes below, for example, represent increasingly higher pitch; the second three, increasingly lower pitch.

The Staff

Although the notes above are obviously higher or lower in a relative sense, the performer must know exactly how much higher or lower. Another part of the notational system, the *staff,* permits exactness in notating pitch. The STAFF is a grid of five lines (with four spaces between them) that we use to position notes and rests. Placing the notes on the staff allows them to be identified more precisely.

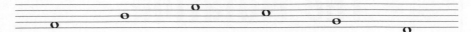

Stem Direction.   When stemmed notes appear on the staff, correct stem direction (up or down) is important. For notes on the third line or above, stems go down from the left side of the notehead. For notes below the third line, stems go up from the right side. Flags are always placed on the right side of the stem.

When several notes are beamed together, stems go up or down according to where most of the notes in the group lie.

Luigi Boccherini, Rondo for Cello and Piano

Larger Rest Values on the Staff.   Larger rest values are associated with a particular line or space on the staff. The half rest lies on the third line; the whole rest extends below the fourth line. Although rarely used today, the breve rest fills the third space.

Half   Whole   Breve

Note Names.   There are seven basic notes, named according to the first seven letters of the alphabet: A B C D E F and G. On the staff, these BASIC PITCHES always appear in order over consecutive lines and spaces. If the name of any one line or space is identified, we know them all because the pattern is invariable. In an ascending series after the note G, A appears again; in descending patterns after A, G is the next note. In the following example, the pitch C is identified with an asterisk.

* = the pitch C

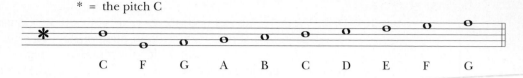

C   F   G   A   B   C   D   E   F   G

The Clef

The asterisk identifies the pitch C on the staff above, but composers tradition-ally use a CLEF to assign notes to specific lines and spaces. The two most common clefs are the *treble clef* and the *bass clef*.

The Treble Clef. The TREBLE CLEF (𝄞), used for relatively higher sounds, identifies the pitch G as being on the second line. If G is on the second line, we know that the pitch A occupies the space above it; the pitch F, the space below it.

G   E F G A B C D E F   F A C E E G B D F

Learning the "ABCs"

Unless you have had previous experience and already know how to read music, now is the time to learn the locations of pitches on the staff. You might think of this process as learning the "ABCs" of music notation. At one point, you learned the alphabet. You probably mastered the letters slowly, learning one or two at a time. Perhaps most important, you received constant feedback on your progress from parents and teachers.

Consider a similar process for learning the note names and their respective staff locations. In fact, a structured approach like that outlined here will help most students master virtually all facets of music funda-mentals.

Step 1   **Theory.** Review the theory behind the material you need to learn. For note locations on the staff, for example, that will mean reviewing symbols such as the staff and the clef.

Step 2   **Limit Your Work.** Ten or fifteen minutes of study three times a day are usually better than an hour of intense study once a day. Avoid the temptation of trying to learn too much at once. Choose a few new items, learn them carefully, then move on to others. In learning notes, for example, begin with about four pitches in the treble clef (G, A, B, and C, for example). Master the locations of these four notes, then add a few more at each study period until you have learned them all. Repeat the pro-cess for bass clef notes.

Step 3 **Drill.** Work for speed and accuracy in your study. Consider constructing your own exercises in addition to those in the text. If you are learning notes, for example, you might copy your target group by hand several times on staff paper, writing the letter name each time as well. In addition, you could rearrange the four notes, then copy and identify them in the new order (C, B, A, and G, perhaps).

Flash cards help most students learn music fundamentals. Write the staff location on one side of a card, the note name on the other.

Step 4 **Self-Test.** In addition to the self-tests in this text, consider creating your own brief quiz (with answers) based on the item or items in question. Take the quiz under test conditions, then assess your progress. Even before you begin learning notes, you might define your current goals, then write several groups of pitches in various orders for later identification. Do the same for note names; then see whether you can provide the staff notation after a period of study. Quiz yourself mainly on new material, but always include a few review questions from earlier study periods. A simple quiz, made up before your first study period, might look like this.

Self-Test for Notes G, A, B, and C

1. Identify notes by name (answers on back of this sheet).

2. Write notes on the staff (answers on back of this sheet).

   A   G   C   B   G   A   C   B   G

Step 5 **Reality Check.** Based on the results of your own quiz (and, perhaps, your score on the chapter self-test from the text), how well do you understand the material? Are you ready to move on to new problems? If so, add a few more notes (or whatever material is under study) to those already learned. If not, you may need to ask your instructor for individual help.

The Bass Clef. The BASS CLEF (𝄢) is used for relatively lower sounds and identifies the position of the pitch F on the fourth line. If F is on the fourth line, the space above is G; the space below is E.

F   G   A   B   C   D   E   F   G   A   A   C   E   G   G   B   D   F   A

Note the identification of several different pitches on the two STAVES (plural of staff) below.

G   D   E   C   D   A   G   E   F   B

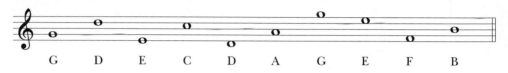

F   G   B   C   E   B   G   A   C   D

EXERCISE 2-1

Fundamental Skills

Notation in Treble and Bass Clefs

Follow the models below and complete the given staff lines with treble and bass clefs.

EXERCISE 2-2 _____

Fundamental Skills

Notating Pitch

A. Write the notes indicated in their proper positions on the treble clef. When note names are repeated (a second pitch A, for example), use a different staff location. Your half notes should have oval heads and correctly placed stems. Refer to page 28 for guidelines on stem direction.

Notate the pitches specified in the bass clef. Use eighth notes with properly placed stems and a single flag attached to the right of each stem. As before, when note names are repeated, vary the staff location.

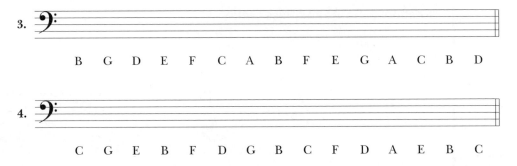

B. Some of the stems and flags in the passages below are incorrectly placed. Use the lower staff to rewrite both passages with correct placement.

Franz Schubert, Quartet No. 15

Tammy Wynette/ Bill Sherrill, "Stand By Your Man"

EXERCISE 2-3 _____

Fundamental Skills

Pitch Identification

Write the name of the note in the blank.

1.

_____ _____ _____ _____ _____ _____ _____ _____

2.

_____ _____ _____ _____ _____ _____ _____ _____

Identify pitches in the following three compositions.

Ottorino Respighi, Suite No. 2

3.

— — — — — — — — — — —

Henry Mancini, "Moon River"

4.

— — — — — — — —

Johann Strauss, *Artist's Life*

5.

— — — — — — — —

The Octave

In line 5 of Skill Exercise 2-3, notice that the pitch F is written in two different places; these pitches are an *octave* apart. An OCTAVE is a natural element upon which virtually all world cultures base their music. Given any note on the staff, the note with the same name immediately above or below is by definition an octave higher or lower. When pitches are an octave apart, the sounds are so similar that they are often incorrectly perceived as being the *same* pitch. The difference (distance) between two pitches is called an INTERVAL; the interval between the bracketed notes below is an octave.

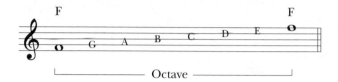

	RECORDED EXAMPLE 1
	TRACK 2
	Octaves

Many popular tunes include one or more prominent octaves. Use the CD that accompanies this text and listen several times to the opening phrase of "Over the Rainbow" (Recorded Example 1). The notes between the words "some" and "where" and also between "-bow" and "skies" lie an octave apart.

Some - where   o - ver the rain - bow,   skies   are   blue.

"Over the Rainbow," by Harold Arlen and E. Y. Harburg. © 1938 (Renewed) Metro-Goldwyn-Mayer Inc. © 1939 (Renewed) EMI Feist Catalog Inc. All Rights Reserved. Used by Permission Warner Bros. Publications U.S. Inc., Miami, FL. 33014.

Ledger Lines

At least in theory, any pitch can be represented on either the treble or the bass staff. The staff can be extended up or down as necessary to accommodate pitches outside the standard five lines and four spaces. These additional lines (which are added only temporarily) are called LEDGER LINES. Ledger lines (and, of course, the spaces between them) are shown in the next two passages.

Since the violin is a soprano instrument, players must become accustomed to reading ledger lines such as those in the next passage.

Alban Berg, *Violin Concerto*

In keyboard music, both bass and treble staves can be extended up and down to accommodate octave ranges as necessary. Notice also that staves may change from treble to bass or from bass to treble as necessary.

Claude Debussy, *Reflections in the Water*

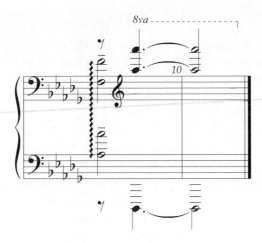

The Octave Sign. Because the octave is so basic in traditional Western notation, we use a special symbol to indicate pitches sounding an octave higher or lower than written. The OCTAVE SIGN (*8va* .....) is used primarily to avoid ledger lines when parts are especially high or low. The Italian word *bassa* is added when the octave sign specifies an octave lower. In addition, when several notes are included in an *ottava* passage (one employing the octave sign), they are delineated by a dashed line. Finally, note that the word *loco* ("in place") is used at the end of an *ottava* section.

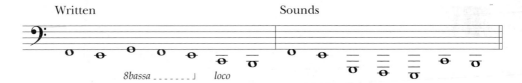

Another type of octave sign is associated with the treble clef. The symbol 𝄞₈ indicates that pitches are to be performed an octave lower than written.

The Grand Staff

A SYSTEM is a set of staves. For notating keyboard music, we use a system consisting of both treble and bass staves. This traditional arrangement is known as the GRAND (or GREAT) STAFF. In the next example, the pitch C occurs in several different locations. Except for those circled (which are identical in sound), each pitch C is an octave from its closest neighbor.

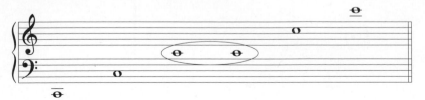

EXERCISE 2-4

Fundamental Skills

Octaves and Ledger Lines

A. Write sixteenth notes both an octave higher and an octave lower than the pitch given. Some pitches will require ledger lines. Name the given pitch. (The other two will have the same pitch name, of course.)

B. Many of the pitches below include ledger lines. Identify them by letter name.

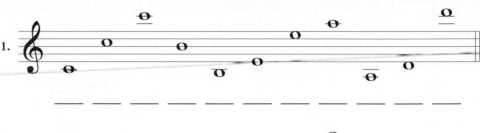

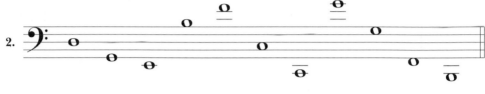

C. Several *ottava* passages are given below. Use the lower staff to rewrite the music as it sounds (an octave higher or an octave lower). Remember that the term *loco* is often used at the end of an *ottava* passage to emphasize a return to "in place" notation. Where blanks appear, name the pitch.

G. M. Cohan, "The Yankee Doodle Boy"

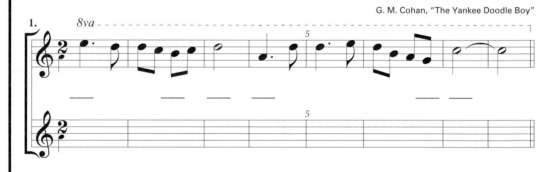

Henry Purcell, Sonata

The following melodies include *ottava* passages. Rewrite the entire line using ledger lines as necessary to eliminate the octave sign. Be prepared to name all pitches.

EXERCISE 2-5

Musicianship Skills

SIGHT SINGING: Matching Pitches

The first step in learning to sing music at sight is matching pitches—that is, hearing a pitch sounded on the piano or another instrument and then singing that same pitch in its correct octave (if possible). Your instructor will play a series of pitches; listen carefully to each new pitch, then sing it in the same octave if you can. The first two lines lie generally within the ranges of most men's voices. Some women will need to sing these pitches one or more octaves higher. Likewise, the second two lines are higher pitches, and men may need to sing them in a lower octave. As a further exercise, write the pitch name of each note in the blank.

1.

_____ _____ _____ _____ _____ _____ _____ _____

2.

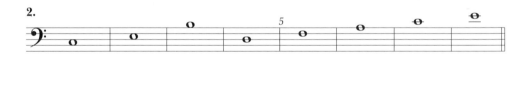

_____ _____ _____ _____ _____ _____ _____ _____

3.

_____ _____ _____ _____ _____ _____ _____ _____

4.

_____ _____ _____ _____ _____ _____ _____ _____

EXERCISE 2-6 ───────────────────────────────────

Musicianship Skills

SIGHT SINGING: Octaves

Sight singing (often called solfège) is an important element in music study. When practicing alone, most students need an instrument (preferably a keyboard instrument) to verify pitch accuracy.

In the lines below, play the first pitch on the piano or another instrument, then match that pitch in your *lower* range. Next, repeat the first pitch, then sing an octave higher. Check the second pitch against the keyboard. Use the blank to name each pitch.

Octave Higher

1.

2.

Octave Lower

3.

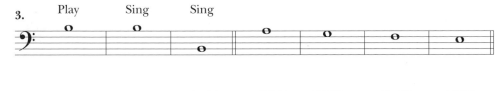

4.

EXERCISE 2-7

Musicianship Skills

EAR TRAINING: Pitch Discrimination

EAR TRAINING is the process of learning *patterns* common to traditional music so that you can recognize, imitate, and notate those patterns when necessary. Immediate reinforcement is crucial in ear training. For that reason, most of the ear-training exercises in this text are followed by the correct answer located just to the right of a blank or a series of choices. You will need a mask to cover the answers. Your cover sheet can be a piece of paper, an index card, or any other opaque material.

RECORDED EXAMPLE 2
TRACK 3
Ear Training

In Recorded Example 2, you will listen to a series of three pitches and indicate whether the last pitch is the same as (S), higher than (H), or lower than (L) the first pitch. There are four different patterns in each line. Cover the answer; circle your choice, then move the mask to check your response against the given answer. Move the mask again to cover the next answer and continue throughout the line in the same way.

Circle **S** if the last pitch is the same as the first.

Circle **H** if the last pitch is higher than the first.

Circle **L** if the last pitch is lower than the first.

Three Pitches

```
        Choices  Answer
        /  |  \     |
1. S  H  L    S        S  H  L  H        S  H  L  L        S  H  L  S
2. S  H  L    L        S  H  L  S        S  H  L  L        S  H  L  H
3. S  H  L    H        S  H  L  L        S  H  L  L        S  H  L  H
```

TRACK
04

These patterns have four pitches. As before, compare the first and last pitches.

Four Pitches

```
        Choices  Answer
        /  |  \     |
1. S  H  L    H        S  H  L  L        S  H  L  L        S  H  L  S
2. S  H  L    S        S  H  L  H        S  H  L  L        S  H  L  S
3. S  H  L    L        S  H  L  S        S  H  L  S        S  H  L  H
```

SELF-TEST

1. (30 points) Study the following melody by the Renaissance composer Giovanni Pierluigi da Palestrina (ca. 1525–1594). Several symbols, note values, and pitch names are identified by letters above or below the staff. In the shorter blanks (if any), write the pitch name; in longer blanks, identify the symbol (treble clef, whole note, and so on).

G. P. Palestrina, "*Lauda Sion*"

	Note Name	Symbol Name		Note Name	Symbol Name
a.		_____	d.		_____
b.	____	_____	e.		_____
c.	____	_____	f.	____	_____

2. (20 points) Write the pitch indicated in the given clef.

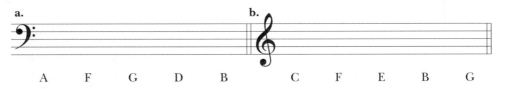

A   F   G   D   B   C   F   E   B   G

3. (20 points) Identify the note given, then write the same basic pitch an octave higher or lower as directed.

	Given note	Write octave higher		Given note	Write octave lower		Given note	Write octave lower		Given note	Write octave lower

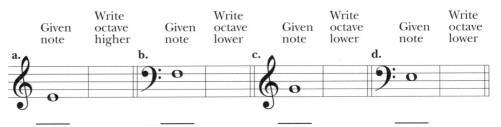

4. (10 points) Circle pairs of notes that are *not* an octave apart.

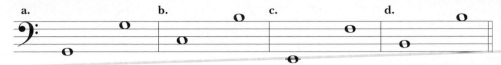

5. (20 points) Using the octave sign, rewrite the following passage to eliminate all ledger lines.

L. van Beethoven, Symphony No. 7

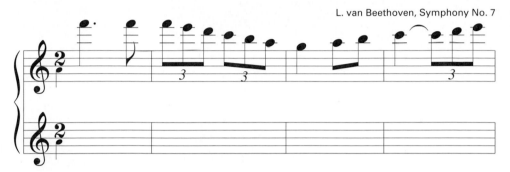

SUPPLEMENTARY STUDIES

Drill Exercises

1. Identify each pitch in the following compositions.

Johann Strauss, *Artist's Life*

a.

Alan Lerner/ Frederick Loewe, *Brigadoon*

b.

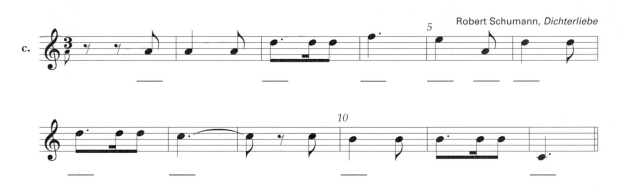

Robert Schumann, *Dichterliebe*

c.

2. Write thirty-second notes an octave above those given. *Do not* use the octave sign; extend the staff as necessary with ledger lines. Identify each given pitch.

3. Again without using the octave sign, write quarter notes that are an octave below those given. As before, identify the given pitches.

NAME _____

Fundamental Skills in Practice

4. The composition that follows is a Gregorian chant dating from before A.D. 800 and representing some of the earliest Western music. On the staff provided, rewrite the chant in more traditional notation using eighth notes. Beam the notes as suggested by the brackets on the upper staff. (If two notes are in brackets, beam those two together in your revision, and so on.) Notice that the treble clef indicates pitches *sounding* an octave lower than written. Write your revised version in the bass clef and notate pitches as they will actually sound.

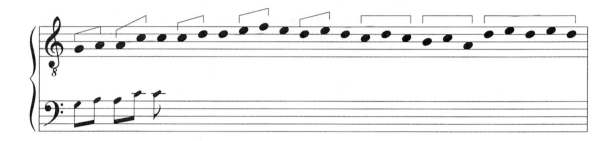

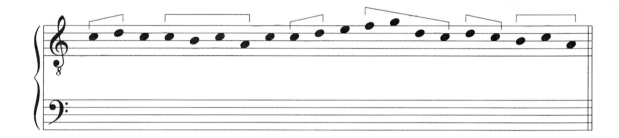

5. The following composition lies in the flute's middle register. Rewrite this music an octave higher to fall within the flute's upper register. Flutists are accustomed to reading ledger lines, so do not use the octave sign. Duplicate all pitch and rhythmic symbols exactly (with pitches an octave higher).

Original Notation

Giuseppe Giordani, "Caro Mio Ben"

Revised Notation for Flute High Register

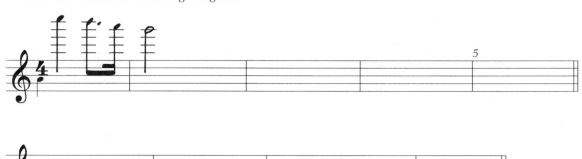

CHAPTER 3

The Keyboard

ESSENTIAL TERMS

- *accidental*
- *barline*
- *double sharp*
- *enharmonic*
- *flat*
- *half step*
- *measure*
- *natural*
- *octave designation*
- *sharp*
- *whole step*

Throughout the world, musical systems are based upon the octave—the simplest and most natural interval. The variations in the way cultures divide the octave into smaller intervals, however, are a primary reason that the music of one culture sounds different from that of another. In the West, the octave is divided into twelve equal smaller intervals called HALF STEPS. Thus, the half step is the smallest interval in Western music. We can illustrate the half step easily by referring to the piano keyboard. Keyboard instruments such as the organ and the piano are constructed so that the interval from one key to the next closest key (above or below) is a half step. As shown here, the distance between any two adjacent keys is a half step regardless of whether the key in question is black or white.

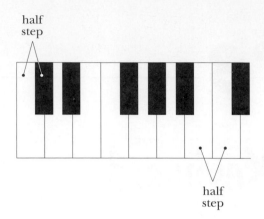

Whole Steps.   Two half steps combine to make a WHOLE STEP—another of the basic intervals of traditional Western music. The distance from any one key to the *second* closest key above or below is a whole step.

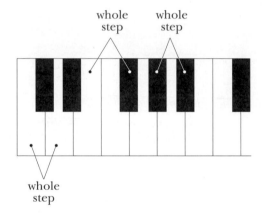

THE KEYBOARD

Since the eighteenth century, fixed-pitch keyboard instruments such as the harpsichord and the piano have dominated Western musical traditions. From the center of the keyboard, notes of increasingly lower pitch are found to the left; to the right are increasingly higher pitches. The standard keyboard is based upon the seven basic pitches, A B C D E F and G. These are the white keys; the black keys fall in between. Observe, however, that black keys do not fall between *every* pair of white keys; they alternate from left to right (lower to higher pitch on the keyboard) in groups of two and three.

The arrangement of black and white keys identifies the notes on the keyboard. The note C is always the white key just below the first (lower) of the two black keys. The note F is always the white key to the left of the lowest of the three black keys. This arrangement is the same in every octave.

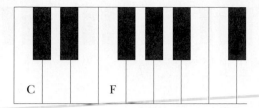

The basic pitches are sequential over adjacent white keys. As is the case with the staff, once any one note is located on the keyboard, the keys that produce the other pitches are easily determined as well.

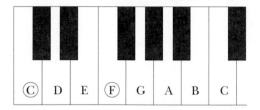

Half Steps and Whole Steps.   The intervals between basic pitches are not the same. Most basic pitches are separated by a whole step, but half steps occur between B and C and between E and F (the two points where black keys do not appear). Half steps between white keys are termed NATURAL HALF STEPS.

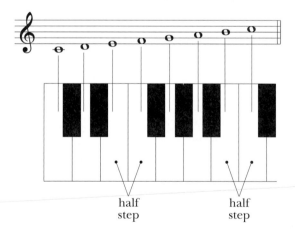

Octave Placement.   The standard keyboard includes more than seven octaves, allowing the performer to choose a high, middle, or low register. Although the names and locations of the notes *within each octave* are exactly the same, the staff notations are different so that the performer knows exactly which octave the composer intended. Notice in the following example that although the pitch C is always to the left of the two black keys on the keyboard, its staff appearance is different in every octave.

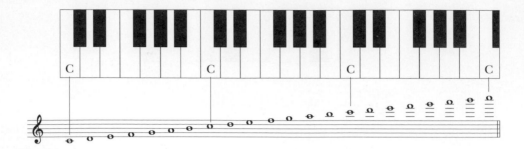

EXERCISE 3-1

Musicianship Skills

KEYBOARD: Locating Pitches

A. Seated at the keyboard, play each of the lines below. Begin with "middle C," in the center of the keyboard; next, locate and play the pitches C that are one, two, and three octaves higher. Repeat the octaves descending from high to low. Remember: C is always the white key to the left of the two adjacent black keys.

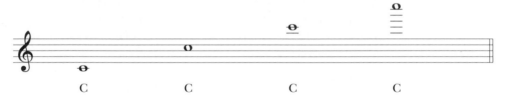

Locate the pitch F immediately above middle C. Play this pitch; then, play the pitches F that fall one, two, and three octaves below it. Repeat the octaves in ascending order.

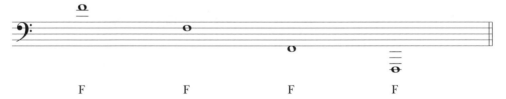

B. This exercise consists of stepwise patterns of eight notes each. Begin by writing the name of each pitch in the blank below it. Refer to the following chart of right- and left-hand fingering patterns. Thumbs are numbered "1"; little fingers, "5."

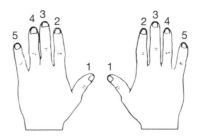

Begin each of the ascending series below with your right thumb. When you have located all the starting pitches, return to the first set and play all eight pitches using a standard fingering pattern. Use the thumb, index, and third fingers for the first, second, and third pitches respectively. For the fourth pitch, turn the thumb under the third finger. Play the fifth through the eighth pitches with the remaining fingers 1–5 of the right hand. Identify each pitch.

Right-Hand Fingering Pattern: Ascending

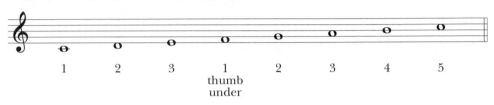

      1   2   3   1   2   3   4   5

thumb
under

1.   **2.**

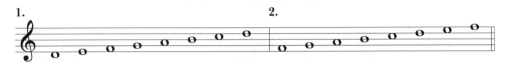

3.   **4.**

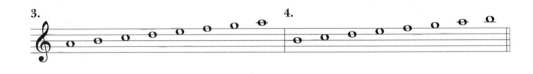

5.   **6.**

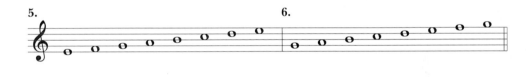

Identify each pitch notated in the bass clef by writing the note name in the blank. Locate and play the first pitch of each ascending series with the fifth finger of the left hand. Turn the third finger over the thumb for the sixth pitch.

Left-Hand Fingering Pattern: Ascending

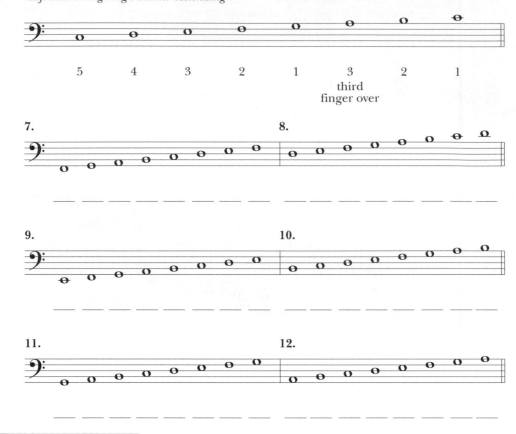

ACCIDENTALS

Basic pitches are sometimes altered to sound higher or lower. ACCIDENTALS are symbols that appear before the note itself and indicate a half- or whole-step alteration in pitch. The three most important accidentals are the sharp, the flat, and the natural.

The Sharp

The SHARP SIGN (♯) indicates that a basic pitch is to be raised one half step. If we want a pitch one half step higher than C, for example, it will be produced by the black key to the immediate right of C. The name of this new note is C-sharp (C♯). Notice that the sharp sign (♯) appears before a note on the staff but *after* the letter name in a written reference.

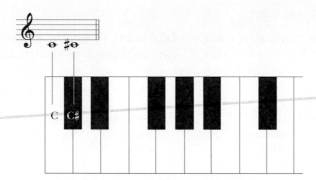

The notes C and C♯ represent two completely different sounds. If a piano or another keyboard instrument is available, play these two notes and listen to the difference. First, play the pitches C and C♯; this interval is a half step. Next, play C and D to hear a whole step. The note D is the white key above C; the black key above D is D♯. Likewise, the black keys above F, G, and A are F♯, G♯, and A♯, respectively.

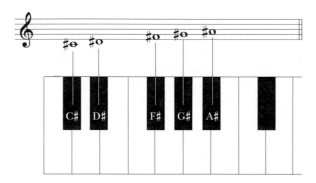

The Flat

The FLAT SIGN (♭) indicates that a basic pitch is to be lowered one half step. The pitch D is played with the white key just above C. The note D♯ is produced by the black key above D. Finally, D-flat (D♭) is the black key to the immediate left of D.

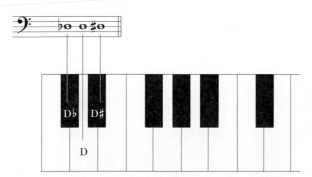

The Natural Sign

The term *natural* in music usually refers to one of the seven (natural) basic pitches. The NATURAL SIGN (♮) cancels a previous flat or sharp and indicates a return to the original basic pitch.

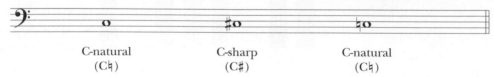

               C-natural   C-sharp   C-natural
                 (C♮)   (C♯)   (C♮)

Measures. As we discussed in the first chapter, vertical lines on the staff (barlines) help a performer separate beats into strong and weak patterns called MEASURES. Although metric patterns and measures will be treated thoroughly in the next chapter, we will preview the symbol here to complete the discussion of accidentals.

Once introduced, accidentals remain in effect *throughout a given measure* and are not repeated for subsequent notes of the same pitch in that measure. In the following passage, the third pitch is D♯—a half step higher than the second

---

Notating Accidentals

Accidentals precede the note they affect and appear close to the note-head on the same line or space. In calligraphy, the sharp symbol is similar to the "number sign" (#). The vertical lines are straight up and down; the horizontal lines slant to the right. A flat sign is like a lowercase letter "b." Of the many approaches to notating a natural sign, perhaps the simplest is a figure of two interlocking uppercase letters "L" (with the second upside down).

    Sharp   Flat   Natural

When you notate notes with accidentals, place the sharp, flat, or natural on the left side and close to the notehead.

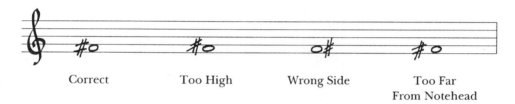

   Correct   Too High   Wrong Side   Too Far
                                                     From Notehead

pitch, D. The next occurrence of the pitch D, however, is in the third measure (the sixth pitch). Crossing the barline into a new measure cancels the effect of the previous sharp sign; consequently, the sixth pitch would be performed D♮. To specify a D♯ for the seventh pitch, the composer must repeat the sharp sign.

César Franck, *Les Eolides*

EXERCISE 3-2

Fundamental Skills

Identifying Half Steps
and Whole Steps

Identify each interval as a half step or a whole step (use "H" for "half" and "W" for "whole").

1.

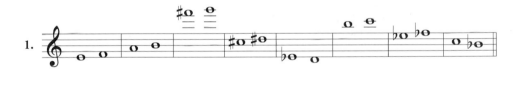

2.

3.

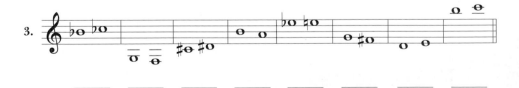

EXERCISE 3-3

Fundamental Skills

Notating Half Steps
and Whole Steps

Write half steps or whole steps *above* the given pitches. In the blanks, provide the letter names of both pitches. Remember that in letter-name notation, the accidental follows the letter (F♯, B♭, and so on).

Ab Bb _____ _____ _____ _____ _____ _____ _____ _____ _____ _____
Whole   Half   Whole   Half   Half   Whole

Whole   Half   Whole   Half   Half   Whole

Write whole steps or half steps *below* the given pitches.

Whole   Half   Whole   Half   Half   Whole

Whole   Half   Whole   Half   Half   Whole

In the following compositions, identify circled intervals as whole steps or half steps.

W. A. Mozart, Sonata, K. 332 (Transposed)

Eddie Miller/ Dub Williams/ Robert Yount, "Please Release Me"

Elizabeth Jacquet de la Guerre, Suite in A Minor

Paul Hindemith, *Ludus Tonalis*

EXERCISE 3-4 ━━━━━━━━━━━━━━━━━━━━━━━━━━━━━━━━━━━━━━

Musicianship Skills

KEYBOARD: Half Steps and Whole Steps

Locate the two pitches of each whole step or half step in Skill Exercise 3-3. Perform each interval at the keyboard. If the first pitch is a white key, use the right thumb and forefinger ascending and the left thumb and forefinger descending. If the first pitch is a black key, use the right or left third and index fingers ascending or descending.

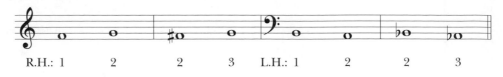

R.H.: 1   2   2   3   L.H.: 1   2   2   3

EXERCISE 3-5 ━━━━━━━━━━━━━━━━━━━━━━━━━━━━━━━━━━━━━━

Musicianship Skills

EAR TRAINING: Hearing Whole Steps
and Half Steps

A. You will hear a series of ascending and descending intervals for identification. As before, cover the answer with a mask; listen to the interval, identify it, then check your answer.

RECORDED EXAMPLE 3
TRACK 5
Whole and Half Steps

Identify the interval by writing either "H" (for half step) or "W" (for whole step) in the blank. Check your answer, then move to the next frame. Most of the intervals in these four lines are half steps. Listen for an interval that sounds different; these are the whole steps.

Predominantly Half Steps

1. ____ H   ____ H   ____ W   ____ H   ____ H   ____ W   ____ H   ____ H

2. ____ H   ____ H   ____ H   ____ H   ____ W   ____ H   ____ W   ____ H

3. ____ H   ____ H   ____ W   ____ H   ____ W   ____ H   ____ H   ____ W

4. ____ H   ____ H   ____ H   ____ W   ____ H   ____ W   ____ H   ____ H

B. These lines are predominantly whole steps, although at least two half steps appear in each line. Identify the interval as before ("W" or "H").

Predominantly Whole Steps

1. _____ W _____ W _____ W _____ H _____ W _____ W _____ H _____ W

2. _____ W _____ H _____ W _____ H _____ W _____ H _____ W _____ H

3. _____ W _____ H _____ W _____ W _____ W _____ H _____ W _____ W

4. _____ W _____ H _____ H _____ W _____ W _____ W _____ H _____ W

C. The final set includes whole steps and half steps in equal numbers. Identify the interval heard.

Whole Steps and Half Steps

1. _____ W _____ H _____ W _____ H _____ H _____ W _____ H _____ H

2. _____ H _____ H _____ W _____ H _____ W _____ H _____ W _____ H

3. _____ H _____ H _____ W _____ W _____ H _____ H _____ W _____ H

4. _____ W _____ H _____ H _____ W _____ W _____ H _____ H _____ W

Double Sharps and Double Flats

Basic pitches can be raised or lowered a whole step through the DOUBLE SHARP (✗) or DOUBLE FLAT (♭♭) signs. Whereas C♯ is played on the black key above C, C–double sharp (C✗) lies yet another half step higher—the same key used for D.

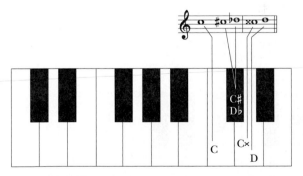

The pitch C♭ is produced by the white key below C (the same one used for B); C–double flat (C♭♭) is found yet another half step lower—the black key also used for B♭.

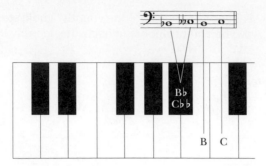

Enharmonic Equivalents

Although the pitches D, D♯, and D♭ all produce different sounds, the same sound can be notated on the staff in a number of ways. Notice, for example, that D♭ is produced by the same key earlier labeled C♯. Obviously, since the two pitches employ the same key, the sounds are identical.

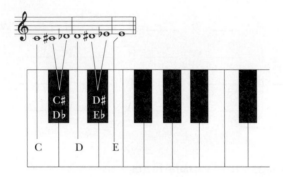

Equivalent pitches such as C♯ and D♭, which *sound the same* but are *notated differently,* are known as ENHARMONICS. Another pair of enharmonic equivalents, F♯ and G♭, is identified below. These two pitches are the same in sound but are written in different places on the staff.

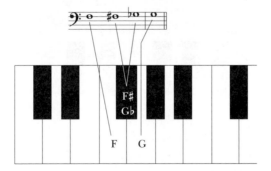

The pitch F♯ is produced by the black key just above F; F♭, however, is a white key—the one just below F, which was identified earlier as the note E. The pitches E and F♭, therefore, are enharmonics. Similarly, E♯ and F are enharmonics. Remember that natural half steps exist between E and F and between B and C.

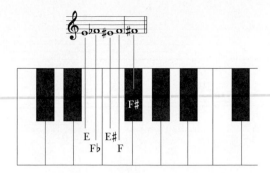

EXERCISE 3-6

Fundamental Skills

Enharmonic Equivalents

A. For each pitch given, provide one enharmonic equivalent. In some cases, more than one answer will be correct. Use the blanks to identify the letter names of the two pitches.

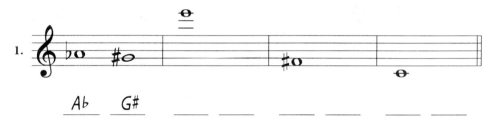

1.

A♭   G♯

2.

3.
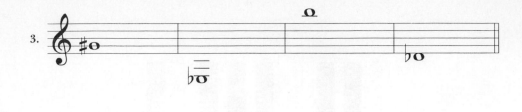

4.
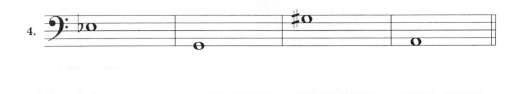

B. Some of these pairs of pitches are enharmonic equivalents; others are not. Circle enharmonic note pairs. Identify all pitches.

1.
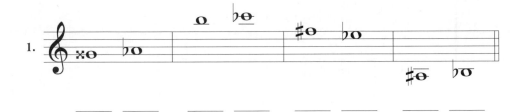

2.
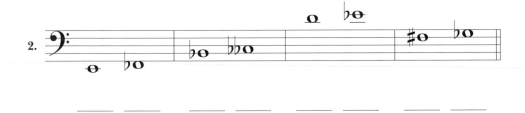

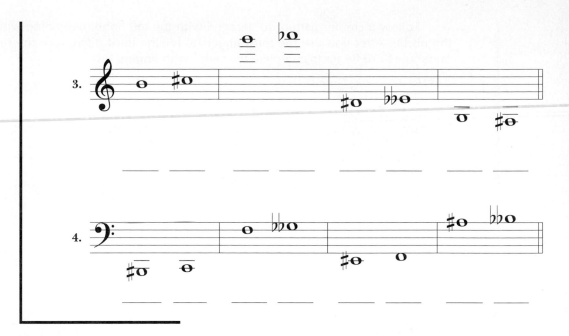

EXERCISE 3-7 ━━━━━━━━━━━━━━━━━━━━━━━━━━━━━━━━━━━━━━

Musicianship Skills

KEYBOARD: Descending Patterns

In Skill Exercise 3-1 you learned and practiced ascending stepwise keyboard patterns. Now reverse the process and descend, beginning with the right little finger (5) and using the fourth (4), third (3), and second fingers (2) for the second, third, and fourth pitches, respectively. When you have played the fifth pitch with your thumb (1), turn your third finger over the thumb to play the last three pitches (3–1).

Right-Hand Fingering Pattern: Descending

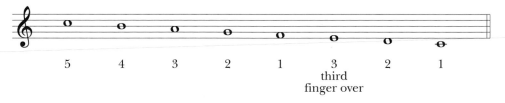

Follow a similar pattern to descend with the left hand, beginning with the thumb (1). After you use the third finger (3) for the third pitch, turn the thumb under the third finger to complete the series with fingers 1–5.

Left-Hand Fingering Pattern: Descending

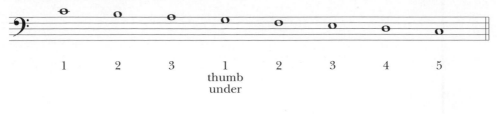

SIGHT SINGING: Whole Steps, Half Steps, and Octaves

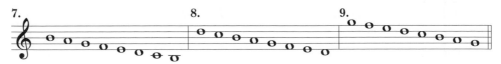

EXERCISE 3-8

Musicianship Skills

SIGHT SINGING: Whole Steps, Half Steps, and Octaves

Play the first note of the interval at the keyboard; match this pitch vocally on a neutral syllable ("la," perhaps), then sing the complete interval. Play both pitches to check your accuracy and repeat the performance several times if necessary. Continue to the second interval and perform it as before. You may need to sing an octave (or two) higher or lower than the pitches notated.

Octaves

Half Steps

3.

4.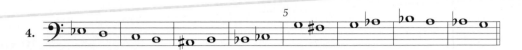

5.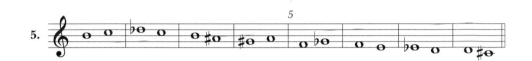

6.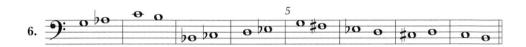

Whole Steps

7.

8.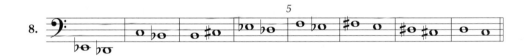

9.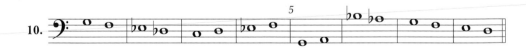

10.

Whole Steps and Half Steps

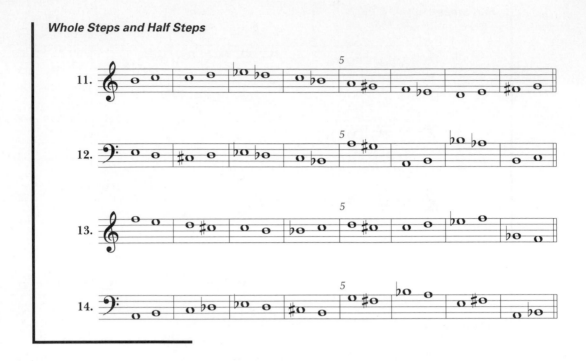

OCTAVE DESIGNATION

As we discussed, each pitch name appears in several different places on the keyboard. These pitches are one or more octaves apart. To avoid the confusion that might result from different notes having exactly the same letter name, a system of OCTAVE DESIGNATION is used to specify an exact octave range. Several systems of octave designation are in use today; the one presented here, recommended by the American Society of Acoustics, has become the most widely used.

The lowest pitch in each octave is C. "Middle C," at the center of the piano keyboard, is identified as "C_4." Other pitches in the same octave are identified with the appropriate uppercase letter and the subscript "4."

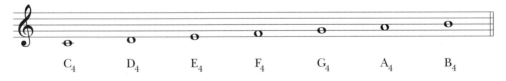

After the pitch B_4, the next higher pitch is C_5, the lowest note in the "C-five" octave. Octaves above C_5 are identified as C_6, C_7, and C_8, respectively.

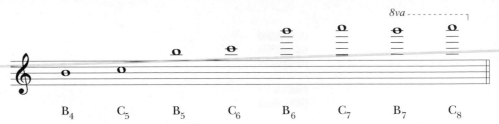

$$B_4 \qquad C_5 \qquad B_5 \qquad C_6 \qquad B_6 \qquad C_7 \qquad B_7 \qquad C_8$$

The pitch an octave below C_4 ("middle C") is C_3. The "C-three" octave extends up to B_3 and includes all the pitches in between.

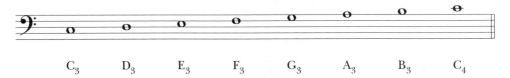

$$C_3 \qquad D_3 \qquad E_3 \qquad F_3 \qquad G_3 \qquad A_3 \qquad B_3 \qquad C_4$$

The octaves below C_3 are C_2 and C_1, respectively. The lowest three notes on the standard piano keyboard are designated B_0, $B\flat_0$, and A_0.

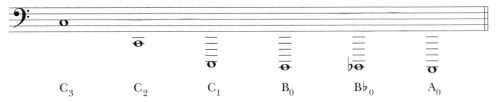

$$C_3 \qquad\qquad C_2 \qquad\qquad C_1 \qquad\qquad B_0 \qquad\qquad B\flat_0 \qquad\qquad A_0$$

When speaking about specific octave ranges, musicians usually say "C-four" (C_4) or "B-three" (B_3). An entire octave can be identified by reference to the lowest pitch: "the C-two (C_2) octave" or "the C-six (C_6) octave," for example.

$$C_2 \text{ Octave} \qquad\qquad\qquad\qquad C_6 \text{ Octave}$$

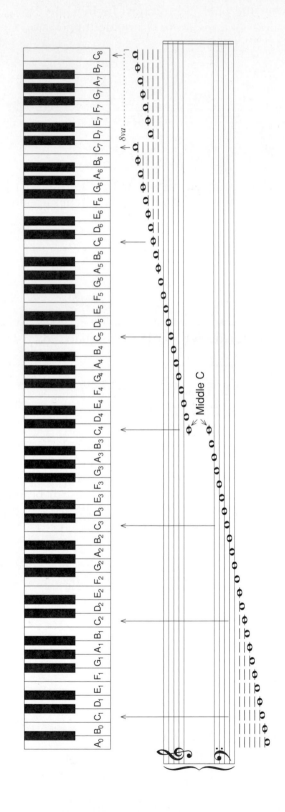

EXERCISE 3-9

Fundamental Skills

Octave Designations

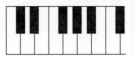

Identify the pitches by letter name and octave designation.

1.

2.

3.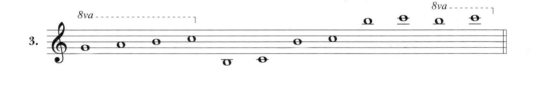

4.

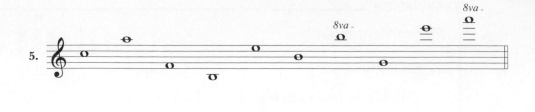

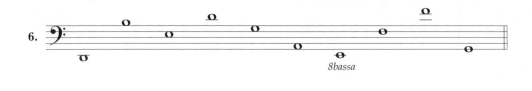

In the following compositions, identify the pitches by letter name and octave designation.

7.   Jean Phillippe Rameau, Gigue

Identify only the pitches where blanks appear. Provide pitch name and octave designation.

Josephine Lang, "God, Be Merciful to Me, a Sinner"

George Frideric Handel, Sonata for Flute

EXERCISE 3-10 ───

Fundamental Skills

Notation in Specific Octaves

Write eighth notes as indicated by pitch name and octave designation. Use ledger lines and add accidentals if necessary. Check for proper stem direction and flag placement.

1.

A_2 $E\flat_4$ D_3 B_3 $F\sharp_1$ G_2 F_2 E_2 $G\sharp_5$ C_2 $D\sharp_2$

2.

F_6 E_4 C_5 B_3 $F\sharp_5$ A_7 D_4 B_5 $D\flat_4$ F_3 $C\sharp_6$

3.

A_2 B_4 $F\sharp_2$ C_3 $D\sharp_1$ $B\flat_0$ D_4 E_2 $E\flat_4$ $B\flat_2$ $G\sharp_4$

EXERCISE 3-11 ───

Fundamental Skills

Intervals and Octave Designations

A. Study the specifications for each item below, then *provide an appropriate clef* and notate the pitch requested, writing the pitch name in the blank (including the octave designation). Write *only* the specified pitch; perform any "calculations" in your head or on a separate sheet. In some cases, more than one answer will be correct and either the treble or the bass clef will be practical. Use the octave sign for pitches in the extreme upper or lower register.

1. An octave above G_3
2. A whole step above C_6
3. A whole step below $D\flat_5$
4. A half step below E_3
5. An enharmonic equivalent for B_2
6. An enharmonic equivalent for $F\sharp_5$
7. A half step below $A\flat_4$
8. A half step below $E\flat_1$
9. An octave below D_3
10. An octave below $G\sharp_5$

(Provide an appropriate clef.)

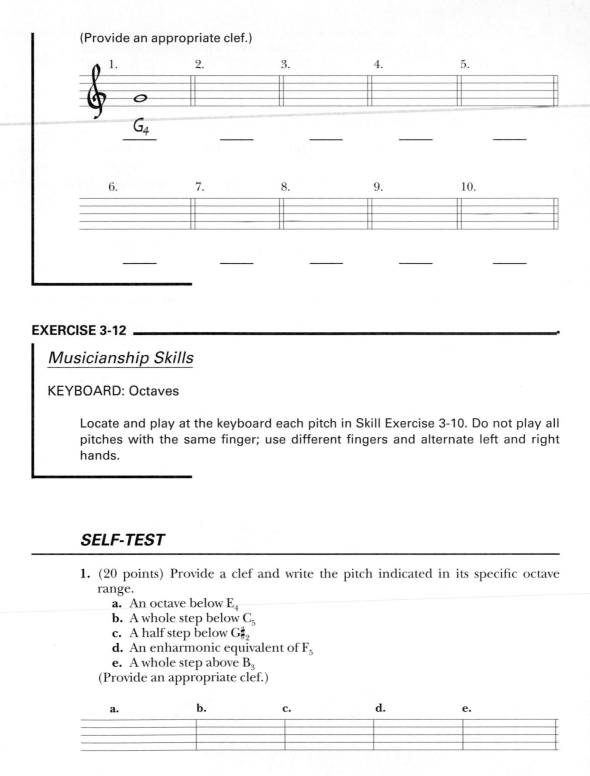

EXERCISE 3-12

Musicianship Skills

KEYBOARD: Octaves

Locate and play at the keyboard each pitch in Skill Exercise 3-10. Do not play all pitches with the same finger; use different fingers and alternate left and right hands.

SELF-TEST

1. (20 points) Provide a clef and write the pitch indicated in its specific octave range.
   a. An octave below E_4
   b. A whole step below C_5
   c. A half step below $G\sharp_2$
   d. An enharmonic equivalent of F_5
   e. A whole step above B_3
   (Provide an appropriate clef.)

2. (20 points) Add an accidental (sharp, flat, or natural) to the second pitch to make the given interval a half step or a whole step as suggested.

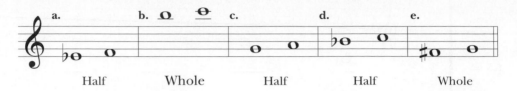

Half   Whole   Half   Half   Whole

3. (20 points) Circle any pitch in each group of three that is *not* an enharmonic equivalent of the first pitch.

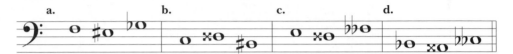

4. (20 points) Identify circled intervals in this passage as whole steps or half steps.

Medieval Song, "If My Face Is Pale"

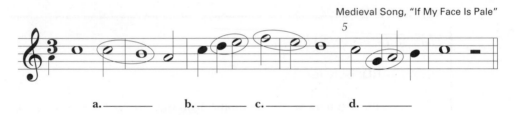

a. _____   b. _____   c. _____   d. _____

5. (20 points) Locate the given pitches on or above the keyboard by writing the pitch name on the appropriate key.

1. D
2. F𝄪
3. G♯
4. E
5. C♭

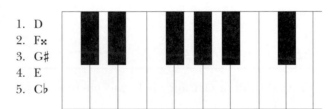

SUPPLEMENTARY STUDIES

Drill Exercises

1. Write the pitch name that forms the designated interval with the note name given. Considering enharmonic equivalents, two or more answers will be correct in each case.

Half Step Above

a. F _____   B♭ _____   C _____   G♯ _____   E _____   A♭ _____

b. D♯ _____   C _____   G _____   F♯ _____   A _____   B _____

Half Step Below

c. C♯ _____   G♭ _____   F _____   D♯ _____   B♭ _____   G _____

d. E♯ _____   A _____   G♯ _____   F _____   C _____   B _____

Whole Step Above

e. C♯ _____   G♭ _____   F _____   D♯ _____   B♭ _____   G _____

f. E♯ _____   A _____   G♯ _____   F _____   C _____   B _____

Whole Step Below

g. G♯ _____   A _____   F♭ _____   D _____   E♭ _____   C _____

h. F _____   C♭ _____   A♯ _____   E _____   B _____   D♯ _____

2. Many of the following pitches include ledger lines or employ the octave sign. Identify each with letter name and octave designation.

a.

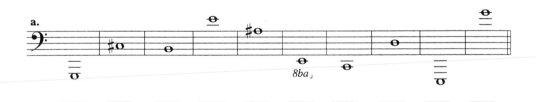

b.

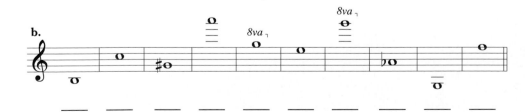

Fundamental Skills in Practice

3. Determining the kinds of intervals present in a melody can tell you a great deal about the music itself. The following melodies include whole steps, half steps, and other intervals that will be discussed later. Locate pitches that lie a half step or a whole step apart and mark them appropriately. Leave other intervals unmarked, then total intervals in the three categories: "whole step," "half step," and "other."

a.   Frédéric Chopin, Prelude, Op. 28

Whole: _____
Half: _____
Other: _____

b.   Anton Bruckner, Symphony No. 7

Whole: _____
Half: _____
Other: _____

c.   Nigerian Folk Song, "I Will Feed My Baby"

Whole: _____
Half: _____
Other: _____

CHAPTER 4

Simple Meters

ESSENTIAL TERMS

- alla breve
- *anacrusis*
- *barline*
- *beat division*
- *beat subdivision*
- *duple meter*
- *measure*
- *meter*

- *quadruple meter*
- *simple division*
- *syncopation*
- *tempo*
- *time signature*
- *transcription*
- *triple meter*

Western music moves in organized series of strong and weak beats. The speed of the beat within a pattern, the TEMPO, may vary from slow to fast, but the beat itself is persistent and inflexible. Although some other cultures prefer distinct groupings of as many as thirty-two beats, we in the West have been content with patterns of two, three, and four beats.

In Chapter 1, we discussed notes and rests as receiving one, two, three, or more beats. You may have gotten the impression, therefore, that all beats are of equal importance. Actually, all beats are *not* equal; some have a more important role than others. Just as the word "not" was italicized in the previous sentence so that you would give it more stress when reading, some beats in music are emphasized, or accented. An ACCENT is a musical stress. There are several types of accent, but the most important in rhythm is *metric accent*.

METRIC ACCENT

Traditional Western music is based on recurring patterns of strong and weak beats called METER. The accents that create different meters are called METRIC ACCENTS. You can feel the effect of meter by singing the beat on a single pitch or counting aloud with a steady pulse. Count "one-two" four times, for example. Speak more loudly on the count of "one" than on the count of "two." This is the effect of a meter with two beats: one strong, the other weak. Notice that the barline, introduced earlier, is used to separate MEASURES, or groups of beats (two beats in this case).

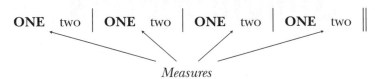

Measures

Next, experience a meter with a three-beat pattern: strong-weak-weak. Again, say or sing at least four of these groups. Stress the metric accent on the first beat of each measure.

ONE two three │ **ONE** two three │ **ONE** two three │ **ONE** two three ‖

Triple Meter

The three-beat (strong-weak-weak) pattern above is known as TRIPLE METER. As you learned earlier, we can notate music using notes of any value to represent the beat. The two lines here, for example, would be performed identically.

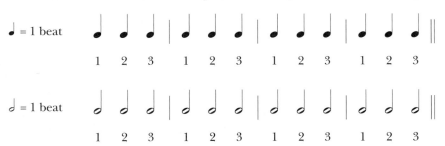

Anacrusis. Many melodies you probably know from childhood are in triple meter. Some, such as "Oh Where, Oh Where Has My Little Dog Gone?", begin with an incomplete pattern called an ANACRUSIS or a PICKUP. The final measure contains the missing portion of the first measure. A single, unaccented beat begins "Oh Where, Oh Where Has My Little Dog Gone?" (notated on page 83). The two remaining beats from the first measure appear at the end (beats 2 and 3).

Oh **WHERE,** oh **WHERE** has my **LIT** - tle dog **GONE?** Oh **WHERE,** oh

WHERE can he **BE?** _____

When a half-note beat is used, only the appearance of the notation is different; a performance would sound exactly the same.

Oh **WHERE,** oh **WHERE** has my **LIT** - tle dog **GONE?** Oh **WHERE,** oh

WHERE can he **BE?** _____

RECORDED EXAMPLE 4

TRACK 8
"Oh Where, Oh Where Has My Little Dog Gone?"

Listen to "Oh Where, Oh Where Has My Little Dog Gone?" (Recorded Example 4). As you read either of the notated lines above, sing along with the recording and feel the triple meter.

Duple Meter

Although many popular songs are written in triple meter, others have a strong-weak, or DUPLE, pattern. Duple and triple are the two basic meters of traditional Western rhythmic structure. In both, the first pulse of each group is accented.

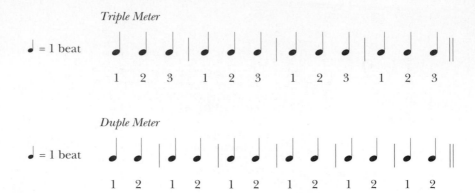

Triple Meter

♩ = 1 beat

1 2 3 1 2 3 1 2 3 1 2 3

Duple Meter

♩ = 1 beat

1 2 1 2 1 2 1 2 1 2 1 2

You probably know the French folk song "Frère Jacques" ("Are You Sleeping, Brother John?"). This melody is often written in a duple meter and without an anacrusis, as shown here.

ARE you **SLEEP**-ing, **ARE** you **SLEEP**-ing, **BRO**-ther **JOHN** - **BRO**-ther **JOHN?**

RECORDED EXAMPLE 5
TRACK 9
"Brother John"

Follow the notation as you listen to Recorded Example 5. Sing along with the performance and feel the accents of duple meter.

Quadruple Meter

Although the two basic metric patterns in Western music are duple (strong-weak) and triple (strong-weak-weak), some melodies are written in QUADRUPLE METER—in which there are four beats in each measure. The difference between two duple patterns and one quadruple pattern is subtle but important. The third beat of two consecutive duple patterns has exactly the same accent as the first beat. In a quadruple pattern, however, the third beat is emphasized, but less so than the first. The symbol (–) is used to indicate this semi-strong accent on the third beat of a quadruple meter.

Duple   *Quadruple*

Strong accents   Strong accent   Lesser accent

The song we know as "Twinkle, Twinkle, Little Star" might be written in either duple or quadruple meter. Sing the melody both ways, performing the accents very carefully to feel the differences between the two versions.

Duple

TWIN-kle, TWIN-kle, LIT-tle STAR_, HOW I WON-der WHAT you ARE_.

Quadruple

TWIN-kle, TWIN-kle, LIT-tle STAR_, HOW I WON-der WHAT you ARE_.

RECORDED EXAMPLE 6
TRACK 10
"Twinkle, Twinkle"

Play Recorded Example 6 at least twice. The first time through, follow the duple-meter notation above. On the second playing, sing along with the quadruple-meter version.

Full Measures of Rest

Composers and music editors use the whole rest to indicate a full measure of silence in *any* meter and with *any* unit of beat. Thus, the whole rest is appropriate in duple and triple, as well as in quadruple meter. This is true without regard to the particular note that serves as the unit of beat. Using a dotted-half rest for a silent measure in ¾ or a half rest for a measure of ² is *incorrect* since the whole rest is preferred in any meter.

Correct   Incorrect   Correct   Incorrect   Correct

EXERCISE 4-1

Fundamental Skills

Using Duple, Triple, and Quadruple Meters

A. Study the following series of notes; then use barlines to divide each line into measures of two, three, or four beats each as indicated.

TRIPLE METER

1.

G. F. Handel, *Fantasia*

L. van Beethoven, Symphony No. 9

DUPLE METER

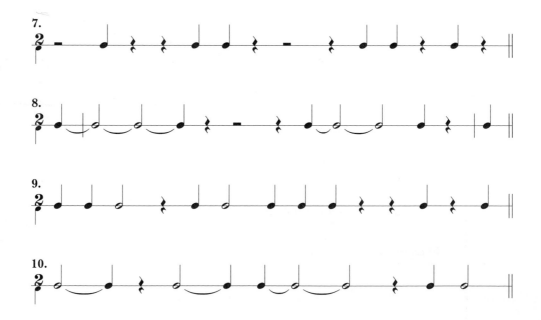

11.   Darius Milhaud, *Creation of the World*

© *1923 Editions Max Eschig. Used By Permission. Sole Representative U.S.A. Theodore Presser Company.*

12.   Roy Harris, Symphony No. 3

QUADRUPLE METER

13.

14.

15.

16.

17.   Jean Sibelius, *King Christian Suite*

18.   Felix Mendelssohn, Fantasy

B. Incomplete Measures. One or more measures in each line is incomplete. Supply *one note* that will complete any measure with fewer than the designated number of beats. (Remember: Some measures are complete as they are.)

TRIPLE METER

1.

2.

DUPLE METER

3.

4.

Continue as before, but add one appropriate *rest* value rather than a note.

QUADRUPLE METER

5.

6.

EXERCISE 4-2

Fundamental Skills

Notating Rhythmic Patterns

A. Complete the following brief rhythmic compositions in duple, triple, and quadruple meters. The first measure is given; provide seven additional measures that are repetitions or variations of the given note or notes. You might vary ♩ ♩, for example, with ♩ ♩ or ♩. Use notes and rests of one or more beats in duration. (Do not use divided-beat patterns at this point.)

DUPLE METER

QUADRUPLE METER

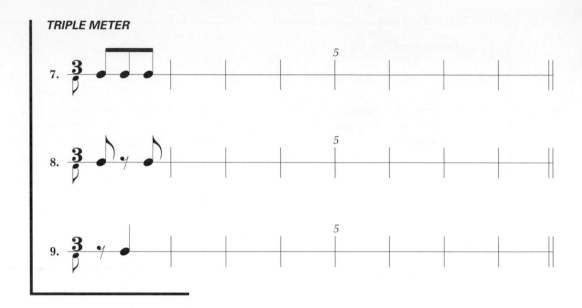

TRIPLE METER

7.
8.
9.

BEAT DIVISION

When composers use notes shorter than one beat, they must divide the beat. In SIMPLE BEAT DIVISION, the beat divides into *two* equal parts.[1] A quarter-note beat, for example, divides into two equal eighth notes.

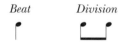

Beat   *Division*

The song "Grandfather's Clock" features a division of the quarter-note beat in a duple meter. The word "grand" receives a full beat; the syllables "fa-" and "ther's," however, share an equally divided beat.

♩ = 1 beat

My   grand – fa- ther's   clock   was too   large   for the   shelf,

If the half note is assigned the value of one beat, the simple division is into two quarter notes.

𝅗𝅥 = 1 beat

Beat   *Division*

---

[1]Compound meter, in which the beat divides into three parts, is discussed in Chapter 5.

Just as effectively, "Grandfather's Clock" could be written using a half-note beat with a simple division into two quarter notes.

Finally, note the *appearance* of the rhythms when the eighth note is assigned the value of one beat and the sixteenth note is the division.

RECORDED EXAMPLE 7

TRACK 11

Simple Beat Division: "Grandfather's Clock"

Listen to "Grandfather's Clock" (Recorded Example 7) several times, following the notation below. First, just sing along and feel the duple meter. Next, tap the beat. Try to hear the division of the beat that occurs in nearly every measure. Finally, tap the beat *division* while you sing or follow along with the notation.

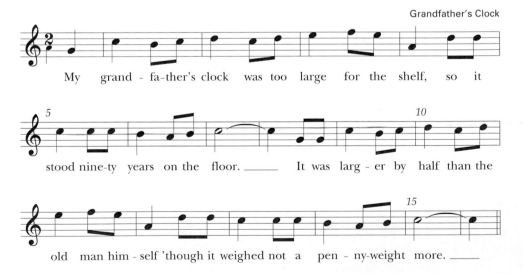

Grandfather's Clock

EXERCISE 4-3 ────────────────────────────────────

Fundamental Skills

Using the Beat Division

A. For each unit of beat given, provide the two notes that make the simple beat division.

B. Provide barlines for the following passages. For those that begin with an anacrusis, the final barline is provided.

TRIPLE METER

César Cui, *The Statue at Czarskoe-Selo*

Felix Mendelssohn, *St. Paul*

DUPLE METER

Giacomo Puccini, *Manon Lescaut*

7.

Sergei Prokofiev, *Romeo and Juliet*

8.

QUADRUPLE METER

9.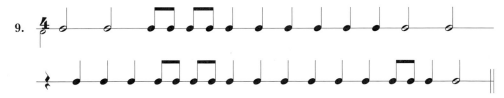

10.

Stevie Wonder, "I Just Called to Say I Love You"

11.

Arcangelo Corelli, Concerto Grosso

12.

Beat Subdivision

Composers sometimes need notes even smaller than those of the beat division. In that case, the division itself can be SUBDIVIDED into two equal parts. If the half note is the beat, for example, the beat division is two quarter notes; the quarter notes *subdivide* into four eighth notes.

The same principle applies when other notes receive the beat. Notice here the simple division and subdivision of the whole-note and eighth-note beats.

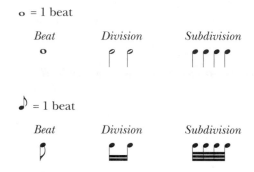

You probably know the folk song "Old MacDonald Had a Farm" (Recorded Example 8). This melody features an interesting mixture of beat, divided-beat, and subdivided-beat units. The meter is duple, and in the notation given below, the quarter note receives one beat.

| RECORDED EXAMPLE 8 TRACK 12 Simple Beat Subdivision: "Old MacDonald" | Listen to Recorded Example 8 ("Old MacDonald") at least three times. Follow the score and tap or sing the beat (quarter note) the first time through. On the second playing, tap the beat division (two eighth notes to the beat). Finally, listen again and tap the beat subdivision (four sixteenth notes to the beat). |

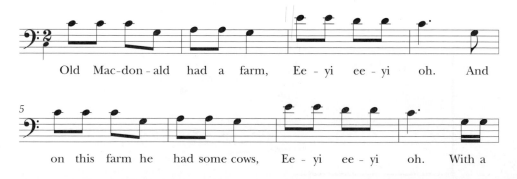

Moo moo here and a Moo moo there, Here a moo there a moo,

Ev-ery where a moo moo Old Mac-don-ald had a farm, Ee-yi ee-yi oh.

EXERCISE 4-4

Fundamental Skills

Notating the Beat, the Division,
and the Subdivision

A. Make a chart that shows the division and the subdivisions of the given beats. The division, of course, will be two notes; the subdivision, four.

Beat	*Division*	*Subdivision*
♪	_____	_____
o	_____	_____
♩	_____	_____
♪	_____	_____
♩	_____	_____

B. Incomplete Measures. Some measures in the following lines are incomplete. As directed, add a note or a rest (it may be dotted or simple) to complete any measure with fewer than the specified number of beats.

Add a note to incomplete measures.

DUPLE METER

TRIPLE METER

Add a rest to incomplete measures.

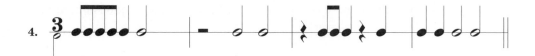

QUADRUPLE METER

SIMPLE TIME SIGNATURES

Through notation, composers give performers a good deal of information about the rhythmic structure of a composition: the note that gets one beat, for example, and the number of beats in a measure. To this point in the text, we have used written-out indications such as "♩ = 1 beat" and "duple meter." We have also employed icons such as 𝄾, 𝄾, and 𝄾 to designate two, three, and four beats per measure, and the quarter-note, eighth-note, and half-note beats, respectively. In effect, you already know quite a bit about simple time signatures.

The TIME (or METER) SIGNATURE consists of two numerals placed at the beginning of the composition.

A time signature comprises an upper and a lower numeral. The upper numeral conveys the metric pattern (duple, triple, quadruple, and so on); the lower numeral designates the note that is to receive one beat. If the quarter note gets one beat, the lower numeral is 4; if an eighth-note or a half-note beat is desired, the lower numerals are 8 and 2, respectively.

Observe the information conveyed by these time signatures:

2/4 = Duple meter   **3/8** = Triple meter   **4/2** = Quadruple meter

2/4 = Quarter-note beat   **3/8** = Eighth-note beat   **4/2** = Half-note beat

EXERCISE 4-5

Fundamental Skills

Simple Time Signatures

A. For each time signature shown, write a word representing the accent pattern (duple, triple, or quadruple) in the first blank. In the second blank, write the actual note that will receive one beat.

1. **3/4** _____TRIPLE_____ ♩   4. **2/4** _____ ____

2. **2/2** _____ ____   5. **4/4** _____ ____

3. **3/8** _____ ____   6. **2/16** _____ ____

7. $\frac{4}{8}$ _____ _____   9. $\frac{4}{2}$ _____ _____

8. $\frac{3}{2}$ _____ _____   10. $\frac{3}{16}$ _____ ____

B. Write a time signature that corresponds to the accent pattern and unit of beat given.

1. _____ Triple meter
Eighth-note beat

2. _____ Duple meter
Eighth-note beat

3. _____ Triple meter
Half-note beat

4. _____ Quadruple meter
Sixteenth-note beat

5. _____ Duple meter
Quarter-note beat

6. _____ Quadruple meter
Eighth-note beat

7. _____ Triple meter
Quarter-note beat

8. _____ Duple meter
Half-note beat

Classification of Simple Meters

Meters are classified according to the accent pattern and the manner of beat division. The meter represented by the time signature $\frac{2}{4}$, for example, is classified as duple-simple,[2] since the accent pattern is duple and the beat division is simple. A meter such as $\frac{3}{8}$ is classified as triple-simple, and $\frac{4}{2}$ is quadruple-simple.

   Alla Breve and Common Time. Sometimes symbols are used to represent certain meters. The meter $\frac{2}{2}$, for example, is often designated by the symbol ¢; this meter is termed *alla breve* (or, less formally, "cut time"). The letter **C**, in reference to common time, is often used as an equivalent for $\frac{4}{4}$.

Counting Rhythms

Counting rhythms with a system of syllables will help you in performance. Several counting systems are available, but the one suggested here has many advantages. Notes that fall on the beat are counted according to the corresponding number in the accent pattern ("one," "two," and so on).

RECORDED EXAMPLE 9
TRACK 13
Counting Rhythms

   Listen to Recorded Example 9 as you study the counting syllables. The symbol ‖, shown in these lines, indicates that the entire passage is repeated from the beginning.

One Two   One Two

One Two Three   One Two Three

---

[2]In many sources, the order of terms is reversed: simple-duple, simple-triple, and so on.

If a note lasts for more than one beat, if it is tied across the barline, or if a rest falls on the beat, the counting is silent.

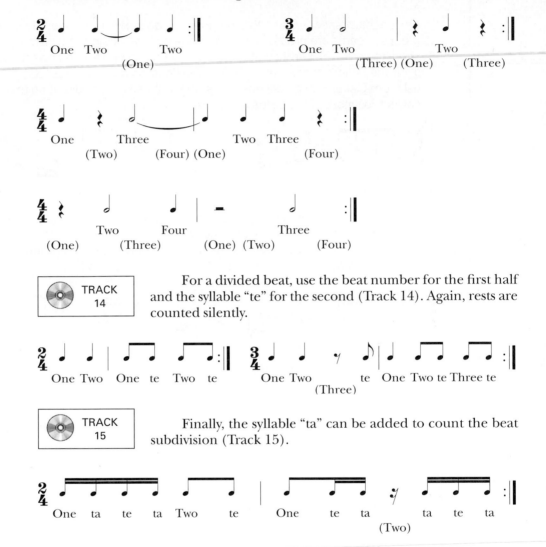

For a divided beat, use the beat number for the first half and the syllable "te" for the second (Track 14). Again, rests are counted silently.

Finally, the syllable "ta" can be added to count the beat subdivision (Track 15).

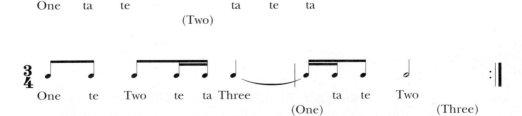

Guidelines for Beaming

As we discussed earlier, the purpose of beaming is to identify beat groups. Beams are placed about an octave above or below the noteheads and should be thicker than stems.* For ascending or descending groups, slant the beams in the direction of the melodic motion. Adhere to individual stem-placement guidelines if possible, but use a stem direction that is correct for *most* of the notes in the group.

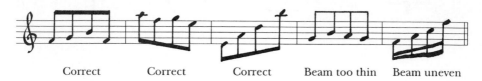

Correct   Correct   Correct   Beam too thin   Beam uneven

In simple meters with quarter-note beat, groups of two eighth notes and four sixteenth notes are commonly beamed. Likewise, beat groups are beamed even with mixed eighth and sixteenth notes. If a group does not begin on the beat, however, beaming is rarely appropriate.

Correct   Correct   Correct   Incorrect   Incorrect

Groups constituting fewer than one beat are rarely beamed unless a dotted note precedes or follows the group.

Incorrect   Correct   Correct

Although groups of a half beat are often beamed, the complete beat unit is usually identified if practical. In a triple meter, a group of notes that fills a measure is often beamed.

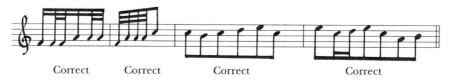

Correct   Correct   Correct   Correct

*See page 28 for information on the proper placement of stems.

Conducting.   You will find traditional conducting patterns helpful in performing rhythms. Conduct with your right hand and keep the beat relatively high—usually no lower than chest level. The first beat of any metric pattern is down; other motions depend upon the accent pattern. The process of arm motion (whether smooth or more jerky, for example) depends upon the style of the music. Finally, ensemble members discern the tempo through the conductor's preparatory beat or beats. These precede the actual first note of music. Study the conducting patterns shown here and practice them until they are familiar.

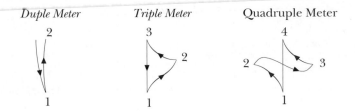

SYNCOPATION

When composers select an accent pattern and make other choices about metric structure, they still must achieve variety in rhythm. One means of varying the rhythmic element is through SYNCOPATION—the intentional misplacement of accents.

In a quadruple-simple meter, there is a strong accent on the first beat, a lesser one on the third beat. These are the natural metric accents. If the emphasis is suddenly shifted to the second and/or fourth beats, however, the effect is invigorating.

The misplacement of accents that creates a syncopated effect can be accomplished in several ways, including note length.

Note Length. When a longer note appears between shorter ones (especially if the longer note is twice the value of the shorter ones), the natural metric accents are disrupted. The following patterns are some of those most often associated with the term "syncopation" in simple meters.

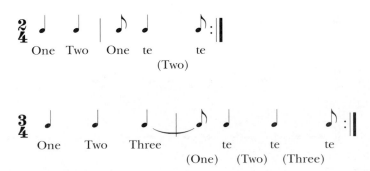

RECORDED EXAMPLE 10

TRACK 16

Syncopation: "You're a Grand Old Flag"

The song "You're a Grand Old Flag" features a distinctive syncopation figure. Listen to two versions of this tune on Recorded Example 10. In the first version, syncopation appears on the words "high FLY-ing flag." The melody begins with an anacrusis.

George M. Cohan

You're a   *GRAND*   old   FLAG   you're a   HIGH *FLY* - ing FLAG

Had the composer, George M. Cohan, chosen natural metric accents, he might have written the passage as follows (second recorded version).

You're a   *GRAND* old   FLAG you're a   *HIGH*   fly - ing FLAG

Without the syncopated "kick" of the original rhythm, however, "You're a Grand Old Flag" is limp and predictable. Skillful composers use strategically placed devices like syncopation to create interest within a traditional meter.

EXERCISE 4-6

Musicianship Skills

RHYTHMIC READING: Simple Meters

Sing each line of music using counting syllables. Conduct as you perform. The syllables have been written under the first two lines; you may want to add them to other lines as well.

DUPLE METER

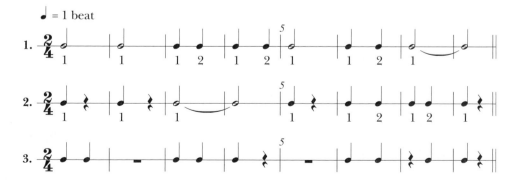

TRIPLE METER

QUADRUPLE METER

EXERCISES WITH SYNCOPATIONS

ENSEMBLES

Ensemble performance poses problems completely different from those encountered when you sing or play alone. The following exercises are intended to be performed by individuals or groups (or perhaps one or more soloists accompanied by a group). There are no tempo or other performance directions, so feel free to add your own.

1.

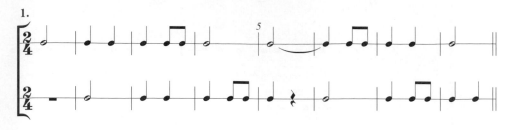

2.

3.

EXERCISE 4-7

Musicianship Skills

EAR TRAINING: Meter Identification

A. (Not Recorded) Your instructor will play a number of melodies. Cover the answer portion of the page, listen to the melody, and identify the meter as "duple" or "triple" by writing that word in the blank (for present purposes, duple and quadruple will be considered equivalent). Check your answer and move to the next frame.

1. _____	duple	**5.** _____	triple
2. _____	duple	**6.** _____	duple
3. _____	duple	**7.** _____	duple
4. _____	triple	**8.** _____	triple

B. Sing the following tunes to yourself and identify the meter as before. If you do not know one or more of these melodies, choose another that you do know and identify its meter.

1. The Star-Spangled Banner   _____

2. Mary Had a Little Lamb   _____

3. Amazing Grace   _____

4. Moon River   _____

5. Yankee Doodle   _____

6. The Marines' Hymn   _____

7. America   _____

8. Happy Birthday to You   _____

SELF-TEST

1. (20 points) The two lines below have no meter signature. Study the beat grouping and determine (1) the accent pattern (duple, triple, or quadruple) and (2) the note representing the beat. More than one answer may be correct.

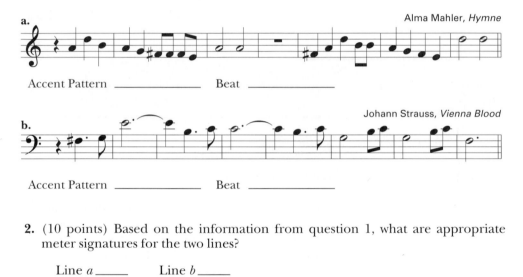

a.   Alma Mahler, *Hymne*

Accent Pattern _____   Beat _____

                                           Johann Strauss, *Vienna Blood*

b.

Accent Pattern _____   Beat _____

2. (10 points) Based on the information from question 1, what are appropriate meter signatures for the two lines?

    Line *a* _____   Line *b* _____

3. (30 points) Given the following meters, write the note receiving the beat, the two that form the beat division, and the four that represent the beat subdivision.

Meter	*Beat*	*Division*	*Subdivision*
a. $\frac{2}{4}$	_____	_____	_____
b. $\frac{3}{2}$	_____	_____	_____
c. $\math혁{C}$	_____	_____	_____
d. $\frac{3}{8}$	_____	_____	_____
e. $\frac{4}{4}$	_____	_____	_____

4. (40 points) Provide barlines for the following passages.

a.

Johannes Brahms, *Love Song*

b.

W. A. Mozart, *The Magic Flute*

SUPPLEMENTARY STUDIES

Drill Exercises

1. The beaming and stem direction in the passages below may not be correct in all measures. Use the given staff to rewrite each line in its entirety, correcting all errors.

a.

G. F. Handel, Chaconne

b.

Norman Dello Joio, Piano Sonata

2. For the notes and rests given, provide the value in beats.

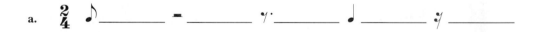

Fundamental Skills in Practice

3. The following composition is notated in $\frac{3}{2}$ meter. Transcribe the time signature to $\frac{3}{8}$ in the first line and $\frac{3}{4}$ in the second line. Revise the notation as necessary. The first measures have been completed as an example.

a.   George Frideric Handel, Suite in D

NAME _____

The following composition is in $\frac{4}{4}$. Transcribe the music to $\frac{4}{2}$ and $\frac{4}{8}$, respectively.

W. A. Mozart, Sonata in C, K. 309

4. On a separate sheet, compose a second part to the rhythmic reduction below. Create a duet for two performers. Give your added part the effect of an accompaniment by keeping rhythms simple and repetitive. Take care with your calligraphy and align beats between the two parts.

Moderato

Ruggero Leoncavallo, *Pagliacci*

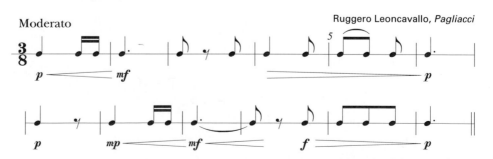

The following passages show two different approaches to beginning the assignment.

1. Given

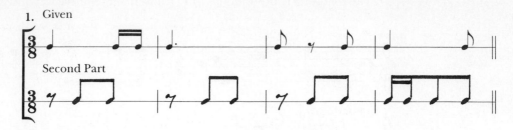

2. Second Part

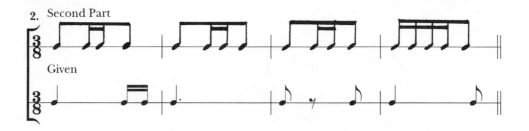

CHAPTER 5

Compound Meters

ESSENTIAL TERMS

- *borrowed beat division*
- *compound meter*
- *duplet*
- *natural beat division*
- *triplet*

A COMPOUND METER is one in which the beat divides into three equal parts. In a simple meter, the beat is always a simple (undotted) note; in a compound meter, on the other hand, the note representing one beat is always a *dotted* note.

Beat Division

The beat in simple meters (an undotted, or simple, note) divides into two parts. As discussed earlier, the quarter-note beat divides into two eighth notes; the sixteenth-note beat divides into two thirty-second notes.

Beat	*Division*	*Beat*	*Division*

Recall, however, that the dot adds one-half the original value to a note or a rest. Whereas the quarter note divides into two eighth notes, the *dotted quarter note* has half again the original value. This permits the characteristic three-part division of a compound meter.

A dotted note can be divided evenly into three parts; similarly, three simple notes can be tied together to make one note with three times their single value. The dotted half note, for example, divides into three quarter notes; the dotted eighth note divides into three sixteenths.

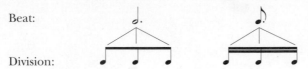

Beat:

Division:

Simple and Compound Meters.   Simple and compound meters are differentiated easily through a simple rule and a single exception:

Rule: If the upper numeral of a time signature is divisible by 3, *the meter is compound* and the beat divides into three parts. If a meter is *not* compound, then it is simple—with a two-part beat division.

Exception: By definition, a meter with 3 as the upper numeral is *simple*.

Any meter that is not simple is compound (there are no other possibilities in traditional Western music). The upper numeral of a compound time signature will always be divisible by 3 (except 3 itself—the exception). Compound time signatures are represented principally by the upper numerals 6, 9, and 12.

EXERCISE 5-1

Fundamental Skills

Simple and Compound Time Signatures

A number of meter signatures are given below. Determine whether the meter is simple or compound by applying the rule and the exception just discussed. Use the blank for your answer ("simple" or "compound").

The Beat in Compound Meters.   Metric (accent) plans in simple and compound meters are identical. Compound meters have two, three, and four beats per measure just as simple meters do. Likewise, they are classified with a word to specify the accent pattern (duple, triple, or quadruple) followed by the word "compound" to designate the three-part beat division. The most common compound meters are duple-compound, triple-compound, and quadruple-compound.

For the time being, we will use the familiar icon introduced earlier to represent complete compound-beat metric plans: , for example.

"Three Blind Mice" is a familiar tune in duple-compound meter. There are two beats per measure, with the beat divided into three parts. The dotted quarter note is the unit of beat in the passage below (Recorded Example 11), although a number of other dotted notes could fulfill this role.

RECORDED EXAMPLE 11
TRACK 17
Duple Compound Meter:
"Three Blind Mice"

Listen to "Three Blind Mice" at least twice. The first time through, feel the duple accent pattern. Each measure has one strong and one weak beat. The second time through, feel the eighth notes. These are the beat *divisions* and define the compound meter. You will hear the divisions most clearly in measures 9, 11, 13, and 14.

♩. = 1 beat

THREE - - Blind - - MICE, - - - - - THREE - - blind - - MICE, - - - - -

SEE - - how - they RUN, - - - - - SEE, - - how - they RUN, - - - - - they

ALL - ran af - ter the FARM - er's wife, who CUT off their tails with a

CARV - ing knife, you've NEV - er seen such a SIGHT in your life - as

THREE - - blind - - MICE - - - - - .

"Three Blind Mice" can also be notated using a dotted-eighth- or a dotted-half-note beat. Compare the following notations with the notation of the first line of the same song given earlier. Assuming that the tempo remains the same, the three transcriptions below would sound exactly alike. Remember that the symbol ‖: indicates that the material within the dots is to be repeated.

THREE - - blind - - MICE- - - - - SEE, - - how - they RUN - - - -

THREE - - blind - - MICE- - - - - SEE, - - how - they RUN - - - -

Beat Subdivision

Although the beat in a compound meter divides into three parts, the subdivision of the beat is still simple—into *two* parts. If the beat is the dotted half note, for example, it divides into three quarter notes; the subdivision is six eighth notes.

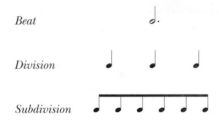

Other compound beats subdivide in a similar manner. The dotted-quarter-note beat divides into three eighths and subdivides into six sixteenth notes. The dotted-eighth-note beat divides into sixteenths and subdivides into thirty-second notes.

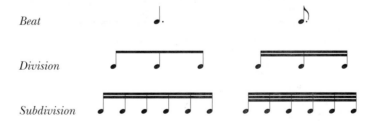

Note Values in Compound Meters

In compound meters, notes receiving more than one beat represent values as they do in simple time (twice the beat, four times the beat, and so on). If the beat is a dotted quarter note, the dotted half note or rest receives two beats; the dotted whole, four beats.

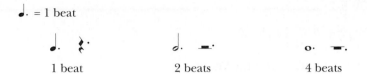

1 beat   2 beats   4 beats

We have no single symbol to represent a unit of three beats in a compound meter. Whereas a single dotted note can stand for three beats in a simple meter, tied notes or consecutive rests are necessary in compound meters. Notice that in the second example below, the larger value precedes the smaller.

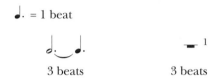

3 beats   3 beats

The beat division and subdivision in a simple meter are one-half and one-quarter the beat's value, respectively. Lesser values in compound meters, however, are more often *thirds* and *sixths* of a beat. If the beat is a dotted quarter note, for example, a single eighth note or eighth rest has the value of one-third of a beat. An undotted quarter note or quarter rest receives two-thirds of a beat.

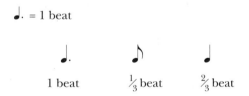

1 beat $\frac{1}{3}$ beat $\frac{2}{3}$ beat

If the dotted half note is the beat, the symbols are different, but the values are the same.

1 beat $\frac{1}{3}$ beat $\frac{2}{3}$ beat

---

[1]A whole rest may be used for an entire measure of silence in *any* meter.

EXERCISE 5-2 ────────────────────────────────────

Fundamental Skills

Note Values in Compound Meters

    A. Given the designated units of beat, write the value for each of the given symbols.

      $\beat.$ = 1 beat

        1.   ℰ· ＿＿＿   ■· ＿＿＿   ♩ ＿＿＿   ℽ ＿＿＿

        2.   ♩· ＿＿＿   ■· ＿＿＿   ♪ ＿＿＿   ♩ ＿＿＿

      = 1 beat

        3.   ℰ ＿＿＿   ■· ＿＿＿   𝅝· ＿＿＿   𝅗𝅥 ＿＿＿

        4.   ℽ ＿＿＿   ♩ ＿＿＿   ♩· ＿＿＿   𝅝 ＿＿＿

      ♪· = 1 beat

        5.   ℽ ＿＿＿   ♩· ＿＿＿   ℽ· ＿＿＿   ℽ ＿＿＿

        6.   ♩ ＿＿＿   ■· ＿＿＿   ℽ ＿＿＿   ♪· ＿＿＿

    B. Several series of notes are shown. Consider the beat specified, then compute the cumulative value of each series in beats or fractions of a beat.

Dotted-Quarter-Note Beat

      ♩· = 1 beat

        1. ♩· ♩ ♪ ♩·   ＿＿   5. ♩ ♪♪♪ ℰ ♩·   ＿＿

        2. ♩ ♪ ♩·‿♩ ♪   ＿＿   6. ♫♪ ℽ ♩ ℽ ♩ ℽ   ＿＿

        3. ♩ ℽ ♩· ♫♫   ＿＿   7. ♩· ♩ ♩ ♪ ♩· ♩   ＿＿

        4. ♩· ♩· ℰ ♪ ♩·   ＿＿   8. ℰ ♪ ℽ ♩ ♩· ♩   ＿＿

Dotted-Half-Note Beat

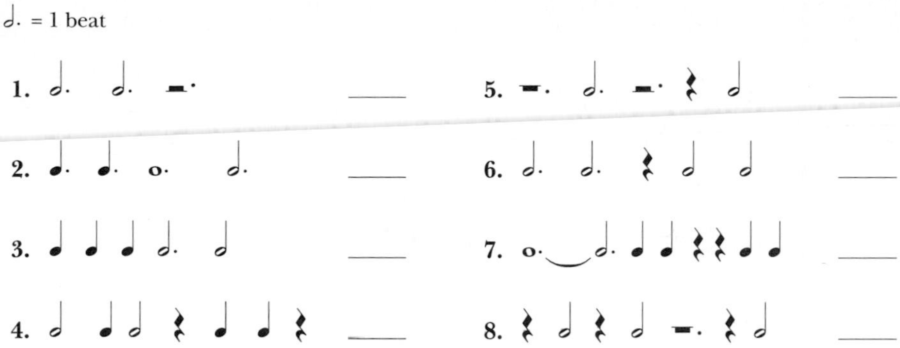

𝅗𝅥. = 1 beat

1. 𝅗𝅥.　𝅗𝅥.　▬.　　　　＿＿＿

2. 𝅗𝅥.　𝅗𝅥.　𝅝.　𝅗𝅥.　　　＿＿＿

3. 𝅘𝅥　𝅘𝅥　𝅘𝅥　𝅗𝅥.　𝅘𝅥　　　＿＿＿

4. 𝅗𝅥　𝅘𝅥𝅘𝅥　𝄾　𝅘𝅥　𝅘𝅥　𝄾　　＿＿＿

5. ▬.　𝅗𝅥.　▬.　𝄽　𝅘𝅥　　＿＿＿

6. 𝅗𝅥.　𝅗𝅥.　𝄽　𝅘𝅥　𝅘𝅥　　＿＿＿

7. 𝅝⌣𝅗𝅥.　𝅘𝅥𝅘𝅥　𝄽𝄽　𝅘𝅥𝅘𝅥　＿＿＿

8. 𝄽　𝅘𝅥　𝄽　𝅘𝅥　▬.　𝄽　𝅘𝅥　＿＿＿

Dotted-Eighth-Note Beat

♪. = 1 beat

1. ♪.　♪♪♪　𝅘𝅥.⌣𝅘𝅥.　　　＿＿＿

2. ♫♫　♪　𝅘𝅥.　　　　＿＿＿

3. ♫　𝄾　♪♪　♪　　　＿＿＿

4. ♪♪♪　♪　♪　𝄾.　　＿＿＿

5. ⅞　⅞♪⅞⅞♪⅞♪　＿＿＿

6. 𝄾　⅞♪♪　♪♪　　＿＿＿

7. ♬♫　𝄾♪♪　　　＿＿＿

8. ♬♫　⅞♪♪　　　＿＿＿

C. Incomplete Measures. Some of these measures are incomplete. Locate incomplete measures, compute the missing value, then add *one rest* that will complete the duple, triple, or quadruple meter.

Duple Meter

♪. = 1 beat

Triple Meter

Compound Time Signatures

As we have discussed, the upper numeral of the time signature in simple meters indicates the accent pattern; the lower numeral specifies the unit of beat. In compound meters, however, the information given in the time signature is not as direct. In a simple meter, the lower numeral represents a specific note (4 = quarter note, for instance). But there is no number understood to represent a dotted note for use in a compound meter signature.

Since a number that can represent a dotted note in a time signature is unavailable, composers indicate with the lower numeral not the beat but the *beat division*. The beat division in a compound meter is always a simple note, which can be indicated by one of the familiar numerals 1, 2, 4, 8, 16, and 32. If the beat is the dotted half note, for example, the lower numeral of the time signature will be 4 because the quarter note is the beat division. If the meter is compound, a lower numeral of 4 indicates not a quarter-note beat but *a dotted-half-note beat*.

Triple-Simple   *Triple-Compound*

$$\begin{matrix}\mathbf{3}\\\mathbf{4}\end{matrix}\qquad\qquad\begin{matrix}\mathbf{9}\\\mathbf{4}\end{matrix}$$

Beat: ♩   ♩.

The lower numeral in a compound meter signature designates not the beat but the beat division. The upper numeral of the time signature is adjusted to reflect that fact. Given a meter with three dotted half notes per measure, we will use the number 4 (standing for a quarter note—the beat division) as the lower numeral of the time signature and the number 9 as the upper numeral. The number 9 indicates that there are *nine quarter notes* in the measure, but since we know that the meter is compound, we know that the number 4 refers not to the beat but to *the beat division*. Furthermore, we know that the number 9 is *three times* the number of beats in a measure.

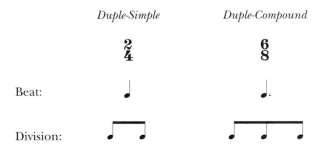

In a duple meter there are two beats in a measure (strong-weak). If the meter is duple-simple (simple-duple) and we want a quarter-note beat, the upper numeral of the time signature is 2; the lower numeral, 4. If the meter is duple-*compound,* however, the upper numeral will be not 2 but 6 (three times the number of beats in a measure). The lower numeral will vary depending upon the unit of beat. If a dotted-quarter-note beat is desired, for example, the lower numeral will be 8 because the beat (which cannot be represented by a number) divides into three eighth notes.

Duple-Simple   *Duple-Compound*

$$\begin{matrix}\mathbf{2}\\\mathbf{4}\end{matrix}\qquad\qquad\begin{matrix}\mathbf{6}\\\mathbf{8}\end{matrix}$$

Beat: ♩   ♩.

Division: ♫   ♫♪

If a duple-compound meter with a dotted-eighth-note beat is desired, the upper numeral will still be 6, but the lower numeral will now be 16 to reflect the division of the dotted-eighth-note beat. The time signature $\begin{smallmatrix}\mathbf{6}\\\mathbf{4}\end{smallmatrix}$ designates a duple-compound meter with a dotted-half-note beat.

$$\begin{matrix}\mathbf{6}\\\mathbf{16}\end{matrix}\qquad\qquad\begin{matrix}\mathbf{6}\\\mathbf{4}\end{matrix}$$

Beat: ♪.   ♩.

For compound meters, the information given in the time signature is the same as for simple meters. First, however, you must "decode" the numbers.

Compound meter because
6 can be divided
evenly by 3

6
8

6 ÷ 3 = 2
Duple accent pattern
Dotted quarter-note
beat

♪⌢♪⌢♪ = ♩.

Beat Division: *compound*

Compound meter because
12 can be divided
evenly by 3

12
2

12 ÷ 3 = 4
Quadruple accent pattern
Dotted whole-note
beat

♪⌢♪⌢♪ = 𝅝.

Beat Division: *compound*

Simplifying Compound Meters

Although the theory behind compound meter signatures may appear somewhat complicated at first, traditional composers have regularly chosen only a few different metric arrangements. You may find it helpful simply to memorize the half dozen most common possibilities.

For accent patterns, the top numbers of 6, 9, and 12 designate duple, triple, and quadruple, respectively. Compositions outside these metric schemes are extremely rare. For the designated beat in a compound meter, the lower numbers 8, 4, and 16 stand for the dotted quarter note, the dotted half note, and the dotted eighth note, respectively. These are virtually the only beat units employed by traditional composers.

Top Numeral	Accent Pattern	Bottom Numeral	Note Receiving One Beat
6	Duple	8	Dotted quarter note
9	Triple	4	Dotted half note
12	Quadruple	16	Dotted eighth note

EXERCISE 5-3

Fundamental Skills

Compound Meter Signatures

A. The meter signatures given below are all compound. First, write the note represented by the lower numeral. This is the beat division. Next, write a dotted note with three times this value. The dotted note is the unit of beat. Finally, determine the accent pattern by dividing the upper numeral of the meter signature by 3. Fill in the blanks as appropriate.

Meter Signature	Note Represented by Lower Numeral	Dotted Note with Three Times This Value	Accent Pattern
1. $\frac{6}{8}$	♪	♩.	DUPLE
2. $\frac{9}{8}$	___	___	___
3. $\frac{6}{4}$	___	___	___
4. $\frac{9}{4}$	___	___	___
5. $\frac{12}{4}$	___	___	___
6. $\frac{9}{16}$	___	___	___
7. $\frac{6}{16}$	___	___	___
8. $\frac{12}{8}$	___	___	___

B. Supply meter signatures that conform to the accent pattern, beat unit, and beat division specified. Some meters are simple; others are compound.

	Accent Pattern	Beat Unit	Beat Division
1. ___	Triple	♩	♪ ♪
2. ___	Duple	♩.	(beamed sixteenth notes)
3. ___	Triple	♩.	♪ ♪ ♪
4. ___	Quadruple	♩.	(three beamed eighth notes)

5. _____ Duple

6. _____ Triple

EXERCISE 5-4

Fundamental Skills

Barlines in Compound Meters

A. The following lines are notated in compound meters. Supply barlines as indicated by the time signatures. If the first barline is supplied, the line begins with an anacrusis. In that case, remember that the final measure will be incomplete and the final barline will be supplied as well.

Modest Mussorgsky, *Pictures at an Exhibition*

1.

G. F. Handel, Concerto Grosso in E Minor

2.

Johannes Brahms, Trio in E-flat

3.

Franz Liszt, *Les Préludes*

4.

Ottorino Respighi, Orchestral Suite

5.

Paul Francis Webster/ Dimitri Tomkin, "The Green Leaves of Summer"

B. Incomplete Measures. Some of these measures are incomplete. Supply one note (simple or dotted) that will complete any incomplete measure.

Beaming in Compound Meters

Whereas groups of two and four equal values are most commonly beamed in simple meters, groups of three and six are commonly beamed in compound meters. Music editors vary in their approaches to beaming the subdivision. The passage on the left accentuates the duple meter, for example; the notation on the right emphasizes the beat division. Both notations are correct, but they should not be mixed in the same composition.

As always, beaming clarifies beats or groups of beats. The pattern on the left is readable, but the beaming suggests a simple meter, such as $\frac{3}{4}$, instead of a compound meter, such as $\frac{6}{8}$. The second notation correctly conveys the three-part division.

| Poor | Correct |

Depending upon the values employed, there are many correct beaming combinations in compound meters. As always, groups of fewer than or more than one beat should not be beamed.

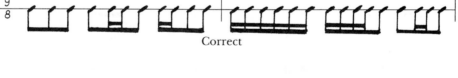

Correct

Incorrect

As in simple meters, complete beat groups can be beamed together regardless of the number of notes involved.

Correct

Music editors today often beam complete beat units despite the occurrence of rests. The older notation, shown in the first example, is also acceptable.

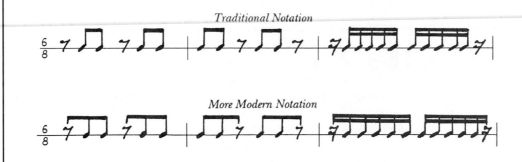

Counting in Compound Meters

In a compound meter, notes on the beat are counted with the beat number just as they are in simple meters. Because the compound beat divides into three parts, however, the counting syllables "la" and "li" (or "le") are used for the second and third divisions, respectively.

RECORDED EXAMPLE 12
TRACK 18
Counting in Compound Meters

Listen to the counting syllables for passages in compound meters (Recorded Example 12). The beat is counted with the beat number as it is in simple meters (Track 18).

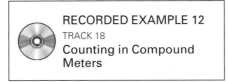

Use the syllables "la" and "li" for counting the compound beat division (Track 19). Notice that rests and ties are counted silently.

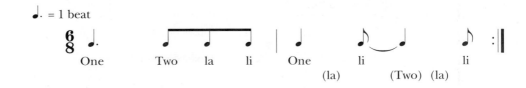

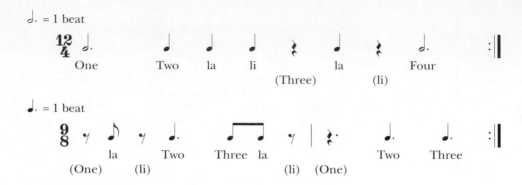

Subdivision. The beat division divides into two parts in both simple and compound meters. Accordingly, the same syllable, "ta," is used in both metric plans (Recorded Example 12, Track 20).

TRACK 20

Follow the score below and listen to the passage that includes compound beat, beat division, and beat subdivision.

Conducting in Compound Meters. Because accent patterns in compound meters are the same basic three employed in simple meters, use the two-, three-, and four-beat patterns shown on page 101 for duple-compound, triple-compound, and quadruple-compound meters, respectively.

EXERCISE 5-5

Musicianship Skills

EAR TRAINING: Identifying Simple
and Compound Meters

A. (Not Recorded) Your instructor will play a number of melodies. Cover the answer portion of the page. Listen to the melody and identify the meter as "duple" or "triple" by writing that word in the blank (again, we will not attempt to differentiate between duple and quadruple). In the second blank, write the word "simple" or "compound" to identify the beat division. Check your answer, then move to the next frame.

1. _____-_____   duple-simple

2. _____-_____   duple-compound

3. _____-_____   duple-compound

4. _____-_____   triple-simple

5. _____-_____ duple-compound

6. _____-_____ duple-simple

7. _____-_____ duple-compound

8. _____-_____ duple-compound

B. Sing the following tunes to yourself and identify the meter as before. If you do not know one or more of these melodies, choose another that you do know and identify its meter.

1. The Impossible Dream _____-_____

2. Hey Jude _____-_____

3. Hail! Hail! The Gang's All Here _____-_____

4. I Saw Three Ships Come Sailing In _____-_____

5. Rock-A-Bye-Baby _____-_____

6. Down in the Valley _____-_____

7. Stars and Stripes Forever _____-_____

8. For He's a Jolly Good Fellow _____-_____

BORROWED DIVISION

In traditional Western musical notation, a composer chooses either a two-part or a three-part beat division. Once the time signature is in place, the performer will interpret the rhythmic symbols accordingly. Although composers may want either a two-part or a three-part beat division primarily, however, there may be occasions when the contrasting division is desired. If the meter is $\frac{6}{8}$, for example, the beat will divide naturally into three parts.

Beat

Division

In addition to the natural beat division in a meter such as $\frac{6}{8}$, the composer may temporarily want a beat divided into *two* equal parts. Traditional rhythmic notation includes a method of indicating the alternate beat division—the "borrowing" of a two-part division for use in a compound meter or a three-part division for use in a simple meter. The beat division specified in the time signature is termed the NATURAL DIVISION; we call the contrasting possibility the BORROWED DIVISION.

The Triplet.   If the meter is simple—$\frac{3}{4}$, for instance—the beat is a quarter note, which divides naturally into two eighth notes. For a three-part division, however, we can mark the notes in question with the numeral 3 to indicate a TRIPLET figure—three notes in the time of two. Since the three eighth notes are all played on one beat, the eighth notes of the triplet are played *faster* than those of the natural division.

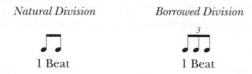

Natural Division   *Borrowed Division*

1 Beat   1 Beat

In other meters, the triplet is performed in the same way. In $\frac{4}{2}$, for example, the beat divides naturally into two quarter notes; the borrowed division is a quarter-note triplet. In $\frac{3}{8}$, the natural division is two sixteenth notes with the triplet comprising three sixteenths.

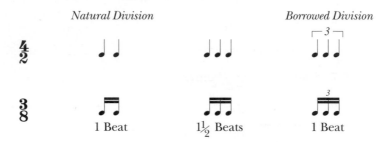

Natural Division   *Borrowed Division*

$\frac{4}{2}$

$\frac{3}{8}$ 1 Beat   1½ Beats   1 Beat

A familiar tune that utilizes a triplet figure is "The U.S. Air Force" (Recorded Example 13). There is no anacrusis, and the triplets occur in the second and seventh measures.

> **RECORDED EXAMPLE 13**
> TRACK 21
> Borrowed Division: "The U.S. Air Force"

Play the recorded passage (Track 21) and listen for the triplet figure that appears twice on the words "in-to the." With text, composers often use rhythms that clarify the importance of individual words and syllables. The syllables "in-to the" are of equal importance and the triplet figure is an appropriate setting. Notice that the more important words "wild" and "sun" have greater length and occur on strong beats.

Off we go - in-to the WILD blue YON-der, FLY-ing high - in-to the SUN.

The eighth-note triplet is certainly the most common, but in other meters, the quarter- and sixteenth-note triplets are performed the same way. Assuming a constant tempo, the following three versions would sound exactly alike.

Off we go — in-to the WILD blue YON - der,

Off we go — in-to the WILD blue YON - der,

Off we go — in-to the WILD blue YON - der,

The Duplet.   The DUPLET is a borrowed division that provides a two-part beat division for use in compound meters. The natural division of the beat in $\frac{9}{8}$ is three eighth notes, and two eighth notes alone do not have a full beat's value. Placing the numeral 2 above or below two eighth notes, however, indicates that they are a duplet and should be performed in one beat—the time normally occupied by three eighth notes.

Natural Division   *Borrowed Division*

1 Beat $\frac{2}{3}$ Beat   1 Beat

Counting the Borrowed Division.   Syllables for counting the triplet in a simple meter correspond to those for the natural division in a compound meter (Recorded Example 14). Likewise, use the beat number and the syllable "te" for the duplet.

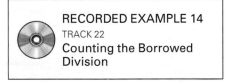

RECORDED EXAMPLE 14
TRACK 22
Counting the Borrowed Division

Follow the score below as you listen to the recording (Track 22). Notice how the use of different syllables for the natural and borrowed beat divisions in simple and compound meters accentuates the inherent differences between those meters.

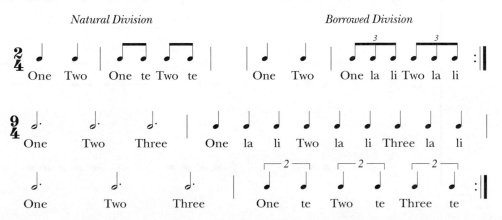

Natural Division   *Borrowed Division*

One Two   One te Two te   One Two   One la li Two la li

One   Two   Three   One la li Two la li Three la li

One   Two   Three   One te Two te Three te

EXERCISE 5-6 _____

Fundamental Skills

Understanding Borrowed Division

A. The borrowed and natural beat divisions are always represented by the same note value. In the following exercise, the natural division is given. Provide the beat and the borrowed beat division.

Meter	Beat	Natural Division	Borrowed Division
1. $\frac{3}{4}$	____		_____
2. $\frac{6}{8}$	____		_____
3. $\frac{2}{2}$	____		_____
4. $\frac{9}{4}$	____		_____
5. $\frac{12}{16}$	____		_____
6. $\frac{4}{4}$	____		_____

B. Incomplete Measures. Some of the following measures are incomplete. Where appropriate, provide *one note* that will complete the measure. Remember: Some measures are complete as notated.

C. Provide barlines for the following passages. If the first barline is supplied, the line begins with an anacrusis. In that case, remember that the final measure will be incomplete.

Glenn Miller, "Moonlight Serenade"

EXERCISE 5-7

Musicianship Skills

Rhythmic Reading

The following exercises employ typical rhythms in compound meters. Study and "decode" the time signature, then set a comfortable tempo for the beat. You may find it helpful to write in the counting below the notes themselves as has been done in the first few lines of each section. Remember to conduct while you perform.

DUPLE METER

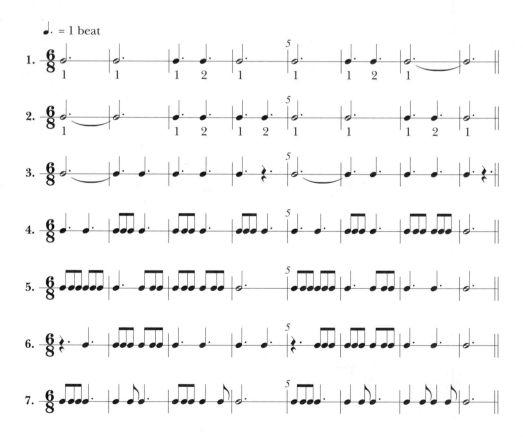

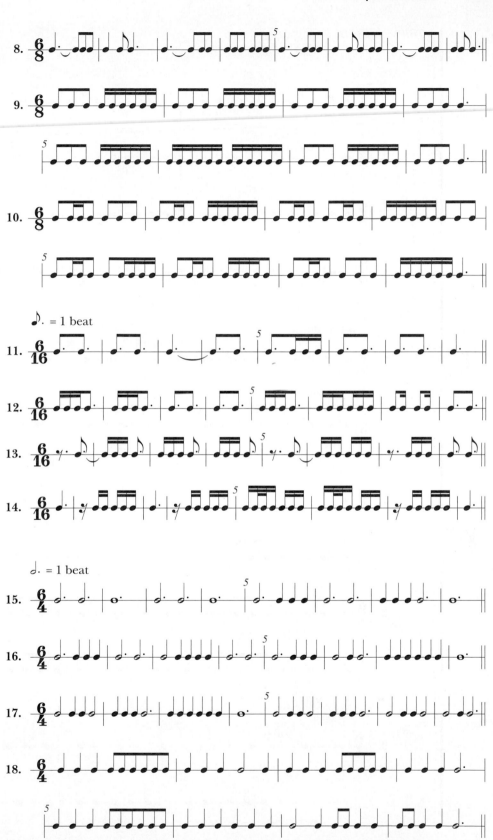

TRIPLE METER

QUADRUPLE METER

The following exercises include *borrowed division.*

TRIPLET PATTERNS

DUPLET PATTERNS

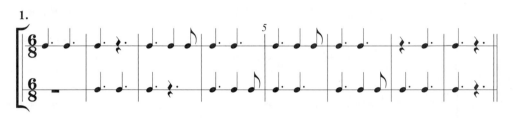

ENSEMBLES

SELF-TEST

1. (10 points) Circle meters that are duple-compound.

a. $\frac{4}{2}$ b. $\frac{6}{4}$ c. $\frac{3}{4}$ d. $\frac{2}{8}$ e. $\frac{6}{16}$ f. $\frac{9}{4}$ g. $\frac{6}{8}$ h. $\frac{2}{2}$ i. $\frac{6}{2}$ j. $\frac{12}{8}$

2. (20 points) Write meter signatures that conform to the given specification, then provide the note that receives one beat (several answers are possible).

Meter	Classification	Beat	Meter	Classification	Beat
a. _____	triple-simple	_____	**d.** _____	duple-compound	_____
b. _____	quadruple-compound	_____	**e.** _____	triple-compound	_____
c. _____	duple-simple	_____			

3. (20 points) For the given meters, write notes that represent the beat, the division, the subdivision, and the borrowed division. In the last blank, classify the meter.

	Beat	Division	Subdivision	Borrowed Division	Classification
a. $\frac{3}{2}$	_____	_____	_____	_____	_____
b. $\frac{9}{4}$	_____	_____	_____	_____	_____

4. (20 points) In beats (or fractional parts) write the values of the given note(s) or rest(s).

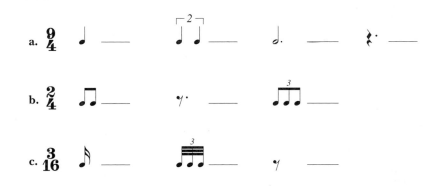

5. (30 points) Provide barlines for the following passages.

P. I. Tchaikovsky, Symphony No. 5

Amy Beach, *Meadow-Larks*

SUPPLEMENTARY STUDIES

Drill Exercises

1. Classify the following meters. For each meter, indicate, first, the accent pattern and, second, whether it is simple or compound.

    a. $\frac{3}{4}$

    _____-_____

    b. $\frac{4}{8}$

    _____-_____

    c. $\frac{12}{8}$

    _____-_____

    d. $\frac{2}{2}$

    _____-_____

    e. $\frac{9}{4}$

    _____-_____

    f. $\frac{3}{1}$

    _____-_____

    g. $\frac{2}{16}$

    _____-_____

    h. $\frac{6}{8}$

    _____-_____

2. Write the note that receives one beat in the following compound meters.

    $\frac{6}{8}$___ $\frac{6}{4}$___ $\frac{9}{16}$___ $\frac{12}{4}$___ $\frac{6}{32}$___ $\frac{9}{8}$___ $\frac{12}{16}$___

3. For the following simple and compound meters, write the note that receives one beat; write the notes that constitute the beat division, beat subdivision, borrowed division; and finally, provide the metric classification.

	Beat	Division	Subdivision	Borrowed Division	Classification
a. $\frac{6}{8}$	___	___	___	___	___-___
b. $\frac{2}{2}$	___	___	___	___	___-___
c. $\frac{3}{2}$	___	___	___	___	___-___
d. $\frac{12}{16}$	___	___	___	___	___-___
e. $\frac{4}{4}$	___	___	___	___	___-___

Fundamentals Skills in Practice

4. Some of the beaming in this passage is incorrect. Study the meter, then use the lower staff to renotate the music with correct beaming.

J. S. Bach, Fugue No. 15 in G Major

5. Use a rhythmic reduction of the preceding passage as one part of a percussion duet. On a separate sheet, construct a two-line system, then recopy the rhythms of Bach's fugue as you renotated them in exercise 4. Next, create a slower-moving second part to complement the first. Where the given part moves basically in eighth and sixteenth notes, use dotted quarter and eighth notes in your second part. One of many possible approaches is given here as an example of score setup.

Renotated Bach Example Here

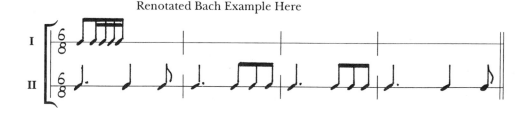

CHAPTER 6

Major Scales and Keys

ESSENTIAL TERMS

- *chromatic half step*
- *diatonic half step*
- *dominant*
- *key*
- *key signature*
- *leading tone*
- *mediant*
- *scale*
- *scale degree*
- *subdominant*
- *submediant*
- *supertonic*
- *tonic*
- *transposition*

Composers in virtually all parts of the world organize music so that the listener can follow transformations of a few pitches throughout the course of a work. A SCALE is a series of pitches that represents not only the inherent organization of a composition (chiefly the relative importance of pitches) but also its potential melodic inventory. Outside the Western world, there are many different scales— some with intervals smaller than a half step. In Western music, however, traditional scales fall into two categories: major and minor. Major scales and keys will be studied in the present chapter; the counterpart, minor scales and keys, will be covered in Chapter 8.

THE MAJOR SCALE

Different types of scales are distinguished by the intervals between pitches. The MAJOR SCALE is composed chiefly of whole steps; half steps (∧) lie between the third and fourth pitches and between the seventh and eighth pitches.

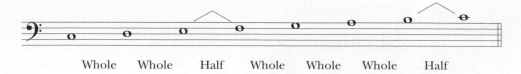

Whole   Whole   Half   Whole   Whole   Whole   Half

Scales can be written and practiced both in ascending and in descending forms. Naturally, the descending form is the reverse of the ascending pattern.

Ascending   *Descending*

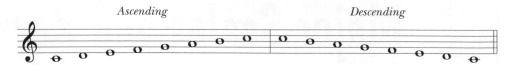

RECORDED EXAMPLE 15

TRACK 23
Major Scale

From Medieval times, the keyboard has been based upon a major scale (the white keys) beginning on the pitch C. Listen to the ascending and descending major scale in Recorded Example 15. Follow the musical notation and the keyboard diagram as you listen. After the scale itself, you will hear the opening phrase of "Joy to the World"—a composition by George Frideric Handel (1685–1759). This melody is a complete descending major scale.

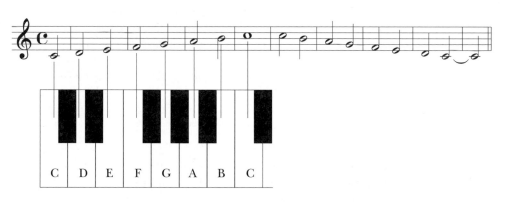

Joy   to   the   world   the   Lord   is   come.

The Tonic.   The first pitch of a scale is important because it serves as the central tone in the composition (or section), to which the other pitches gravitate. The first pitch of a scale is called the TONIC (from the Greek word for "weight"). In the major scale below, C is the tonic. Notice that this pitch is repeated an octave higher to end the scale. Scales are named for their tonics. The tonic of the C major scale is C; G is the tonic of a major scale beginning on G.

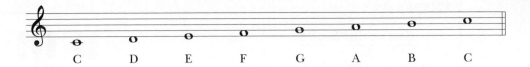

Scale Degrees

Because order is so important in scales, each pitch is assigned a SCALE-DEGREE NUMBER to designate its relationship to the tonic pitch. The tonic is the first scale degree. The second scale degree is the second pitch of the ascending scale; the fourth scale degree is the fourth pitch; and so on.

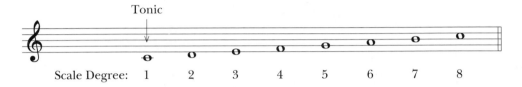

Scale-Degree Names. Just as the first (and eighth) scale degree is also known as the "tonic," the other scale degrees have names as well. Shown here, these names refer to a pitch's relationship to the tonic.

Tonic   Supertonic   Mediant   Subdominant   Dominant   Submediant   Leading Tone

Diatonic and Chromatic Half Steps

Two categories of half steps occur in traditional Western music. If the half step comprises pitches with *different* letter names (F♯ and G, for example), we term the half step DIATONIC. A CHROMATIC half step, on the other hand, involves pitches with the *same* letter name (F and F♯, for example). All the intervals below are half steps; note the important difference between those labeled diatonic and those labeled chromatic.

Both diatonic and chromatic half steps appear in many melodies, but chromatic half steps are *never* used in writing major scales. No traditional scale, for example, has two consecutive pitches named G (even if one is G and the other is G♯).

EXERCISE 6-1

Fundamental Skills

Diatonic and Chromatic Half Steps

A. Several half steps are shown. In the blank, write "D" if the half step is diatonic and "C" if it is chromatic. Write "W" if the interval is a whole step.

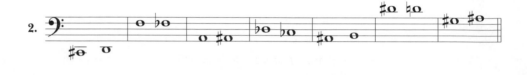

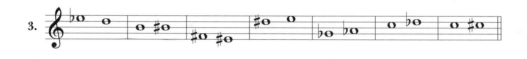

B. Write diatonic or chromatic half steps as directed *above* the given pitch.

Above

Diatonic   Chromatic   Chromatic   Diatonic   Chromatic   Diatonic   Chromatic

Above

Diatonic   Chromatic   Chromatic   Diatonic   Chromatic   Diatonic   Chromatic

Write diatonic or chromatic half steps as directed *below* the given pitch.

Below

3.

Diatonic   Chromatic   Chromatic   Diatonic   Chromatic   Diatonic   Chromatic

Below

4.

Diatonic   Chromatic   Chromatic   Diatonic   Chromatic   Diatonic   Chromatic

C. Provide a letter name (with an accidental if necessary) that forms the designated interval above or below the one given.

1. D ____ E♭ ____   F♯ _____   A _____   B♭ _____   G _____
      diatonic half   whole step   diatonic half   chromatic half   whole step
      step above   below   step above   step above   above

2. G♯ _____   E _____   B _____   C♯ _____   D♭ _____
     whole step   chromatic half   diatonic half   whole step   chromatic half
     below   step above   step above   above   step below

3. C _____   A♭ _____   G _____   F _____   G♭ _____
     diatonic half   chromatic half   chromatic half   diatonic half   chromatic half
     step below   step above   step below   step below   step below

4. E♭ _____   D♯ _____   G♭ _____   E _____   C♭ _____
     whole step   whole step   chromatic half   diatonic half   whole step
     above   above   step above   step below   below

The Major and Minor Modes

Although the tonic is the most important pitch of a scale, the third scale degree (the mediant, also called the MODAL DEGREE) is important as well. An essential difference between major and minor scales lies in the distance between the first and third scale degrees. This interval imparts much of the characteristic major or minor "flavor" to a melody. A MAJOR MODE is created when the third degree is two whole steps above the tonic. In the MINOR MODE, the first and third scale degrees are separated by a whole step plus a *diatonic* half step.

RECORDED EXAMPLE 16
TRACK 24
Major and Minor Modes

Study the notation and keyboard diagrams on the next page and play Recorded Example 16 (Track 24). Listen to the half-step difference between the first and third scale degrees of the major and minor modes.

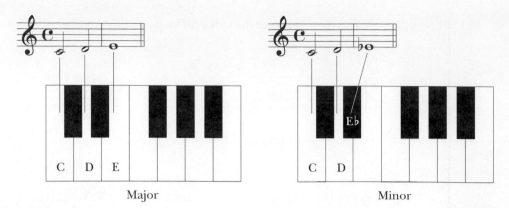

Major   Minor

Now listen to "Brother John" played first in the major mode (as you probably know it), then in the minor mode. Notice that although only the third (modal) scale degree is different, the effects of the two passages are quite different.

Major

Are you sleep-ing, Are you sleep-ing, Broth-er John, Broth-er John?

Minor

Are you sleep-ing, Are you sleep-ing, Broth-er John, Broth-er John?

Remember that the distance between the first and third scale degrees determines whether a scale is major or minor. If the distance is two whole steps, the scale is major; if the span is a whole step plus a diatonic half step, the scale is minor.[1]

---

[1]In Western music before about 1675 and after about 1875, there are other possibilities besides major and minor.

EXERCISE 6-2

Musicianship Skills

EAR TRAINING: Major and Minor Modes

A. In this exercise (Recorded Example 17), you will hear several patterns that employ scale degrees 1, 2, and 3. Listen to each pattern and determine whether the mode is major or minor. Cover the answer portion with a mask. Listen to the musical fragment, respond, then check your answer by sliding the mask to the right.

RECORDED EXAMPLE 17
TRACK 26
Major/Minor Patterns

Write an appropriate letter in the blank: "M" for "major" or "m" for "minor." In the first two lines, scale degrees 1-2-3 ascend. In lines 3 and 4, the patterns descend (3-2-1). There are six different patterns in each line.

Ascending

1. _____ M   _____ m   _____ M   _____ m   _____ M   _____ m

2. _____ m   _____ m   _____ M   _____ m   _____ M   _____ M

Descending

3. _____ m   _____ m   _____ m   _____ M   _____ M   _____ m

4. _____ M   _____ m   _____ M   _____ M   _____ m   _____ M

TRANSPOSITION

If a traditional composition is based on the C major scale, the work will be constructed so that the listener hears the pitch C as more important than any of the others. TRANSPOSITION is the process of moving a series of pitches (a major scale in this case) so that although it centers on another tonic, *the original pattern of intervals among pitches is maintained.*

If we want to transpose the C major scale to begin on the pitch D, for example, D will be the tonic. Although a series of basic pitches beginning on D includes two half steps, these do not occur between scale degrees 3 and 4 and between scale degrees 7 and 8 as they do in a major scale. Unless the original order of intervals is the same, the transposition is not complete.

C Major Scale   D Major Scale?

Transpose the C major scale to begin on D by first writing the basic pitches from D to D as shown above. To complete the transposition, however, you must add accidentals to duplicate the intervallic pattern for the major scale.

Now, check the existing interval pattern and adjust as necessary. The second scale degree (E) is a whole step above D; this interval conforms to the major-scale pattern and you will add no accidental. The third scale degree (F), however, is not a whole step but a half step above the second. Because a whole step is needed to conform to the pattern, the F must become F♯.

The interval between F♯ and G is a half step, and since that corresponds to the major-scale pattern, leave the G♮. Likewise, the fifth and sixth pitches (A and B) need no accidental.

The seventh pitch of the scale, C, lies not a whole step but a half step above B (the sixth scale degree). To conform to the major-scale pattern, the C must be made C♯ (because the interval between the sixth and seventh scale degrees must be a whole step); this accidental also creates the necessary half step between the seventh and eighth scale degrees. The D major scale is now complete and includes two accidentals—F♯ and C♯.

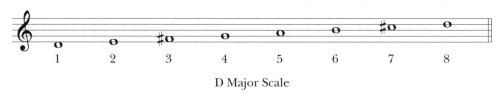

D Major Scale

If the C major scale is transposed to begin on E♭, three flats are necessary to reproduce the intervallic pattern.

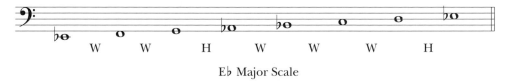

E♭ Major Scale

Five of the basic pitches must be sharped in a B major scale.

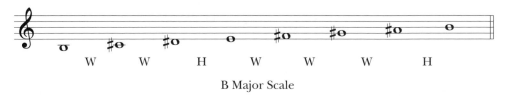

B Major Scale

EXERCISE 6-3

Fundamental Skills

Recognizing Transposed
Major Scales

Each of the following scales has seven different pitches, with the tonic pitch duplicated an octave higher. Some of the scales are transposed major scales, but others do not conform to the whole-step–half-step major-scale pattern and are *not* major (other types of scales will be discussed in later chapters). Analyze the interval pattern of each scale. If the pattern follows that for a major scale, write "Major" in the blank. If, however, there is any deviation from the pattern, circle the first discrepancy and write "Other." *Note:* If you find even one deviation from the major-scale pattern, you need go no further; the scale is not major.

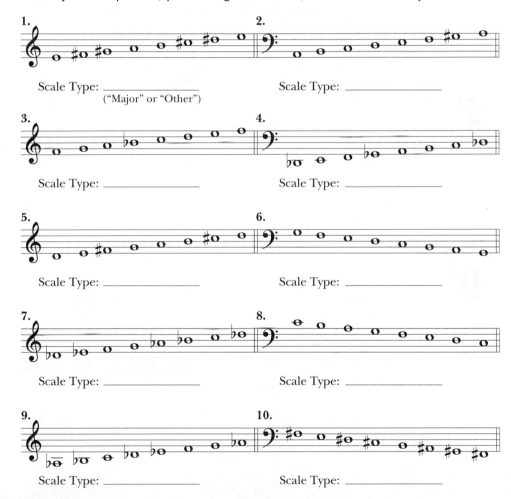

1.

Scale Type: _____
("Major" or "Other")

2.

Scale Type: _____

3.

Scale Type: _____

4.

Scale Type: _____

5.

Scale Type: _____

6.

Scale Type: _____

7.

Scale Type: _____

8.

Scale Type: _____

9.

Scale Type: _____

10.

Scale Type: _____

Constructing Major Scales

To construct major scales, you need to recall and apply the whole-step–half-step pattern: W W H W W W H. Any sequence of intervals that conforms to this pattern will be a major scale; any sequence that does not conform cannot be a major scale. Consider the following steps to construct a B♭ major scale.

1. Beginning with the tonic (B♭ in this example), write in basic pitches up to and including the octave above the tonic. (Because the tonic has an accidental, we automatically add that same accidental to the octave.)

2. Write the whole-step–half-step pattern between pitches. (If you can visualize this pattern without writing it, all the better.)

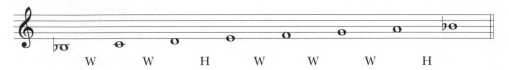

3. Add accidentals as necessary to make the interval sequence conform to the major-scale pattern.

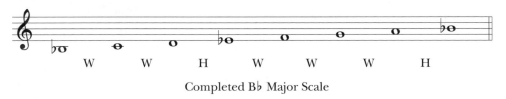

Completed B♭ Major Scale

Descending Scales.   Write a descending scale simply by reversing the interval pattern.

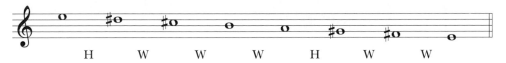

Another (and perhaps better) approach to writing descending scales is to think through or sketch the scale in its ascending pattern, then write the pitches in reverse order.

EXERCISE 6-4 ――――――――――――――――――――――――――――――

Fundamental Skills

Writing Major Scales

A. Write ascending scales on the tonics shown. Begin with basic pitches up to and including an octave above the tonic. (If the tonic has an accidental, remember to add this accidental to the octave as well.) Next, write (or abbreviate) "Whole" or "Half" between pitches as appropriate. Finally, add accidentals to match the interval pattern.

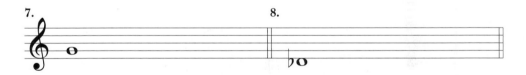

B. Write descending major scales beginning with the tonics given. Proceed as in the preceding exercise, but reverse the interval pattern (H W W W H W W).

5.

6.

7.

8.

C. Letter Names. In addition to notating scales on a staff, you should be able to write scales using pitch names. The process is the same.

Problem: Write an E major scale with letter names.

1. Write the E major scale with basic pitches.

E	F	G	A	B	C	D	E

2. Apply the interval pattern.

E	F	G	A	B	C	D	E
W	W	H	W	W	W	H

3. Add accidentals as needed.

E	F♯	G♯	A	B	C♯	D♯	E
W	W	H	W	W	W	H

Complete major scales beginning on the tonics shown.

1. D ____ ____ ____ ____ ____ ____ D

2. B♭ ____ ____ ____ ____ ____ ____ B♭

3. A ____ ____ ____ ____ ____ ____ A

4. F ____ ____ ____ ____ ____ ____ F

5. D♭ ____ ____ ____ ____ ____ ____ D♭

6. B ____ ____ ____ ____ ____ ____ B

7. G ____ ____ ____ ____ ____ ____ G

8. C ____ ____ ____ ____ ____ ____ C

9. E♭ ____ ____ ____ ____ ____ ____ E♭

10. F♯ ____ ____ ____ ____ ____ ____ F♯

EXERCISE 6-5 _____

Musicianship Skills

SIGHT SINGING: Major-Scale Patterns

A. Using the method specified by your instructor, sing the following scale patterns. Play the first note on the piano, then sing the pattern both ascending and descending. Try not to let your pitch go flat as you sing; this is a natural tendency for most beginners. After you have sung the passage, play the tonic on the keyboard to see if you ended on the correct pitch.

  This exercise centers on scale degrees 1–3.

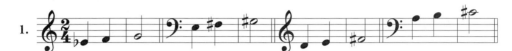

B. Now try singing scale degrees 1–5. Play the tonic on the piano as before, hear the scale mentally, then sing the first five scale degrees both ascending and descending.

C. First, write the scale specified, including any necessary accidentals. Next, sound the tonic pitch on the keyboard and sing the entire scale both ascending and descending. Check your final pitch again on the keyboard. Only eight scales are suggested here; write and practice others as well.

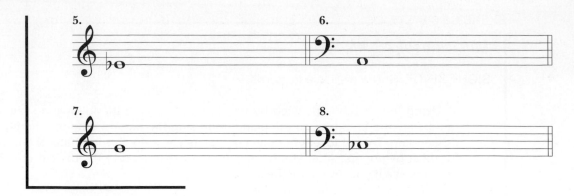

MAJOR KEYS

Authorities disagree about the best definitions of words such as "key" and "tonality." We probably could make certain distinctions between the two terms, but for our purposes, KEY and TONALITY connote the psychological perception that the tonic pitch of a scale is more important than any of the others. The skillful composer creates the sensation of tonality; the listener perceives it. If the scale is G major, the *key* is G major. Likewise, if A♭ is the tonic and the scale is major, the key is A♭ major.

If a composer wants to create a feeling for the key of E major, for example, the pitches of that scale will predominate in the melody. As you have learned, the scale of E major includes four accidentals: F♯, C♯, G♯, and D♯.

E Major Scale

If the E major scale is to be used extensively, a sharp sign will be necessary for every F, every C, and so on. Rather than inserting accidentals each time these pitches are used, however, composers identify the accidentals at the beginning of the composition in the *key signature*.

Key Signatures

As the name suggests, a KEY SIGNATURE is a list of the accidentals associated with a given key. These accidentals are listed at the beginning of a composition between the clef sign and the time signature, and are repeated at the beginning of each subsequent line. Accidentals in a key signature are *always* in effect unless marked otherwise (with a natural sign, for example). The following melody is in the key of E major.

Carl Ditters von Dittersdorf, Quartet

E Major Melody with Accidentals

With a key signature, the same accidentals are specified at the beginning of every line, making the notation easier to read.

E Major Melody with Key Signature

Nullifying a Key Signature.   Performers assume that accidentals stated in a key signature are *always* in effect. The composer, therefore, must specify any return to a basic pitch. Because we assume that the key signature will be correct most of the time, *an accidental in one measure is automatically canceled in the next measure.* Although accidentals within a given measure need not be repeated, the performer will return to pitches specified in the key signature for the next and all following measures.

Study the melody of the Beatles song "When I'm Sixty-Four," shown here. The key is D major; the two sharps in the key signature specify that every pitch F and every pitch C will be played sharp.

In addition to the pitch inventory specified by the key signature, the composers of this popular song used several accidentals. The second pitch, for example, is E♯ rather than the basic pitch E. In the fifth measure, the pitch series C♯-D-D♯-E occurs twice. The C♯ is specified by the key signature, but a D♯ is also used as an accidental. Notice that because the same pattern occurs twice in a single measure, a natural sign is necessary to return the melody to D♮ (the sixth pitch). Likewise, to repeat the D♯, the sharp sign must be repeated for the seventh pitch (the sharp having been canceled by the natural sign).

cautionary

Cautionary Accidentals.   In the sixth measure of "When I'm Sixty-Four" given above, the composers employ a C♮ to cancel the C♯ specified in the key signature. In the next measure, a CAUTIONARY ACCIDENTAL (also called a courtesy accidental) appears with the C as a reminder of the key signature. Theoretically, the sharp sign is not necessary, since the C♮ from the previous measure was canceled by the barline. Most composers and arrangers, however, make every effort to clarify notation and to anticipate performer errors. Cautionary accidentals are useful to that end.

Order of Sharps and Flats

If the scale that produces the effect of a certain key has one sharp, that sharp will be F♯. If the scale has two sharps, they will be F♯ and C♯. There is no major or minor scale or key that has two sharps named G♯ and D♯, for example. With flats, the sequence of appearance is just as rigid; one flat will always be B♭; two will be B♭ and E♭; and so on.

The order of flats spells out the word "BEAD," and the additional flats are "GCF." The sharps occur in the reverse of this order. Learning the order of the flats, therefore, produces the order of the sharps if the sequence can be written (or visualized) backward.

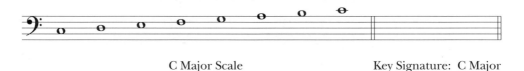

Order of Flats: | B♭ | E♭   A♭   D♭   G♭   C♭   F♭

Order of Sharps: F♯   C♯   G♯   D♯   A♯   E♯ | B♯

When sharps or flats are written on the staff as a key signature, they appear left to right in the order given above—generally alternating between higher and lower choices of octave.

The key of C major has no accidentals; this fact is reflected in the key signature, which contains no sharps or flats.

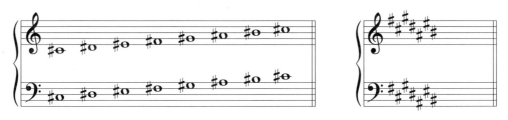

C Major Scale   Key Signature: C Major

The key of C♯ major has all seven sharps in its scale and key signature. Notice the placement of the seven sharps on the grand staff.

C♯ Major Scale   Key Signature: C♯ Major

The key of C♭ major has all seven flats in its key signature. You may find it helpful to remember that "the Cs" have no accidentals (C major), all sharps (C♯ major), and all flats (C♭ major).

Cb Major Scale   Key Signature: Cb Major

The positions of the sharps and the flats on the staff are traditional; deviations, such as those below, constitute notational inaccuracies.

Incorrect   Incorrect

EXERCISE 6-6

Fundamental Skills

Key Signatures

A. Return to the eight major scales in Skill Exercise 6-5C on page 161, and use the lines below to write a key signature in both treble and bass clefs based on the accidentals present in each scale. Be sure to use the correct order and staff placement for the sharps or flats. (If, for some reason, you did not complete this exercise earlier, you will first need to notate the scales.) Write the name of the key in the blank.

1.   2.   3.   4.

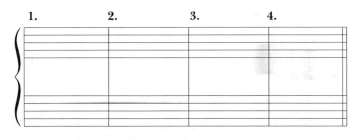

_____ _____ _____ _____

5.   6.   7.   8.

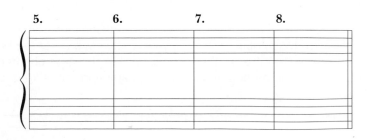

_____ _____ _____ _____

Learning Key Signatures

If you take the time to memorize all fifteen major key signatures, you will find your future work in music fundamentals much easier. It may not seem fair, but some students just memorize more easily than others. For some, merely associating the key names and the appropriate accidentals will be sufficient. For others, making written lists of key signatures will help. Most students will profit from making flash cards. On one side of the card, write the key name ("G Major" or "E♭ Major," for example). On the reverse side of the card, *notate the accidentals on the grand staff* (as opposed to writing "1 Sharp" or "3 Flats").

TRICKS OF THE TRADE

You might note also that in sharp keys, the key name is a diatonic half step above the last sharp (in the order of sharps). In B major, the last sharp is A♯—a diatonic half step below B. Likewise, if "some" key has five sharps, A♯ will be the last sharp. The key name, B, is a diatonic half step above the last sharp.

The formulas are different for flat keys. For example, in the key D♭, the key name (D♭) is the *penultimate* flat. If we want to know the key signature of D♭ major, we assume that D♭ is the penultimate flat, move higher (to the right) one step on the order of flats to G♭, and arrive at the last flat in the key of D♭ major. This tells us that D♭ major has five flats. Reversing the process, if we know that "some" key has five flats, the name of the key will also be the name of the penultimate flat (D♭).

The keys of C major (no sharps/no flats) and F major (one flat) are exceptions to these guidelines; you will simply have to remember their key signatures without any other association. In the next chapter, however, you will learn a method of associating major and minor keys through the Circle of Fifths.

Major Key Signatures

Enharmonic duplications (B = C♭, D♭ = C♯, and G♭ = F♯) create fifteen, rather than twelve, major keys. Study these keys and memorize the key signatures. (See also "Learning Key Signatures" in the box on page 166.)

C major   G major   D major   A major   E major   B major   F♯ major   C♯ major

F major   B♭ major   E♭ major   A♭ major   D♭ major   G♭ major   C♭ major

---

EXERCISE 6-7

Fundamental Skills

Scale Degrees in Major Keys

A. The ability to name or identify a particular scale degree within a given key—especially without first constructing the entire scale—is an important skill. Asked to name the fourth scale degree of F major, for example, you would respond, "B♭." The pitch B is the fourth basic pitch above F, and since the key of F major has one flat, the fourth scale degree is B♭. The sixth scale degree of G♭ major is E♭; the second scale degree of D major is E.

Write the pitches indicated. Be sure to include any necessary accidental(s). In addition, write the scale-degree name (the second scale degree is the supertonic, and so on).

	G major	B♭ major	E major	C major	D♭ major	F major	A♭ major
1.	𝅝						
	2	5	6	5	6	3	7

SUPERTONIC   ___   ___   ___   ___   ___   ___

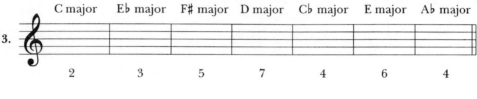

	D major	B major	F major	C# major	A major	G major	G♭ major
2.	3	7	2	4	6	2	5

_____ _____ _____ _____ _____ _____ _____

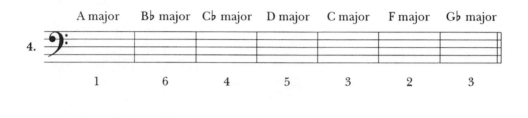

	C major	E♭ major	F♯ major	D major	C♭ major	E major	A♭ major
3.	2	3	5	7	4	6	4

_____ _____ _____ _____ _____ _____ _____

	A major	B♭ major	C♭ major	D major	C major	F major	G♭ major
4.	1	6	4	5	3	2	3

_____ _____ _____ _____ _____ _____ _____

B. This exercise centers on scale-degree names. Write the appropriate letter name, including any accidental.

1. G major, supertonic   _____   6. A♭ major, tonic   _____

2. F major, dominant   _____   7. D major, submediant   _____

3. E♭ major, leading tone   _____   8. E major, leading tone   _____

4. A major, subdominant   _____   9. D♭ major, subdominant   _____

5. B major, mediant   _____   10. C major, dominant   _____

C. If we need to identify a pitch relative to the tonic of a given key, the task is more simple than in previous exercises. The pitch B is the third scale degree in G major and *also* the seventh scale degree in C major. In these exercises, you may assume that the given pitch actually appears in the specified key.

In the first blank, write the scale-degree number that identifies the given pitch in the specified key. In the second blank, write the scale-degree name (tonic, supertonic, and so on).

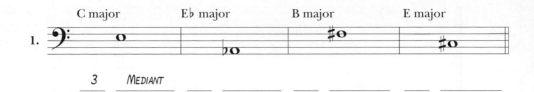

1.   C major   Eb major   B major   E major

    _3_   MEDIANT   ___   ___

2.   B major   Ab major   C major   F major

    ___   ___   ___   ___

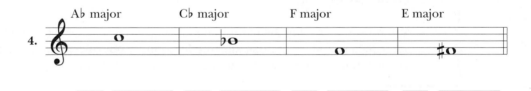

3.   Bb major   G major   D major   Db major

    ___   ___   ___   ___

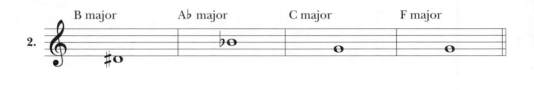

4.   Ab major   Cb major   F major   E major

    ___   ___   ___   ___

D. A single pitch serves in various roles depending upon the key. For each pitch, name three different major keys that include that pitch. Identify the scale-degree position of the pitch in the second blank.

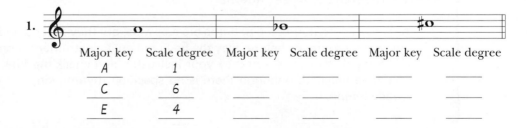

1.

Major key	Scale degree	Major key	Scale degree	Major key	Scale degree
A	1				
C	6				
E	4				

2.

Major key	Scale degree	Major key	Scale degree	Major key	Scale degree
___	___	___	___	___	___
___	___	___	___	___	___
___	___	___	___	___	___

3.

Major key	Scale degree	Major key	Scale degree	Major key	Scale degree
___	___	___	___	___	___
___	___	___	___	___	___
___	___	___	___	___	___

EXERCISE 6-8

Musicianship Skills

KEYBOARD: Ascending Major Scales

At the keyboard, play the eight major scales in the third part of Skill Exercise 6-5, page 161. You need not use specific fingerings, but resist using the same finger for each note. In addition, do not use the thumb on a black key.

EXERCISE 6-9

Musicianship Skills

SIGHT SINGING: Stepwise Patterns

A. These short, nonmetric patterns are stepwise, but they ascend and descend in various contours. As before, play the first note on an instrument, sing the pattern using the method suggested by your instructor, and check the final pitch when you have finished. Although there is no specified rhythm, sing the pitches at a steady tempo.

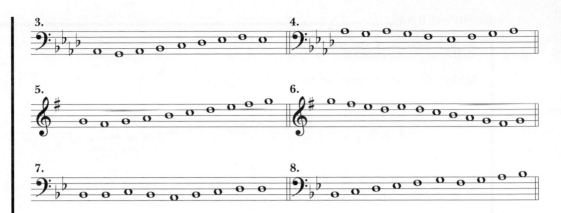

B. These melodies are based on intervals from the stepwise patterns above. First, practice the rhythm on a neutral syllable. When you can perform the rhythm accurately (and without breaking the tempo), sing the melody from beginning to end.

EXERCISE 6-10 ━━━━━━━━━━━━━━━━━━

Musicianship Skills

Melodies and Ensembles for Sight Singing

STEPWISE PHRASES FROM MUSIC LITERATURE

L. van Beethoven, Symphony No. 9

D Major

Giles Farnaby, *His Conceit*

G Major

G. F. Handel, *Royal Fireworks Music*

6.

D Major

Engelbert Humperdinck, *Hansel and Gretel*

7.

C Major

Johannes Brahms, *The Little Sandman* (simplified)

8.

A Major

ENSEMBLES

1.

G Major

2.

Bb Major

SELF-TEST

1. (10 points) Rearrange each set of notes to correspond to correct sharp or flat order.

    a. B♯ A♯ E♯   ____   ____   ____

    b. A♭ B♭ E♭   ____   ____   ____

    c. C♯ G♯ F♯   ____   ____   ____

    d. F♭ C♭ G♭   ____   ____   ____

    e. A♯ G♯ D♯   ____   ____   ____

2. (40 points) Write the major scales indicated. Use accidentals rather than a key signature.

3. (10 points) Several melodic fragments follow. Consider the given pitches as scale degrees 1-2-3 ascending or 3-2-1 descending. Identify the mode of each fragment, then circle "Major" or "Minor" as appropriate.

Major   Minor   Major   Minor   Major   Minor   Major   Minor   Major   Minor

4. (20 points) Identify the scale-degree name (tonic, dominant, and so on) and number of each of the pitches given. Write the number in the first blank and the name in the second.

    a. A Major   **b.** E♭ Major   **c.** C Major   **d.** B Major

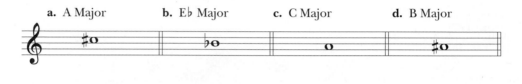

_____ _____   _____ _____   _____ _____   _____ _____

5. (10 points) Write the letter name (and accidental, if any) that appears as the specified scale degree in the key indicated.

    a. B major, subdominant   _____

    b. E♭ major, dominant   _____

    c. F♯ major, leading tone   _____

    d. A major, mediant   _____

    e. C♭ major, supertonic   _____

6. (10 points) Identify the following intervals as whole step (W), diatonic half step (D), chromatic half step (C), or "none of the above" (N).

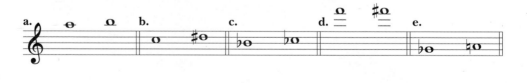

_____   _____   _____   _____   _____

SUPPLEMENTARY STUDIES

Drill Exercises

1. Several fragments of adjacent pitches are shown. For each frame, circle the *one* key that is *not* appropriate for that fragment, The pitches C-D-E-F, for example, appear in the keys of C major and F major, but *not* in the key of G major (the F would be F♯).

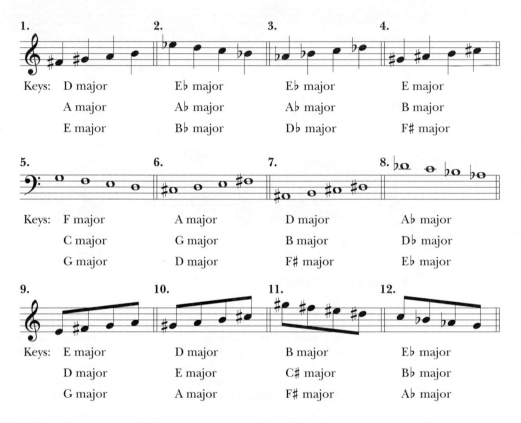

Keys:	D major	Eb major	Eb major	E major
	A major	Ab major	Ab major	B major
	E major	Bb major	Db major	F# major

Keys:	F major	A major	D major	Ab major
	C major	G major	B major	Db major
	G major	D major	F# major	Eb major

Keys:	E major	D major	B major	Eb major
	D major	E major	C# major	Bb major
	G major	A major	F# major	Ab major

2. Write major scales beginning on the *specific* pitches indicated. Choose an appropriate clef and use accidentals or a key signature as you prefer. Use the octave sign if necessary to avoid ledger lines.

a. D₅

b. Eb₂

c. F₄

d. C#₃

e. Gb₆   **f.** B₂

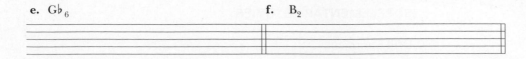

g. Ab₅   **h.** Db₂

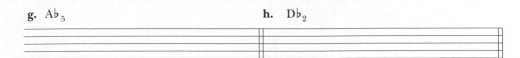

3. Identify the major keys represented by the given signatures.

Fundamental Skills in Practice

4. Each of the following melodies and phrases is based on one of the fifteen major keys but is notated with accidentals rather than a key signature. Determine the key of each melody by building a key signature from the accidentals involved. Write the key signature in the blank staff preceding the melody, and write the name of the key in the blank. Be aware that some compositions begin, and even end, on pitches other than the tonic. Finally, remember that unless canceled by a natural sign, an accidental is in force for an entire measure.

a.   W. A. Mozart, *The Marriage of Figaro*

NAME _____

b.

Robert Schumann, *Dedication*

c.

W. A. Mozart, Quartet, K. 499

5. As directed, choose one or more of the preceding melodies and analyze the pitch content. Begin by writing the appropriate major scale using letter names. Next, tally the number of occurrences of each pitch. Count the total number of pitches in the melody and determine how often each pitch is used. Which, if any, pitches are not used at all? Comment on which pitches seem most and least important in the construction of the melody. As you did in an earlier chapter, analyze the melodic contour and draw a graphic representation showing relative ascending and descending motion.

CHAPTER 7

Intervals

An INTERVAL is the distance (or difference) between two pitches. In previous chapters, several intervals have been discussed: the octave, the unison, the whole step, and the half step. As shown below, intervals can be either *harmonic* or *melodic*. A HARMONIC INTERVAL is formed from the simultaneous occurrence of two pitches; MELODIC INTERVALS occur consecutively.

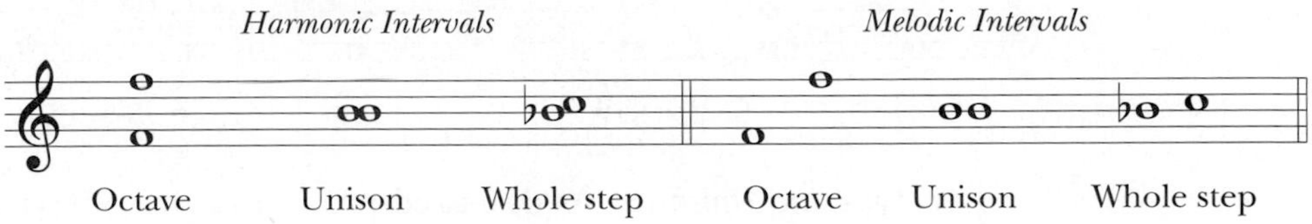

Harmonic Intervals   *Melodic Intervals*

Octave   Unison   Whole step   Octave   Unison   Whole step

INTERVAL TYPE

We classify intervals according to their type and their quality. The TYPE of an interval is an arithmetic distance determined simply by reckoning the number of steps (lines and spaces) between the two pitches. Begin with the lower pitch; then, count lines and spaces, ending with the upper. If the upper pitch is one line or space above the lower, the interval is a SECOND. The intervals previously discussed as whole steps and half steps are more accurately termed *seconds,* because the upper pitch lies on the line or space directly above the lower pitch. Seconds always involve a line *and* a space.

Seconds

A THIRD is an interval formed when two pitches appear on adjacent lines *or* adjacent spaces. Thirds, like those shown here, always involve either lines *or* spaces—not a combination.

Thirds

FOURTHS, like seconds, always involve a line *and* a space. The arithmetic type of the harmonic intervals below is a fourth.

Fourths

A FIFTH is like a third in that the two pitches lie on either lines *or* spaces—not both. The following melodic intervals are fifths.

Fifths

SIXTHS and SEVENTHS follow a similar pattern. The upper pitches are six and seven lines or spaces, respectively, above the lower pitch. Sixths are formed by pitches on lines *and* spaces; sevenths occur between pitches on lines *or* spaces.

Sixths   Sevenths

Octaves and Unisons. As discussed previously, the OCTAVE is the "duplication" of the original pitch name either higher or lower. The UNISON (or PRIME) results from the duplication of exactly the *same* pitch in another voice (or a melodic repetition of the same pitch in the same voice). The following intervals are either octaves or unisons. Octaves are written on lines *and* spaces and, like unisons, are made up of the same pitch name, including any accidental.

Octaves   Unisons

EXERCISE 7-1

Fundamental Skills

Interval Type

A. Construct melodic intervals of the type indicated above the given pitch. Do not employ accidentals.

1.

Second Fourth Third Seventh Sixth Fifth Octave Second Fifth Seventh

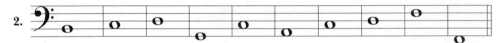

2.

Octave Third Fourth Sixth Seventh Fifth Unison Sixth Third Seventh

3.

Second Third Sixth Fifth Third Fourth Octave Third Fifth Fourth

Write a pitch below the one given that creates the specified interval type. Accidentals are unnecessary.

4.

Unison   Third   Seventh   Sixth   Fifth   Third

5. Second   Fourth   Third   Second   Fifth   Fourth

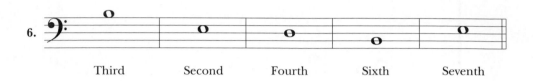

6.   Third   Second   Fourth   Sixth   Seventh

B. Identify the arithmetic interval type.

1.

___   ___   ___   ___   ___

2.

___   ___   ___   ___   ___

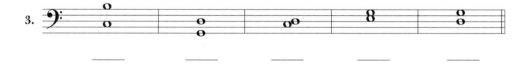

3.

___   ___   ___   ___   ___

4.

___   ___   ___   ___   ___

5.

6.

EXERCISE 7-2

Musicianship Skills

KEYBOARD: Interval Type

A. Use the blank to write the note that makes up the specified interval above the given pitch. At the keyboard, play the first pitch in the octave designated; then, play the second pitch above or below the one given. Since this exercise involves no accidentals, you should use the thumb and second finger for a second, the thumb and third finger for a third, and so on. Use the thumb and fifth finger for the sixth, seventh, and octave. Reverse the fingering pattern for descending intervals. Practice the intervals both harmonically and melodically.

1. A third above G_5 _____
2. A fourth below C_3 _____
3. A fifth below B_5 _____
4. A seventh above D_2 _____
5. A second above E_3 _____

6. A fourth below F_1 _____
7. An octave above A_0 _____
8. A sixth above G_3 _____
9. A sixth below C_6 _____
10. A fifth below B_4 _____

B. Return to Part B of Exercise 7-1 and play each interval at the keyboard.

INTERVAL QUALITY

Arithmetic interval type is a general way of classifying sounds as seconds, sixths, or whatever. In fact, however, many different sounds are classified in the same arithmetic category. The following intervals, for example, have both been discussed; they are *seconds*, yet they have different sounds.

Whole step   Half step

SECONDS

Identifying an interval by *quality* as well as by type provides an exact description of the sound produced. Intervals occur basically in one of two quality categories: perfect and major.

Perfect Intervals

Four simple interval types are classified as perfect: the unison, the octave, the fifth, and the fourth. Other types belong in the category of major intervals and can *never* be perfect in quality. Major intervals will be discussed later in this chapter.

Unison and Octave.   A UNISON is the sounding of an identical pitch. When two tones are identical, the interval is classified as a PERFECT UNISON (abbreviated P1). Each of the intervals below is a perfect unison.

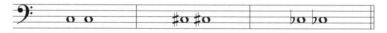

Perfect Unisons

Likewise, when a tone is exactly an octave above or below a given pitch (including the duplication of any accidental), the interval is a PERFECT OCTAVE (P8).

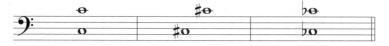

Perfect Octaves

Perfect octaves are separated by twelve half steps as shown here.

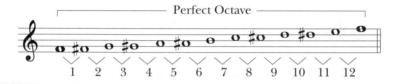

Fourths and Fifths.   Pitches a fourth apart are perfect in quality if there are five half steps between the two pitches. Fifths are classified as perfect when the two pitches are separated by seven half steps.

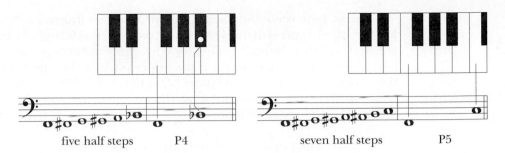

| five half steps | P4 | | seven half steps | P5 |

Review the widths (sizes) of the four perfect intervals in terms of half steps.

Interval	Number of Half Steps between Pitches
P1	0
P4	5
P5	7
P8	12

Perfect Intervals in the Major Scale

Not only is counting half steps time-consuming, but the approach also offers considerable potential for error. Fortunately, you can determine interval quality quickly by another method. As they occur above the tonic of a major scale, unisons, octaves, fourths, and fifths are *always perfect in quality*. Simply determine if the upper pitch is a diatonic pitch in the *key* represented by the lower pitch. Especially in the beginning, however, you may still choose to verify your response by counting half steps.

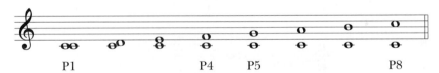

| P1 | | | P4 | P5 | | | P8 |

Diminished and Augmented Intervals. If an octave, a unison, a fourth, or a fifth is not perfect, then it must be wider or narrower than the corresponding perfect interval. If the interval is one half step *narrower* than perfect, it is DIMINISHED (d). If the interval is a half step *wider,* it is AUGMENTED (A).

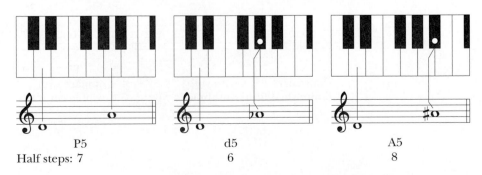

| P5 | d5 | A5 |
| Half steps: 7 | 6 | 8 |

As we have seen, the upper pitch of a perfect interval corresponds to the key signature represented by the lower pitch. Considering the previous example, we know that the pitches D–A form a *perfect fifth* because the upper pitch (A) falls within the key of D major. If the upper pitch of the interval is A♭, however, the quality of the fifth is *diminished* because it is a half step narrower than perfect. For the same reason, we immediately recognize the fifth formed by the pitches D–A♯ as wider than perfect and therefore *augmented* in quality.

Constructing Intervals.   Build intervals above a given pitch first by providing the appropriate arithmetic type, then adjusting the upper pitch *if necessary.* Study the following two examples.

1. *Construct a perfect fourth above D.* First, write the pitch G (the arithmetic type). Next, check that pitch against the key of D. Because G is a diatonic pitch in the key of D, no further step is necessary. The fourth is perfect and includes five half steps.

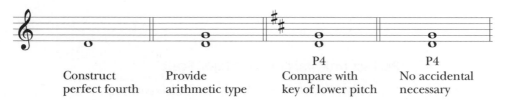

| Construct perfect fourth | Provide arithmetic type | P4 Compare with key of lower pitch | P4 No accidental necessary |

Verify by counting half steps.

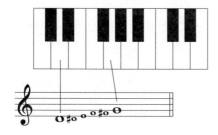

2. *Construct a diminished fifth above E.* Write the pitch B, which is an arithmetic fifth above E. Compare this pitch with the scale of E major. We find that B is a diatonic pitch and therefore forms a perfect fifth with E. Create a diminished fifth by changing the B to B♭.

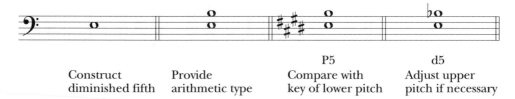

| Construct diminished fifth | Provide arithmetic type | P5 Compare with key of lower pitch | d5 Adjust upper pitch if necessary |

Verify by counting half steps.

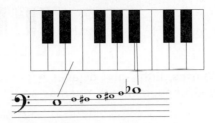

When we classify intervals as "perfect," "diminished," or "augmented," we are differentiating among *sounds*. Listen to Recorded Example 18, in which you will hear octaves, unisons, fourths, and fifths of various sizes.

RECORDED EXAMPLE 18
TRACK 27
Perfect Intervals

Follow the score below as you listen first to the four perfect intervals. The two pitches are played first melodically, then sounded together (harmonic intervals).

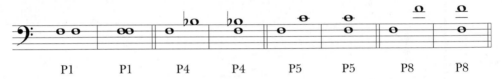

P1	P1	P4	P4	P5	P5	P8	P8

TRACK
28

We rarely hear intervals that would be described as "augmented octaves" or "diminished unisons." Fourths and fifths, however, are often augmented or diminished. Listen to the series of fourths shown here and compare their distinctive sounds.

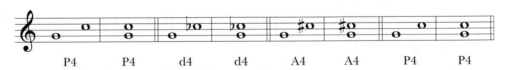

P4	P4	d4	d4	A4	A4	P4	P4

TRACK
29

Fifths appear in various qualities as well. Listen to perfect, diminished, and augmented fifths on Track 29 of Recorded Example 18.

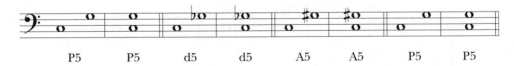

P5	P5	d5	d5	A5	A5	P5	P5

EXERCISE 7-3

Fundamental Skills

Interval Quality

A. Identify the unisons, fourths, fifths, and octaves below by type and quality (they are perfect, diminished, or augmented). You may want to count half steps to verify your response.

1.

2.

3.

4.

B. Note the given interval type and quality. If necessary, use an accidental to adjust the *upper pitch* so that the interval conforms to its description. Remember: Some of the intervals are correct as notated.

1.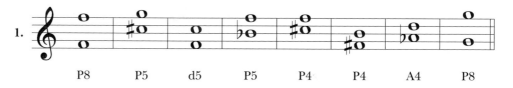

P8   P5   d5   P5   P4   P4   A4   P8

2.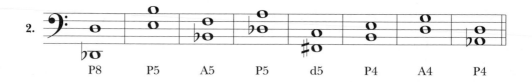

P8   P5   A5   P5   d5   P4   A4   P4

P4 P1 P8 P5 A5 A4 d4 P8

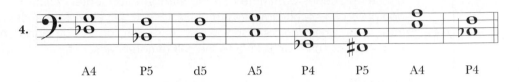

A4 P5 d5 A5 P4 P5 A4 P4

C. Construct the specified interval above the given pitch. Tally half steps to check your answer.

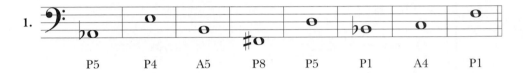

P5 P4 A5 P8 P5 P1 A4 P1

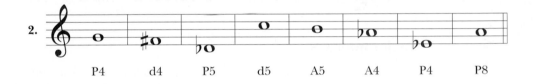

P4 d4 P5 d5 A5 A4 P4 P8

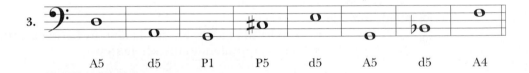

A5 d5 P1 P5 d5 A5 d5 A4

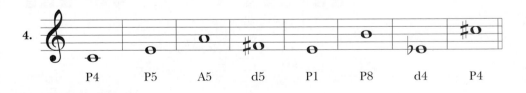

P4 P5 A5 d5 P1 P8 d4 P4

Notating Harmonic Seconds

Correct placement of accidentals is crucial in music notation. Harmonic seconds pose special problems in our system. In melodic seconds, any accidentals are placed before the notehead. When seconds are written harmonically, however, an accidental associated with either or both pitches precedes *both* notes on the staff. An accidental beside the second pitch of a second implies a melodic (consecutive) performance. If the interval is a harmonic second, write sharp, flat, or natural signs on the same line or space and close to the pair of noteheads.

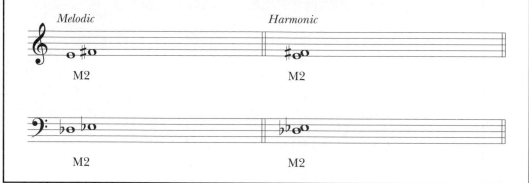

Major Intervals

Fourths, fifths, octaves, and unisons can be classified as perfect in quality. The remaining intervals, however (seconds, thirds, sixths, and sevenths), can *never* be classified as perfect and are known instead as *major*. Perfect and major intervals are entirely separate categories; perfect intervals can *never* be major, and major intervals can *never* be perfect.[1]

The MAJOR SECOND (M2) includes two half steps between pitches. Notice that the major second is equivalent to the whole step.

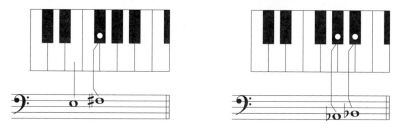

Major seconds

---

[1]The distinction between the terms "perfect" and "major" is Medieval in origin. Although the original meanings of these and similar terms pertain only marginally to today's music, the words are included in the standard vocabulary that we use in discussing music fundamentals.

The MAJOR THIRD includes four half steps between pitches.

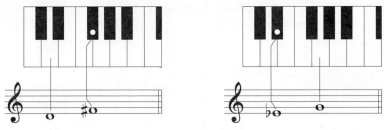

Major Thirds

The MAJOR SIXTH comprises nine half steps.

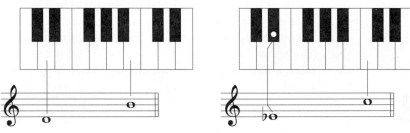

Major Sixths

A SEVENTH is major if the upper pitch is eleven half steps higher than the lower pitch.

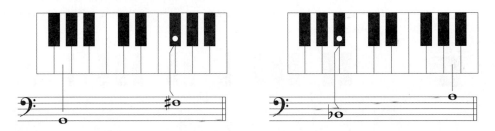

Major Sevenths

The half-step count is useful for comparison and verification of major intervals, but as with perfect intervals, the key signature of the lower pitch is a better measure of quality. If the upper pitch of a second, a third, a sixth, or a seventh corresponds to the major key of the lower pitch, *the interval is major.*

We can tell almost at a glance that the first interval below (B♭–G) is a *major sixth*, since G is a diatonic pitch in the key of B♭ major. Likewise, we know immediately that the second interval (F–D♭) is *not* a major sixth, since the key of F major has a D♮, not a D♭.

Minor and Augmented Intervals.   Seconds, thirds, sixths, and sevenths that are one half step narrower than major are MINOR (abbreviated m2, m3, and so on). If the interval is a half step wider than major, it is AUGMENTED (A).

Looking at the first of the two harmonic intervals below (a third), we can see immediately that the quality is not major. The key of B major includes a D♯, and the upper pitch of the third is a D♮. Because the interval in question is a half step narrower than major, it is minor in quality. Likewise, in considering the sixth (the second interval), we know that C major has an A♮, not an A♯. Because this sixth is a half step wider than major, it must be augmented in quality.

Diminished Intervals.   The only similarity between perfect and major intervals is that they both can be augmented or diminished in quality. As discussed, decreased a half step, major intervals become minor. If a minor interval is *further narrowed* by another half step, however, it becomes DIMINISHED in quality (abbreviated d).

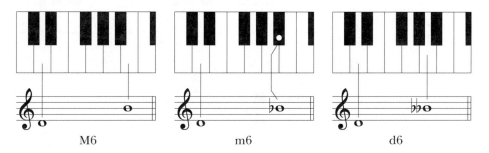

To construct major intervals and their variants, we rely on the same principle learned earlier: A major (or perfect) interval corresponds to the key represented by the lower pitch. If we need a minor, a diminished, or an augmented interval, we must adjust that upper pitch. Study the following two problems.

1. *Construct a major seventh above A.* Write the basic pitch G (the arithmetic type). Next, check this pitch against the key of A. Because G♯ is a diatonic pitch in the key of A, the upper pitch of the major seventh must likewise be G♯.

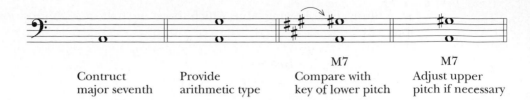

Contruct major seventh	Provide arithmetic type	Compare with key of lower pitch	Adjust upper pitch if necessary
		M7	M7

Verify by counting half steps.

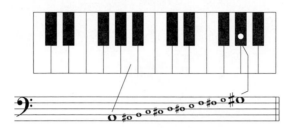

2. *Construct a diminished sixth above F.* First, write the pitch D—an arithmetic sixth above F. Next, comparing the upper pitch with the scale of F major, we find that D forms a *major* sixth above F. Since we want a *diminished* sixth, we must lower the upper pitch by two half steps. By adding the first flat to the D, we create a *minor* sixth. The second half-step decrease (to D♭♭) creates the diminished quality we want.

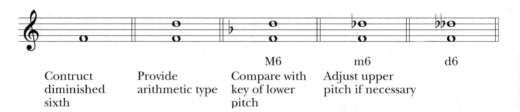

Contruct diminished sixth	Provide arithmetic type	Compare with key of lower pitch	Adjust upper pitch if necessary	
		M6	m6	d6

Verify by counting half steps.

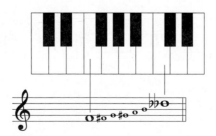

Study the following table, which shows the half-step composition of various intervals.[2]

Interval	Half Steps between Pitches
P1	0
m2	1
M2	2
m3	3
M3	4
P4	5
P5	7
m6	8
M6	9
m7	10
M7	11
P8	12

RECORDED EXAMPLE 19

TRACK 30

Seconds, Thirds, Sixths, and Sevenths

Intervals that are major in the major scale have equally distinctive sounds when they are altered to become augmented, minor, or diminished. Study the notated seconds below as you listen to the intervals played (Recorded Example 19).

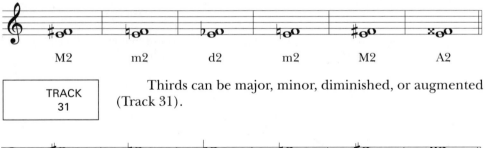

M2   m2   d2   m2   M2   A2

TRACK 31

Thirds can be major, minor, diminished, or augmented (Track 31).

M3   m3   d3   m3   M3   A3

---

[2]The half-step count of augmented or diminished fourths, fifths, unisons, or octaves will be one half step more or fewer, respectively, than the number listed for perfect. Likewise, an augmented second, third, sixth, or seventh will have one more half step than major. The same intervals diminished in quality will have one fewer half step than those that are minor.

Sixths (Track 32) and sevenths (Track 33) follow a similar pattern of qualities.

M6   m6   d6   m6   M6   A6

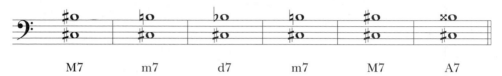

M7   m7   d7   m7   M7   A7

EXERCISE 7-4

Fundamental Skills

Focus on Major Intervals

A. The following intervals are major, minor, diminished, or augmented. Identify interval type and quality as usual. You may want to verify some responses by counting half steps.

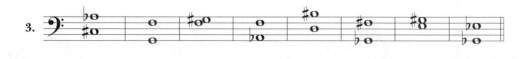

B. Note the given interval type and quality. If necessary, adjust the *upper pitch* (with an accidental) so that the interval conforms to its description. Remember: Some of the intervals are correct as notated.

1.

M3 m2 M6 m6 m3 M7 m7 M2

2.

m7 m6 M2 m3 M7 m2 A2 M3

3.

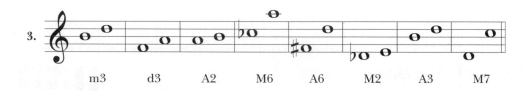

m3 d3 A2 M6 A6 M2 A3 M7

4.

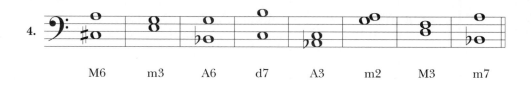

M6 m3 A6 d7 A3 m2 M3 m7

C. Construct the specified interval above the given pitch. Tally half steps to check your answer.

1.

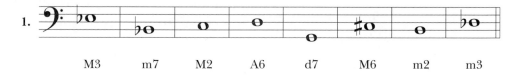

M3 m7 M2 A6 d7 M6 m2 m3

2.

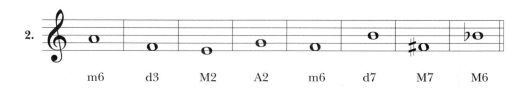

m6 d3 M2 A2 m6 d7 M7 M6

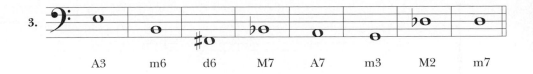

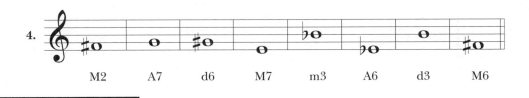

EXERCISE 7-5

Musicianship Skills

KEYBOARD: Intervals

Return to the first four lines of Skill Exercise 7-4. If you have not already completed this exercise, you will need to do so now. Play each interval on the keyboard exactly as notated. Use two different fingers of the same hand for the two pitches (even for a unison). The exact fingering pattern will depend upon the size of the interval and the pitches involved. As in earlier keyboard exercises, use the left hand for the bass-clef octaves; use the right hand for intervals in the treble clef.

EXERCISE 7-6

Fundamental Skills

Notating All Intervals

In this exercise, choose an appropriate clef and write the *one* pitch specified (you may want to use scratch paper to notate both pitches). Observe the given pitch and octave, then write the designated interval *above* it.

1. M2 above D_3
2. M6 above $E\flat_5$
3. P5 above G_1
4. d5 above B_4
5. P4 above $F\sharp_5$
6. M7 above E_2

7. d5 above $B\flat_3$
8. A6 above C_4
9. m2 above $A\flat_1$
10. P8 above $G\flat_6$
11. A2 above $A\flat_5$
12. A3 above B_2

13. P5 above A_4
14. M6 above F_4
15. M2 above $A\flat_4$
16. M7 above $C\sharp_1$
17. P4 above $F\sharp_2$
18. M6 above D_6

19. P5 above $D\flat_2$
20. d7 above $C\sharp_4$
21. d3 above A_5
22. A6 above $F\sharp_6$
23. P8 above A_0
24. A4 above B_4

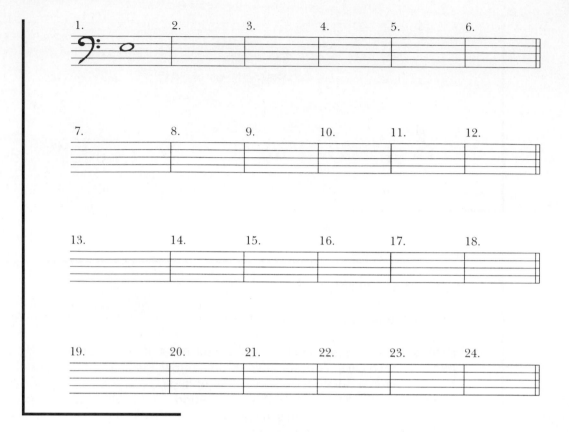

EXERCISE 7-7

Musicianship Skills

EAR TRAINING: Hearing Interval Quality

In Chapter 3, you differentiated between whole steps and half steps. Those intervals, of course, are also known as major and minor seconds. The present exercise centers on seconds as well as four additional categories of intervals: major and minor thirds and perfect fourths and fifths.

MAJOR AND MINOR THIRDS

RECORDED EXAMPLE 20
TRACK 34
Hearing Intervals

Use an index card or a sheet of paper to cover the answer portion of the lines below. As you did in Chapter 3, listen to the interval, write your answer in the blank, then move the mask to compare your response with the interval played in Recorded Example 20. There are four lines, with six frames per line. Move from left to right across each line.

1.	_____ M3	_____ m3	_____ m3	_____ M3	_____ m3	_____ M3
2.	_____ m3	_____ M3	_____ M3	_____ M3	_____ m3	_____ m3
3.	_____ M3	_____ M3	_____ m3	_____ m3	_____ M3	_____ M3
4.	_____ m3	_____ M3	_____ m3	_____ M3	_____ m3	_____ M3

PERFECT FOURTHS AND PERFECT FIFTHS

 TRACK 35

These intervals are either perfect fourths or perfect fifths.

1.	_____ P5	_____ P5	_____ P4	_____ P5	_____ P4	_____ P5
2.	_____ P4	_____ P5	_____ P4	_____ P4	_____ P5	_____ P4
3.	_____ P4	_____ P4	_____ P5	_____ P4	_____ P5	_____ P4
4.	_____ P4	_____ P5	_____ P5	_____ P4	_____ P4	_____ P5

ALL INTERVALS STUDIED

 TRACK 36

These lines include seconds, thirds, fourths, and fifths.

1.	_____ M2	_____ m2	_____ P4	_____ P5	_____ M2	_____ m2
2.	_____ M3	_____ m3	_____ P5	_____ M3	_____ M2	_____ m3
3.	_____ P4	_____ P5	_____ m2	_____ M3	_____ M3	_____ m3
4.	_____ M2	_____ m2	_____ P5	_____ M3	_____ P4	_____ P5

OTHER ASPECTS OF INTERVAL CONSTRUCTION AND IDENTIFICATION

Occasionally, an interval will be narrower than diminished or wider than augmented. Such intervals are identified as DOUBLY DIMINISHED (dd) or DOUBLY AUGMENTED (AA). The interval B to F, for example, comprises six half steps and is a diminished fifth; the interval B to F♭ is a *doubly diminished fifth* (with five half steps). Likewise, C to F♯ has six half steps and is an augmented fourth; C♭ to F♯ (with seven half steps) is a *doubly augmented fourth*.

d5   dd5   A4   AA4

Enharmonic Spellings

Enharmonic equivalents, you will remember, are pitches that have the same sound but different notations. Intervals can be written as enharmonic equivalents as well. The interval D to G♯, for example, is an augmented fourth (six half steps); another pitch, A♭, is also six half steps above D. The intervals D to G♯ and D to A♭ are enharmonic equivalents; they sound exactly the same. In notation, however, the two intervals are completely different. The pitches D to G♯ constitute an augmented *fourth*, whereas D to A♭ is a diminished *fifth*.

Understanding that intervals are always identified and written according to interval *type* is crucial. If you were asked to write a diminished fifth above D, the pitch G♯ would *never* be acceptable; G♯ is a fourth above D—not a fifth. Similarly, if you identified the interval D to A♭ as an augmented fourth, your answer would be incorrect; D to A♭ is a diminished fifth.

Compound Intervals

Intervals larger than an octave are termed COMPOUND INTERVALS. An octave plus a second, for example, is a NINTH; an octave plus a third is a TENTH; and so on. Observe that the quality of a compound interval is the same as the quality of the corresponding simple interval.

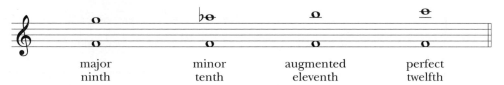

| major ninth | minor tenth | augmented eleventh | perfect twelfth |

Problem Intervals

Sometimes the lower pitch of an interval may not correspond to one of the fifteen major keys. The interval between E♯ and B♯ is a problem, for example, because we have no key of E♯ major. If both pitches of the interval are affected by the *same accidental*, however (*not* a combination), the accidentals *can be ignored*. If we need to calculate the interval between E♯ and B♯, we can simply discount the sharps and determine the interval between E and B in the usual manner.

Identify	Delete sharps	Calculate interval between basic pitches	Original interval will be same type and quality
?		P5	P5

The same situation exists if our pitches are E𝄫 and B𝄫. When basic pitches are altered *in the same way,* the interval type and quality are unchanged (the sound, of course, is different).

Identify	Delete double flats	Calculate interval between basic pitches	Original interval will be same type and quality

?   P5   P5

Discounting and Restoring Accidentals.   When the two pitches of a problem interval are not affected by the same accidental, and the lower pitch does not correspond to one of the major keys, a second approach may be helpful. First, discount the accidental of the lower pitch so that it represents one of the fifteen major keys; next, calculate the quality in the usual way. Finally, *adjust the result* to reflect the accidental discounted earlier. Remember that sharping the lower pitch decreases interval size; if a flat is added to the lower pitch, the interval will be larger.

Identify	Delete sharp	Calculate quality	Note effect of sharp on basic interval	Adjust quality as necessary

?   P5   decreased half step   d5

The Circle of Fifths

Several aspects of traditional Western music theory hinge on the perfect fifth. The power of this interval in establishing a feeling for key and in controlling harmonic flow is easily documented (although such a discussion lies outside the scope of a fundamentals text). You may find series of perfect fifths, called THE CIRCLE OF FIFTHS, convenient for remembering the major (and, later, minor) key signatures. If we begin a circle with C major at "twelve o'clock" and progress clockwise by ascending perfect fifths, we move to keys with one sharp, two sharps, three sharps, and so on. Moving counterclockwise by descending perfect fifth, we progress through a series of flat keys (one flat, two flats, and so on). Notice on the following diagram that the last three sharp keys (B, F♯, and C♯) overlap with the last three flat keys (D♭, G♭, and C♭). These pairs of keys are enharmonic equivalents.

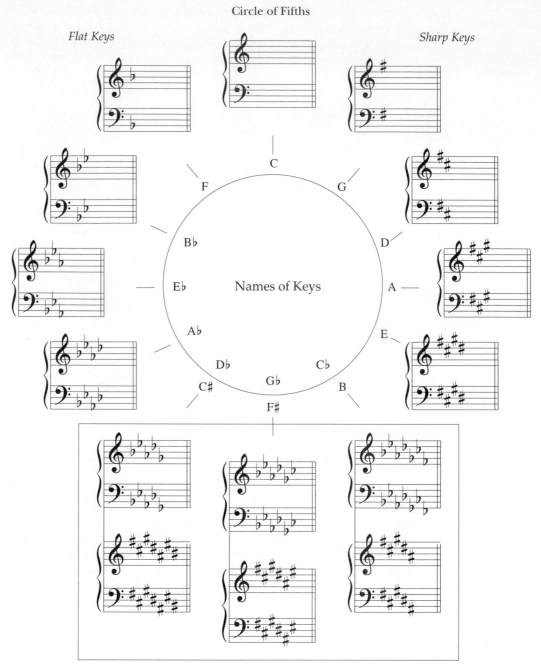

Circle of Fifths

Flat Keys   *Sharp Keys*

Names of Keys

Enharmonic Keys

EXERCISE 7-8

Fundamental Skills

Interval Construction and Identification

A. Identify the type and the quality of the following intervals.

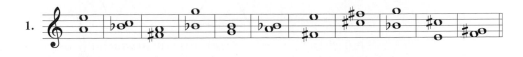

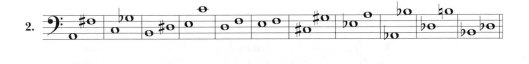

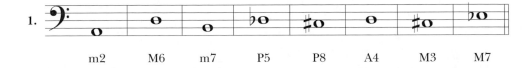

B. Write the designated interval above the given pitch.

m2	M6	m7	P5	P8	A4	M3	M7

P8	M2	M6	P5	P8	m3	P4	d5

A2	P5	d3	m7	A6	dd4	P5	A2

INTERVAL INVERSION

The word *inversion* suggests that some change in a relationship has taken place. An inverted pyramid, for example, is one that has been turned upside down and rests on its point.

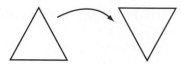

Similarly, an INVERTED INTERVAL is one in which the original positions of the two pitches have been reversed. Interval inversion can be accomplished in either of two ways: (1) by raising the lower pitch an octave so that it appears above the upper, or (2) by lowering the upper pitch an octave so that it lies below the lower.

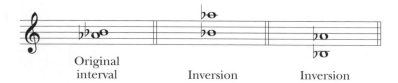

| Original interval | Inversion | Inversion |

When intervals are inverted, type and quality usually change. In the preceding example, the major second inverts to a minor seventh. Notice also the additional inversions below. Except when the original quality is perfect, *both* type and quality change (perfect remains perfect).

| Interval | Inversions | Interval | Inversions | Interval | Inversions |
| M3 | m6 | P4 | P5 | A4 | d5 |

Changes in interval type that result from inversion are predictable. Seconds invert to sevenths; sevenths invert to seconds. Thirds invert to sixths, and sixths invert to thirds. Likewise, fourths and fifths invert. Notice that numerically, a given interval and its inversion add up to nine (2 + 7 = 9, 7 + 2 = 9, and so forth).

Inversion of interval quality is equally straightforward. If the original quality is major, the inverted interval will be minor; likewise, minor intervals inverted become major. The same is true of augmented and diminished intervals: An augmented interval becomes diminished when inverted; diminished intervals become augmented. Inverted perfect intervals, however, remain perfect. Study the table of inversion and the examples shown on the next page.

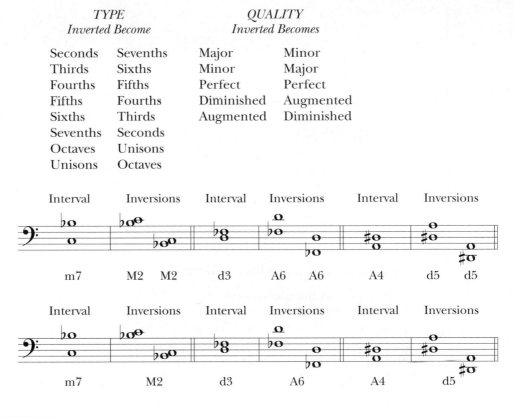

TYPE		QUALITY	
Inverted Become		*Inverted Becomes*	
Seconds	Sevenths	Major	Minor
Thirds	Sixths	Minor	Major
Fourths	Fifths	Perfect	Perfect
Fifths	Fourths	Diminished	Augmented
Sixths	Thirds	Augmented	Diminished
Sevenths	Seconds		
Octaves	Unisons		
Unisons	Octaves		

EXERCISE 7-9

Fundamental Skills

Interval Inversion

Invert the following intervals. First, write the upper pitch of the original interval an octave lower; next, reverse the process and move the lower pitch of the original interval an octave higher. Identify both the original interval and the inversion.

1.

<u>P5</u>   <u>P4</u>
        Inversions   Inversions   Inversions

2.

        Inversions   Inversions   Inversions

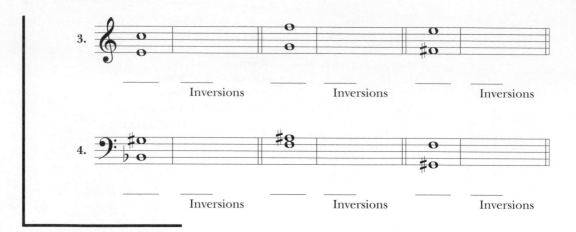

Inversions   Inversions   Inversions

Inversions   Inversions   Inversions

Writing Intervals below a Given Pitch

The type and the quality of an interval are always identified by calculating from the lower pitch. At times, however, it may be necessary to write an interval below one given. Asked to write a major sixth below F, we could always count down nine half steps, or we could write the interval type (F to A♭), identify it in the customary way, and then adjust the lower pitch as necessary.

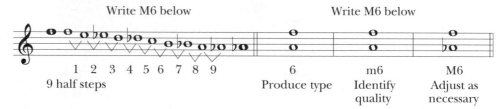

Although these methods may be satisfactory, they offer the potential for error, since there are several steps. The theory of interval inversion provides a simple, two-step method of writing intervals below a given pitch. Since intervals invert in a predictable way, an interval below a given pitch can be produced by first writing the inversion above (in the usual way) and then lowering this pitch an octave. If we want a major seventh below D, for example, we would calculate a minor second (the inversion of a major seventh) *above* the given pitch and then write this pitch an octave lower.

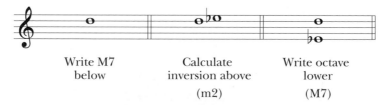

As long as the inversion is determined correctly, and assuming there are no errors in notation, interval inversion combined with octave transposition will always produce the correct pitch below a given note. The fastest and simplest way to determine a diminished sixth below the pitch G, for instance, is through interval inversion. We would figure the inversion (an augmented third) above G, then write the resulting pitch an octave lower. Remember: You can always verify your work by counting half steps between the two pitches.

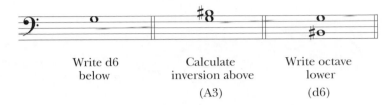

| Write d6 below | Calculate inversion above (A3) | Write octave lower (d6) |

EXERCISE 7-10

Fundamental Skills

Intervals below a Given Pitch

Using inversion, construct intervals below the pitches given. Check your answer by calculating the half steps between pitches.

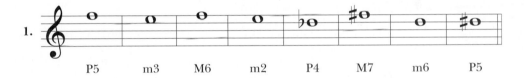

1. P5   m3   M6   m2   P4   M7   m6   P5

2. m3   A4   P8   m7   d5   M6   m2   A6

3. M3   d5   P4   M7   m6   P5   A4   m3

SELF-TEST

1. (20 points) Identify the type and the quality of the marked intervals in this melody. Write your answers in the blanks beneath the score.

Paul Hindemith, *Mathis der Maler*

a. _____   b. _____   c. _____   d. _____   e. _____

2. (20 points) If necessary, adjust the *upper pitch* of each interval so that it corresponds to the specified quality.

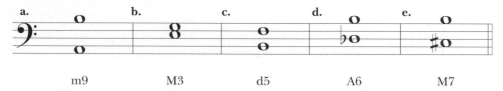

m9   M3   d5   A6   M7

3. (20 points) Construct the specified intervals above the given pitches.

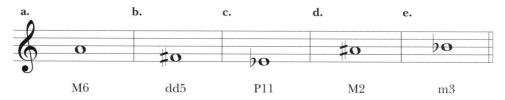

M6   dd5   P11   M2   m3

4. (20 points) Some of the following interval pairs are enharmonic equivalents; others are not. Use the blanks to identify the type and the quality of the intervals in each measure. Circle the measure if interval pairs form enharmonic equivalents (A4–d5 or A6–m7, for example).

_____ _____   _____ _____   _____ _____   _____ _____

5. (20 points) Write the designated pitches *below* the one given.

M7   m3   P5   d6

SUPPLEMENTARY STUDIES

Drill Exercises

1. Identify the given interval by type and quality; then write and identify another interval that is the enharmonic equivalent of the first. (More than one answer may be correct.)

a.

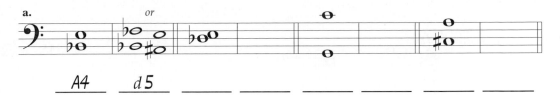

A4   d5   ___ ___ ___ ___ ___ ___

b.

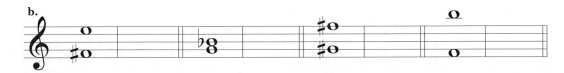

___ ___ ___ ___ ___ ___ ___ ___

2. The following interval exercises include complexities such as (theoretical) keys like G♯ major or F♭ major, double sharps and flats, and unusual intervals. Write the specified interval above the given pitch.

a.

P5   m6   M2   AA4   P4   M7   A8   m3

b.

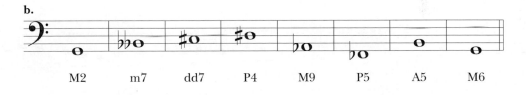

M2   m7   dd7   P4   M9   P5   A5   M6

c.

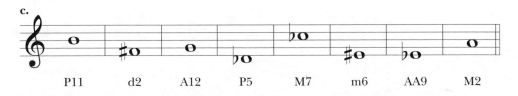

P11   d2   A12   P5   M7   m6   AA9   M2

Write an interval *below* the given pitch.

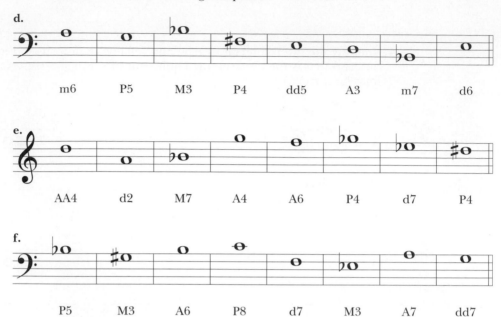

d.

m6   P5   M3   P4   dd5   A3   m7   d6

e.

AA4   d2   M7   A4   A6   P4   d7   P4

f.

P5   M3   A6   P8   d7   M3   A7   dd7

Fundamental Skills in Practice

3. An interval exists between each pair of adjacent pitches in a melody. For the following melodies, identify the type and the quality of intervals.

Amy Beach, *Meadow-Larks*

Carl Pandolfi, *On Lockwood*

Johannes, Brahms, *Love Song*

NAME _____

4. Transpose the melody by duplicating each pitch a perfect fifth higher. You might also consider trying other transpositions (a major second higher, for example, or a perfect fifth lower).

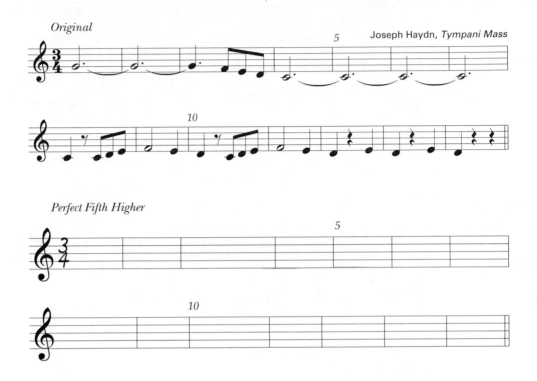

Original

Joseph Haydn, *Tympani Mass*

Perfect Fifth Higher

5. Examine the interval content of the following duet. First, analyze each part melodically and make a list of the intervals used most and least frequently. Next, do the same for the harmonic intervals *between* pitches. Notice that if one part remains stationary and the other moves, the harmonic interval has changed.

   Do certain interval types occur typically on strong or weak beats? Concerning the melodic line, is the motion of each voice mostly by step? By leap? Speculate on whether this duet was written for voice or for an instrument.

Jan P. Sweelink, *Rules of Composition*

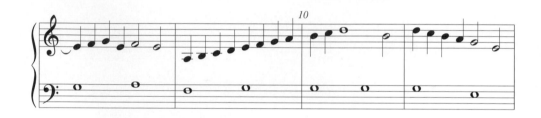

CHAPTER 8

Minor Scales and Keys

Most traditional Western music is either major or minor in mode. Although a number of other scales existed theoretically during the Common Practice Period, composers between about 1675 and 1875 limited themselves to only two "modes" of melodic composition. As you learned in Chapter 6, an essential difference between major and minor is the interval between the first and third scale degrees. In major, this interval is two whole steps (M3); in minor, the first and third scale degrees are separated by a whole step plus a diatonic half step (m3).

The Minor Scale

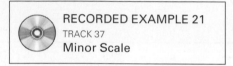

RECORDED EXAMPLE 21
TRACK 37
Minor Scale

The MINOR SCALE is found on the white keys of the piano beginning on the pitch A. Listen to the ascending and descending A minor scale heard on Track 37 of Recorded Example 21. Follow the score and the keyboard diagram as you listen.

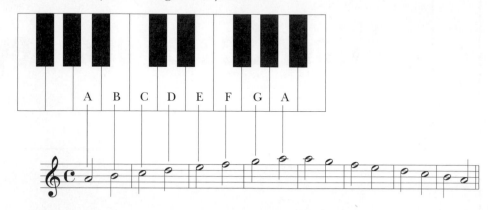

Return to Track 23 (Recorded Example 15, page 150). Listen again to the major scale and the melody "Joy to the World." Concentrate on the difference in "color" between this scale and the minor scale you just heard (Recorded Example 21).

Like the major scale, the minor scale has a fixed pattern of intervals—one that you will need to memorize: W H W W H W W.

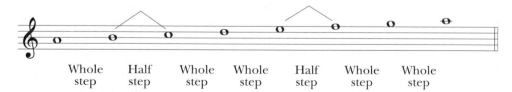

If the scale descends, of course, the pattern is reversed (W W H W W H W).

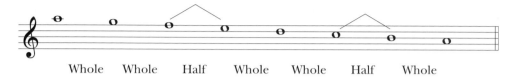

RECORDED EXAMPLE 22
TRACK 38
Major and Minor Scales

Before playing Recorded Example 22, study the differences between the C major and C minor scales, and between the A major and A minor scales as shown below. Listen for the half steps; they fall between the third and fourth and between the seventh and eighth scale degrees in a major scale. In minor, half steps lie between the second and third and between the fifth and sixth degrees.

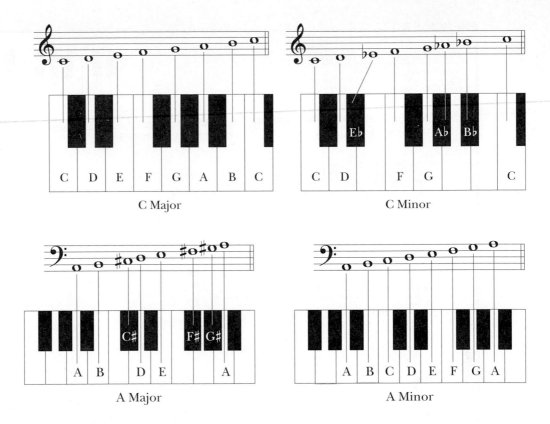

Transposing Minor Scales. Minor scales are transposed exactly as major scales are: Begin with the given tonic, write basic pitches up to and including the octave above the tonic (including any accidental), and then add accidentals to the basic pitches as necessary to duplicate the minor scale pattern (W H W W H W W). If the tonic is D, for example, a B♭ is necessary to create a minor scale.[1]

If the tonic is B, two sharps are necessary to create a minor scale.

---

[1]Later in this chapter, we will write minor scales using *key signatures* and employ the same fast and accurate methods we used for major scales and intervals. For the present, however, write minor scales with accidentals, by duplicating the whole-step–half-step pattern.

EXERCISE 8-1

Fundamental Skills

Minor Scales

A. Duplicate the minor scale pattern (W H W W H W W) to begin on the given tonics. Mark the half steps and add accidentals as necessary.

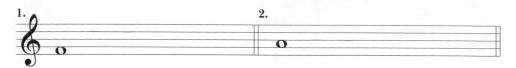

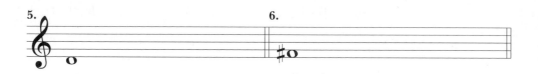

B. Using letter names, spell the ascending minor scales specified.

1. B	____	____	____	____	____	____	B
2. E	____	____	____	____	____	____	E
3. Db	____	____	____	____	____	____	Db
4. G♯	____	____	____	____	____	____	Gb
5. D	____	____	____	____	____	____	D
6. G	____	____	____	____	____	____	G
7. Bb	____	____	____	____	____	____	Bb
8. Eb	____	____	____	____	____	____	Eb

EXERCISE 8-2

Musicianship Skills

KEYBOARD: Minor Scales

There are definite fingering patterns for minor scales, but for the time being you may practice them on the keyboard with any convenient fingering pattern. Do not use the same finger for every note, however, and as always, avoid using the thumb on a black key. Return to Skill Exercise 8-1 and practice those scales ascending and descending. Write out other scales and practice them as well.

VARIATIONS IN MINOR

Whereas traditional Western composers did not regularly alter the intervals in major scales, three different forms of the minor scale are common. Distinct forms of minor are known as *natural, harmonic,* and *melodic.* These scale patterns reflect the choices made most often by traditional composers. Performers practice three different forms of minor to become familiar with the most typical melodic patterns. In actual composition, however, the three forms are adhered to less rigidly, and two of them may even be employed simultaneously (one form in the melody, for example, and a different one in the harmony).

Natural (Pure) Minor

The minor scale derived from the application of the intervallic formula we learned earlier is NATURAL (or PURE) MINOR. If we transpose the A minor scale to begin on the pitch E, an F♯ is necessary to duplicate that intervallic pattern. The resulting scale is known as E natural (pure) minor. At this point, you might want to replay Recorded Example 21 (Track 37) to review the sound of the minor scale.

W H W W H W W	W H W W H W W	
A Natural Minor	E Natural Minor	

Leading Tone and Subtonic. In addition to the interval between the first and third scale degrees, an important difference between major and natural minor scales concerns the seventh degree. As we discussed in Chapter 6, a "leading tone" is defined both as the seventh degree of a scale *and* as a pitch that lies a diatonic half step below the tonic. In a natural minor scale, however, a *whole step* separates the seventh and eighth scale degrees. The seventh degree of a major scale is a leading tone, but in natural minor, the seventh scale degree lies a whole step below the tonic and is called a SUBTONIC.

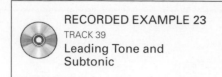

RECORDED EXAMPLE 23
TRACK 39
Leading Tone and
Subtonic

Play Recorded Example 23 and listen first to an E major scale, then to the E natural minor scale that follows. As you listen to the two scales, follow the score and keyboard diagrams below. Pay particular attention to the leading tone in the major scale and the subtonic in minor.

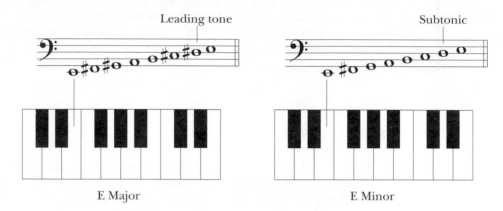

The subtonic, which results in minor from applying the interval pattern given earlier, is especially associated with the natural (pure) form. In the F natural minor scale, for example, the seventh degree, E♭, is a whole step below the tonic and, therefore, a subtonic.

F Natural Minor

Harmonic Minor

Composers of traditional Western music have favored the sound of the leading tone over that of the subtonic. Even when writing in the minor mode, composers create a leading tone by raising the seventh degree a half step. This new scale is known as HARMONIC MINOR (Recorded Example 24). As discussed, the seventh degree in natural minor is a subtonic; in *harmonic* minor, the seventh degree is a leading tone—just as it is in major.

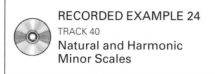

RECORDED EXAMPLE 24
TRACK 40
Natural and Harmonic
Minor Scales

In Recorded Example 24, hear both natural and harmonic minor scales beginning on the pitch A. The effect of the subtonic in ascending natural minor is relatively weak, but listen to the dramatic emphasis on the tonic created by the leading tone (harmonic minor).

A Natural Minor

A Harmonic Minor

Construct a harmonic minor scale, beginning with natural minor (from the intervallic pattern), then raising the seventh degree a half step. If the seventh degree is a flattened pitch, it will become natural in harmonic minor; if it is a basic (natural) pitch, it will become sharp; if sharp, it will be raised to a double sharp.

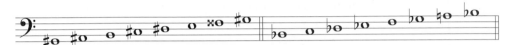

Harmonic Minor Scales

EXERCISE 8-3

Fundamental Skills

Harmonic and Natural Minor Scales

A. In the space provided, use accidentals to complete ascending natural and harmonic minor scales on the tonics given.

1.   Natural   Harmonic

2.   Natural   Harmonic

3.   Natural   Harmonic

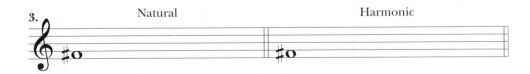

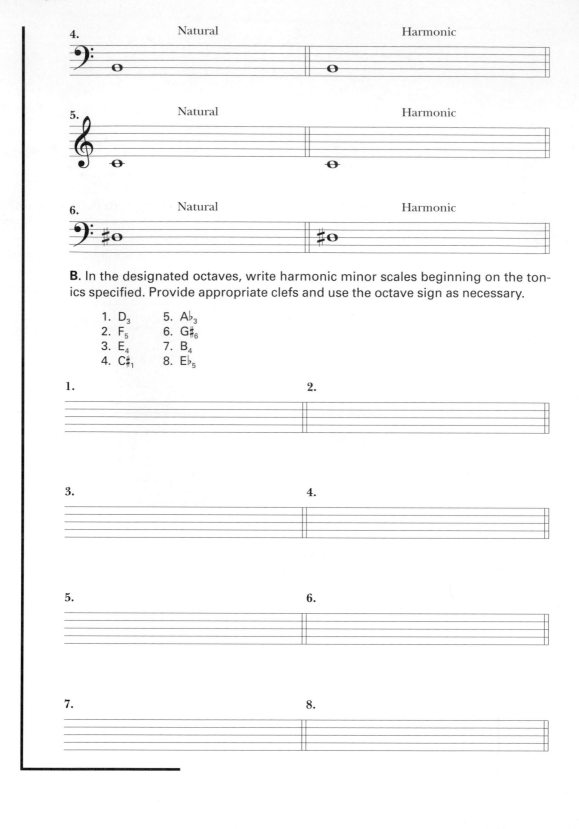

B. In the designated octaves, write harmonic minor scales beginning on the tonics specified. Provide appropriate clefs and use the octave sign as necessary.

1. D_3 5. $A\flat_3$
2. F_5 6. $G\sharp_6$
3. E_4 7. B_4
4. $C\sharp_1$ 8. $E\flat_5$

Melodic Minor

Although the raised seventh degree in harmonic minor provides a leading tone, it also creates a melodic problem for traditional composers: the AUGMENTED SECOND, an interval including a whole step plus *a chromatic half step*. An augmented second occurs between the sixth and raised seventh degrees of a harmonic minor scale.

C Harmonic Minor Scale

For both theoretical and stylistic reasons, traditional composers have avoided the augmented second in melodies. The practice that evolved from this preference resulted in the third form of minor: *melodic*. In a MELODIC MINOR SCALE, the sixth and seventh degrees are *both* raised a half step from the natural minor pattern. Since the seventh degree is raised a half step, the melodic minor scale has a leading tone; the raised sixth degree that characterizes melodic minor eliminates the augmented second.

A harmonic minor

A melodic minor

Descending Melodic Minor.   Major, natural, and harmonic minor scales are written the same ascending and descending. Melodic minor has two forms, however. The ascending form, with raised sixth and seventh degrees, has already been discussed. The traditional descending form of melodic minor is the same as natural minor. Whereas the sixth and seventh degrees are raised in ascending melodic minor, they return to their natural (pure) pitches descending.

RECORDED EXAMPLE 25
TRACK 41
Harmonic and Melodic Minor Scales

When you play Recorded Example 25, listen closely to the augmented second in the ascending harmonic form and the *absence* of this awkward interval in ascending melodic minor. Listen as well to the difference in ascending and descending forms of melodic minor, shown on the next page.

Harmonic

Melodic

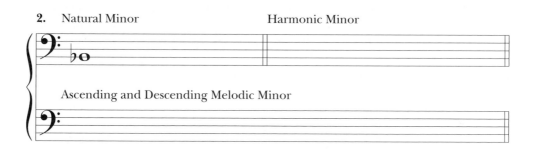

EXERCISE 8-4 _____

Fundamental Skills

Melodic Minor Scales

A. Begin by writing a *natural* minor scale in the first measure. Follow this with *harmonic* minor in the second measure. Finally, use the second line to write a complete ascending and descending melodic minor scale.

1.   Natural Minor   Harmonic Minor

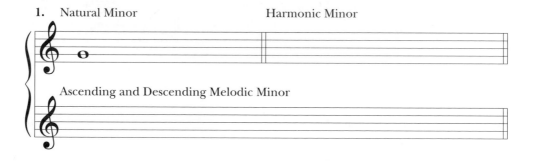

Ascending and Descending Melodic Minor

2.   Natural Minor   Harmonic Minor

Ascending and Descending Melodic Minor

3.   Natural Minor   Harmonic Minor

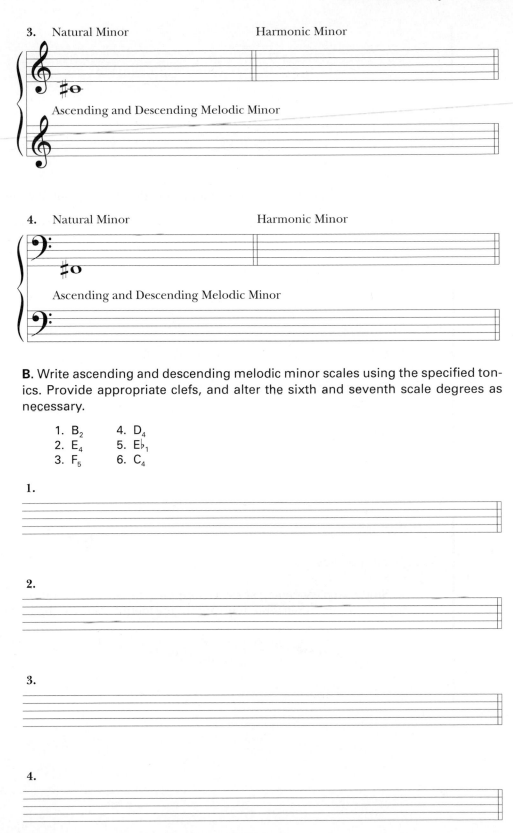

Ascending and Descending Melodic Minor

4.   Natural Minor   Harmonic Minor

Ascending and Descending Melodic Minor

B. Write ascending and descending melodic minor scales using the specified tonics. Provide appropriate clefs, and alter the sixth and seventh scale degrees as necessary.

1. B_2 4. D_4
2. E_4 5. Eb_1
3. F_5 6. C_4

1.

2.

3.

4.

5.

6.

C. Use letter names to write ascending and descending melodic minor scales.

	Ascending			*Descending*	
1.	D♯ __ __ __ __ __ __ __	D♯	D♯	__ __ __ __ __ __ __	D♯
2.	G __ __ __ __ __ __ __	G	G	__ __ __ __ __ __ __	G
3.	D __ __ __ __ __ __ __	D	D	__ __ __ __ __ __ __	D
4.	E __ __ __ __ __ __ __	E	E	__ __ __ __ __ __ __	E
5.	C __ __ __ __ __ __ __	C	C	__ __ __ __ __ __ __	C
6.	A __ __ __ __ __ __ __	A	A	__ __ __ __ __ __ __	A
7.	C♯ __ __ __ __ __ __ __	C♯	C♯	__ __ __ __ __ __ __	C♯
8.	A♯ __ __ __ __ __ __ __	A♯	A♯	__ __ __ __ __ __ __	A♯

EXERCISE 8-5

Fundamental Skills

Recognizing Scales

A. Study each ascending scale. Determine whether it is major or one of the three forms of minor; then write the appropriate identification in the blank.

1.

A MELODIC

2.

_____ _____

3.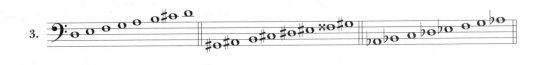

_____ _____

4.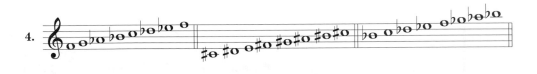

_____ _____

B. The following melodies are constructed from a major scale or from one of the three forms of minor. Analyze the scale with the given tonic; then, identify the scale type in the blank. One of the melodies employs two different forms of minor. Locate this melody and speculate on why the composer used the two different forms.

1. Tonic

Joseph Haydn, Symphony No. 104

2. Tonic

Robert Schumann, "The Wild Horseman"

3. Tonic   P. I. Tchaikovsky, Symphony No. 4

4. Tonic   Ludwig van Beethoven, Sonata, Op. 2, No. 4

5. Tonic   Giovanni Pergolesi, *Stabat Mater*

6. Tonic   W. A. Mozart, Symphony No. 40

7. Tonic   César Franck, Symphony in D Minor

8. Tonic   Jewish Folk Song, "Havah Nagilah"

EXERCISE 8-6

Musicianship Skills

EAR TRAINING: Hearing Major and Minor Modes

A. In Chapter 6, you worked through Recorded Exercise 17 (Track 26), in which you differentiated between major and minor modes based on scale degrees 1–3. Before moving on, repeat that exercise using the blanks below. Listen to the ascending or descending pattern, then write "M" for major or "m" for minor as appropriate.

(Replay Recorded Example 17, Track 26.)

Ascending

1. _____ M   _____ m   _____ M   _____ m   _____ M   _____ m

2. _____ m   _____ m   _____ M   _____ m   _____ M   _____ M

Descending

3. _____ m   _____ m   _____ m   _____ M   _____ M   _____ m

4. _____ M   _____ m   _____ M   _____ M   _____ m   _____ M

B. These recorded passages include scale degrees 1–5 in major and minor. Some of the passages are ordered (1-2-3-4-5 or 5-4-3-2-1); others are unordered. In all cases, however, the tonic is the first or the final pitch heard (Recorded Example 26).

> **RECORDED EXAMPLE 26**
> TRACK 42
> Scale Degrees 1–5

Listen to the recorded passage, then write "M" for major or "m" for minor to identify the mode.

1. _____ M   _____ m   _____ m   _____ M   _____ m   _____ M

2. _____ m   _____ m   _____ M   _____ M   _____ m   _____ m

3. _____ m   _____ M   _____ m   _____ m   _____ M   _____ M

TRACK 43

C. Scale degrees 5–8 help us differentiate among the three forms of minor. If you hear a leading tone, for example, the scale is harmonic or melodic minor. If there is a subtonic, on the other hand, the scale must be natural minor. You will hear several stepwise patterns that represent the *final* four ascending pitches of a scale (degrees 5-6-7-8). Listen to the final two pitches and determine whether the seventh degree is a **leading tone** (write "LT" in the blank) or a **subtonic** (write "ST").

1. _____ LT   _____ LT   _____ ST   _____ LT   _____ ST   _____ ST

2. _____ LT   _____ ST   _____ LT   _____ LT   _____ LT   _____ ST

D. "Sing" the following melodies to yourself silently. Is the mode major or minor? Write the appropriate word in the blank. If you do not know one or more of these songs, think of others you know, sing them to yourself, and identify the modes.

1. "We Three Kings"   _____

2. "America"   _____

3. "God Rest Ye Merry, Gentlemen"   _____

4. "When Johnny Comes Marching Home"   _____

5. "When We Played Our Charade"   _____

6. "Oh! Susanna"   _____

KEYS AND KEY RELATIONSHIPS

You probably have noticed that the keys (and the scales) of C major and A minor have the same key signature (no sharps or flats). This means that there are *two* keys with identical pitch inventories—one major, the other minor. Key signatures in minor are formed exactly as they are in major; the accidentals necessary to produce *natural* minor are grouped at the beginning of a composition and are always in effect unless canceled. In addition to A minor, note the key signatures for the keys of D minor, B minor, E minor, and F minor. These scales appear on pages 217, 219, and 220, respectively).

A minor   D minor   B minor   E minor   F minor

Minor Key Signatures

When compositions begin in minor, the key signature always reflects *natural* minor. In the actual music, however, harmonic and melodic forms of minor occur regularly as accidentals effect the raised sixth or seventh. Sometimes, as in the next example, two or more forms of minor occur in the same composition—even simultaneously.

Frédéric Chopin, Mazurka, Op. 67, No. 2

Study the following table, which shows the signatures for all fifteen minor keys. Notice that the order of sharps and flats and their placement on the grand staff are the same as for major keys.

A minor   E minor   B minor   F♯ minor   C♯ minor   G♯ minor   D♯ minor   A♯ minor

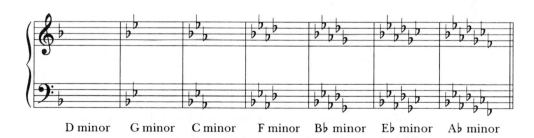

D minor   G minor   C minor   F minor   B♭ minor   E♭ minor   A♭ minor

The Circle of Fifths for Minor Keys. As is the case in major keys, clockwise movement by ascending perfect fifth produces each successive new minor key on the sharp side; moving counterclockwise by the same interval displays minor keys with increasing numbers of flats.

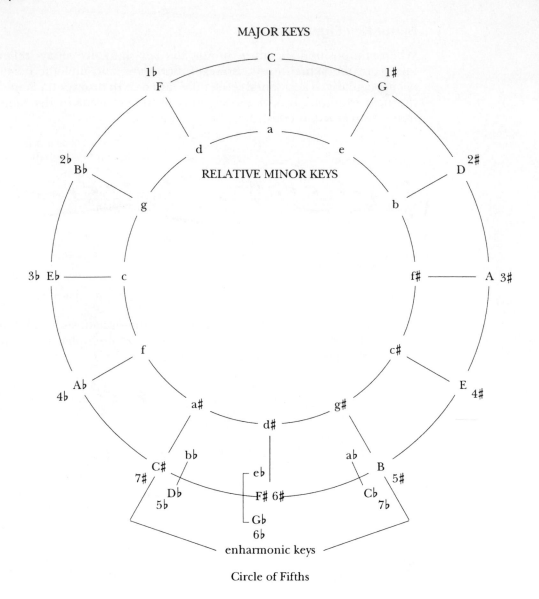

Circle of Fifths

You will probably have more success in your studies of music fundamentals if you memorize the minor key signatures. However, if you know the major keys thoroughly, you can quickly find a minor key signature by associating it with its relative major, as discussed on page 233.

The keys of A minor and C major are related in that they contain the same *pitches*. The keys of C major and C minor, on the other hand, have *different* key signatures and a number of different pitches; the relationship between these two keys centers on their having the same *tonic pitch*. These two close relationships—of key signature and tonic pitch—are important in traditional music.

The Parallel Relationship

When major and minor keys have the same tonic, we term the relationship between them PARALLEL. The parallel relationship is complementary; C major is the parallel major of C minor, just as C minor is the parallel minor of C major. Parallel major and minor keys always have the same tonic pitch. The key of B♭ minor, therefore, is the parallel minor of B♭ major. Parallel major and minor keys have the same tonic, but they have different key signatures.

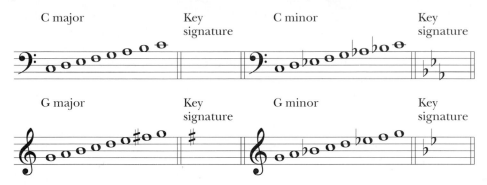

The Relative Relationship

Major and minor keys with the same key signature share a complementary RELATIVE RELATIONSHIP. The key of C major is the relative major of A minor; A minor is the relative minor of C major.

Determining Relative Minor Keys. Relative major and minor keys *do not* have the same tonic. The tonic of the relative minor of a given major key is the sixth scale degree of the corresponding major scale. Put another way, the tonic of the relative minor lies a major sixth above the tonic of the major key. As we have discussed, the relative minor of C major is A minor. The pitch A is the sixth scale degree of C major and, likewise, A is a major sixth above C. Note the relationship between major and relative minor as shown here.

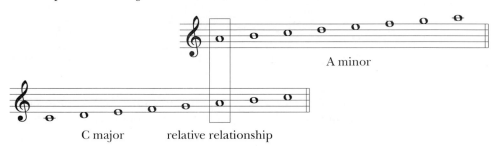

Find the relative minor of a given major key simply by naming the sixth scale degree of that major scale (*including* any accidental, of course); this pitch will be the tonic of the relative minor. The key signature of this minor key will be the same as that of its relative major.

If we can count from the tonic up to the sixth scale degree to find a relative minor, logic suggests that we can also *count down*—from the tonic down to the sixth scale degree. If you elect this approach, remember to apply the key signature of the major key to the process (as you would do when counting up to the sixth degree from the tonic). To verify your answer, make sure that the sixth scale degree lies a *minor third* below the tonic of the major key.

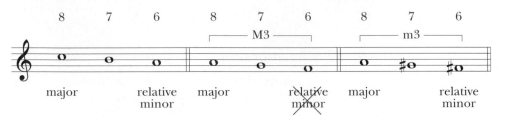

Problem: *Find the relative minor of D major.*

1. Locate the sixth degree of the D major scale. This can be done by counting up six pitches or down three within the tonic key. If you are comfortable with intervals, find the tonic of the relative minor key by calculating a major sixth *above* or a minor third *below* the tonic of the major key.

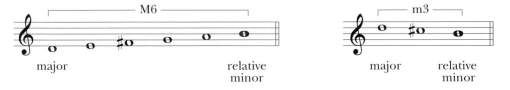

2. Assume the key signature of the major key for the minor as well. The tonic of the minor key is the sixth scale degree of the relative major.

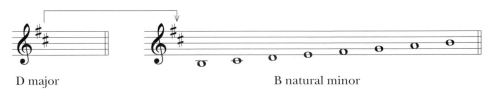

More Tricks of the Trade

For those with no prior experience, music fundamentals may be daunting at times. Fortunately, several logical associations make the task of understanding keys easier. For example, a parallel minor key will always have three flats more than the corresponding major key. If we begin with C major (no sharps, no flats), and add three flats (B♭, E♭, and A♭, of course), we arrive at the key signature for *C minor*—the parallel minor.

C major   + 3♭   C minor

In many ways, flats and sharps in music exist just like positive and negative numbers in mathematics. If we begin with E major (with four sharps), then add three flats to those four sharps to determine the key signature of the parallel minor, the remainder is one sharp. The parallel minor of E major is E minor; the key signature is one sharp. Likewise, if we want the key signature of the parallel minor of E♭ major (three flats), we add three more flats and arrive at a six-flat key signature for the minor key.

E major   + 3♭   E minor   E♭ major   + 3♭   E♭ minor

EXERCISE 8-7 ──────────────────────────────

Fundamental Skills

Relative Minor Keys

    A. For the following major keys, determine the relative minor and write the name of that key in the blank. Write the key signature, which is the same for both keys.

Major	*Relative Minor*	*Key Signature*
1. B♭	_____	
2. G	_____	
3. F	_____	
4. B	_____	
5. C	_____	

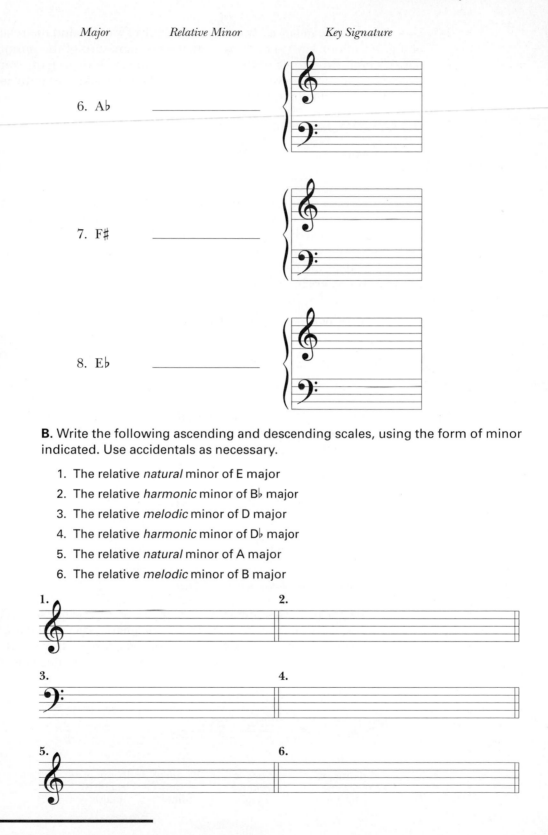

	Major	*Relative Minor*	*Key Signature*
6.	A♭	_____	
7.	F♯	_____	
8.	E♭	_____	

B. Write the following ascending and descending scales, using the form of minor indicated. Use accidentals as necessary.

1. The relative *natural* minor of E major
2. The relative *harmonic* minor of B♭ major
3. The relative *melodic* minor of D major
4. The relative *harmonic* minor of D♭ major
5. The relative *natural* minor of A major
6. The relative *melodic* minor of B major

Determining Relative Major Keys. When you want to find the relative major of a given minor key (to find or verify the key signature of the minor key, perhaps), employ the tonic of the minor key as the sixth degree of "some" major scale. Remember, however, that the intervals between sixth, seventh, and eighth scale degrees in major are inflexible:

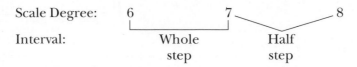

The tonic of the given minor key is the sixth scale degree of the relative major. Count up a whole step (to reach the seventh scale degree), then a diatonic half step to arrive at the tonic of the relative major. If we want the relative major of B minor, for example, we ascend first a whole step (B to C♯) and in addition, a diatonic half step higher (C♯ to D). The relative major of B minor is D major; both keys have two sharps in their key signatures.

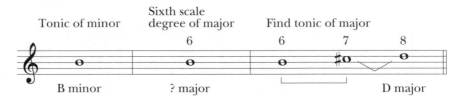

Another, one-step method of finding the relative major is to ascend a minor third from the tonic of the minor key. This process also produces the tonic of the relative major.

Problem: *Find the relative major of C♯ minor.*

1. Assume the pitch C♯ as the sixth scale degree of some major scale. Find the tonic of this major scale by determining the intervals between sixth, seventh, and eighth scale degrees as they appear in a major scale. If you prefer, calculate a minor third above the tonic of the minor key to produce the same result.

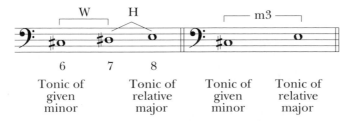

2. The new tonic located through this process is the name of the relative major key.

E major   C♯ minor

EXERCISE 8-8

Fundamental Skills

Relative Major Keys

A. Using the formula outlined previously, determine the relative major for each given minor key. Next, produce the key signature that applies to both minor and relative major.

Minor	Relative Major	Key Signature
1. E♭	_____	
2. F♯	_____	
3. B	_____	
4. G	_____	

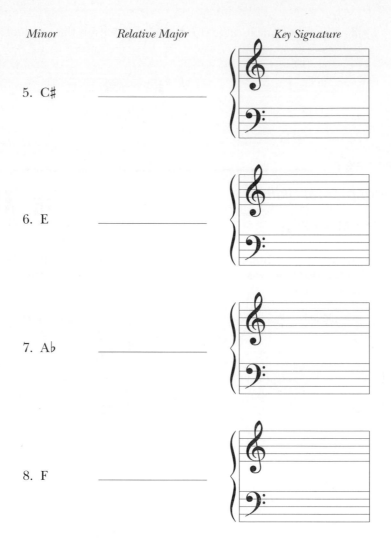

	Minor	*Relative Major*	*Key Signature*
5.	C♯	_____	
6.	E	_____	
7.	A♭	_____	
8.	F	_____	

B. If you need to find the parallel minor of a given major key, you may want first to find the relative major of that minor. This will provide the key signature of the minor key. Remember: In the parallel relationship, two keys have the same tonic; unless you happen to know the key signature, you must still find the relative major to determine the key signature of the parallel minor.

Write the ascending and descending scales as indicated.

1. The parallel natural minor of C major
2. The parallel *harmonic* minor of E major
3. The parallel major of B minor
4. The relative *melodic* minor of E♭ major
5. The relative *natural* minor of B♭ major
6. The relative major of D♯ minor
7. The parallel *harmonic* minor of A major
8. The relative *harmonic* minor of F major

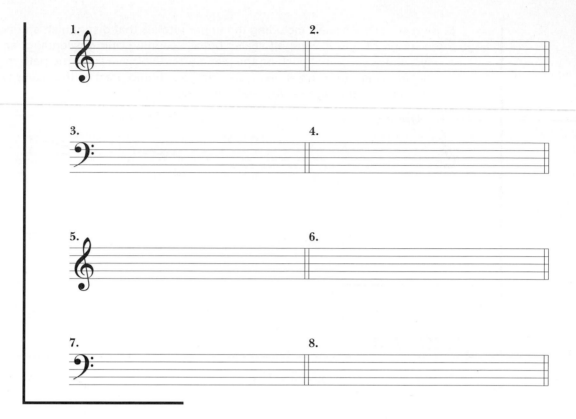

EXERCISE 8-9

Musicianship Skills

SIGHT SINGING: Minor Scale Patterns

A. Using syllables or another method specified by your instructor, sing the following five-note patterns. Play the first pitch on the keyboard, then match that pitch and sing the pattern ascending and descending. Be conscious that only the third scale degree is different.

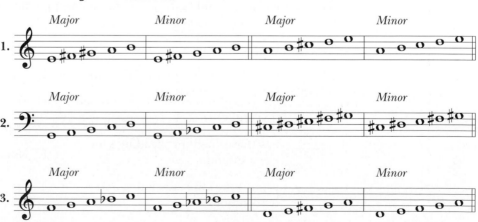

B. Sing complete scales, including the upper pitches that distinguish among the three forms of minor. Sing all scales both ascending and descending, and as always, check your final pitch on the piano after you have sung the pattern. The pitches for scales on F are shown here, but you should practice the scales with a variety of tonics throughout your natural range.

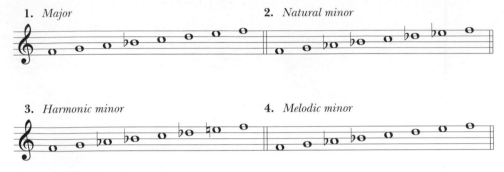

1. *Major*   **2.** *Natural minor*

3. *Harmonic minor*   **4.** *Melodic minor*

SELF-TEST

1. (40 points) On the grand staff, provide signatures for the major key specified. In addition, use the blank to name the relative minor key.

a.   **b.**   **c.**   **d.**

D♭ major ____ minor   B♭ major ____ minor   F♯ major ____ minor   G♭ major ____ minor

2. (10 points) In the space provided, match the letter or letters identifying the scale form *or forms* that correspond to the given statement. In some cases, you will write two or more letters in the blank.

a. _____ has (have) a leading tone

b. _____ include(s) an augmented second

c. _____ has (have) two whole steps between first and third scale degrees

d. _____ has (have) neither a leading tone nor a subtonic

e. _____ is (are) the same ascending and descending

A. Major

B. Natural minor

C. Harmonic minor

D. Melodic minor

E. None of these

f. _____ has (have) raised sixth scale degree

g. _____ has (have) the same descending form as natural minor

h. _____ has (have) the same last four pitches as major (and *not* major)

i. _____ has (have) the same first five pitches as major (and *not* major)

j. _____ has (have) a subtonic

3. (20 points) Identify the tonic pitch and the scale type and form (if minor).

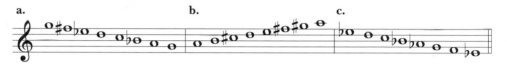

4. (30 points) Write the ascending scales indicated.
   a. The parallel harmonic minor of B major
   b. The relative melodic minor of E major
   c. The relative major of D minor

SUPPLEMENTARY STUDIES

Drill Exercises

1. Review the definitions of a leading tone and a subtonic; then, write the pitches that represent those alternative possibilities in the scales given. Although the subtonic is not customarily associated with a major scale, it is commonly found in music before about 1675 and after about 1875.

	Scale	*Leading Tone*	*Subtonic*
a.	C major	_____	_____
b.	G major	_____	_____
c.	G minor	_____	_____
d.	B major	_____	_____
e.	A♭ major	_____	_____
f.	A minor	_____	_____
g.	F♯ major	_____	_____
h.	F♯ minor	_____	_____
i.	B♭ major	_____	_____
j.	E minor	_____	_____

2. Write ascending natural minor scales on the given tonics. Provide your own clefs and use the octave sign as necessary.

a.	E♭$_2$	**d.**	C♯$_3$
b.	B$_4$	**e.**	G$_1$
c.	F♯$_5$	**f.**	D$_6$

a.

b.

c.

d.

e.

f.

3. Using pitch names, write ascending harmonic minor scales on the given tonics. Circle the augmented second.

a. D♯ _____ _____ _____ _____ _____ _____ D♯

b. E _____ _____ _____ _____ _____ _____ E

c. G♯ _____ _____ _____ _____ _____ _____ G♯

d. A _____ _____ _____ _____ _____ _____ A

e. B♭ _____ _____ _____ _____ _____ _____ B♭

f. C _____ _____ _____ _____ _____ _____ C

g. C♯ _____ _____ _____ _____ _____ _____ C♯

h. F _____ _____ _____ _____ _____ _____ F

4. Write ascending and descending melodic minor scales on the given tonics.

a.

b.

c.

d.

NAME _____

5. The following scales are either major or natural, harmonic, or melodic minor. Identify the scale type and form (if minor).

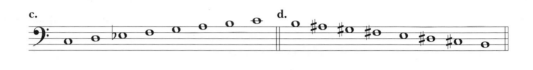

Fundamental Skills in Practice

6. Analyze the following melodies as you did in Chapter 6. As before, the tonic is given. Your task will be to make an inventory of the pitches present and determine which are used most and least frequently. Some of the melodies are major, others are minor. If the melody is minor, determine the predominant form and if directed to do so, comment on the use of the raised sixth or seventh (or both).

CHAPTER 9

Root-Position Triads

ESSENTIAL TERMS

- bass
- diminished triad
- doubling
- fifth
- harmony
- major triad
- minor triad
- root
- root position
- spacing
- tertian triad
- third
- triad
- triad quality

HARMONY is the vertical aspect of musical line that occurs simultaneously with melody, rhythm, and form. Of several fundamental elements that separate Western music from that of other cultures, perhaps our concept of a planned and regimented harmony is one of the easiest to understand. In Africa, for example, a simple musical line may be "thickened" through recurring rhythmic and melodic patterns called *ostinatos*. In India, many compositions feature a *drone*—two or three crucial pitches heard over and over again as a static accompaniment. In still other cultures, many different melodies are heard simultaneously in a layered texture. But in the West, at least since 1600, we have preferred a harmony that is clearly accompanimental and, at the same time, separable into stereotypical patterns.

The basic unit of Western harmony is the TRIAD—a collection of three pitches. In the context of traditional harmony, the term "triad" is understood to mean a TERTIAN TRIAD—one built of consecutive thirds. Although other types of triads exist, the tertian triad is the only one employed in traditional music.

Tertian Triads

The tertian triad involves three elements: the *root,* the *third,* and the *fifth.* The ROOT is the lowest of the three pitches when the triad appears over consecutive lines or spaces. Above the root is the THIRD; the upper pitch of the triad is the FIFTH. The terms "third" and "fifth," of course, refer to the intervals that these pitches form above the root.

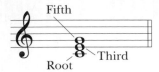

Root Position

The root is the lowest of the three pitches when the triad occurs over consecutive lines or spaces. When the root of the triad is also the BASS (the lowest-sounding pitch), the triad is in ROOT POSITION. If a triad is not in root position, it is *inverted.* Inverted triads, in which the root is above the bass, will be discussed in the next chapter. The four triads shown here are all in root position.

Root-Position Triads

Triad Quality

Like intervals, triads occur in a number of qualities—each with a distinct "flavor." The quality of a triad is determined by the qualities of its three component intervals. In traditional music, there are only four triad qualities: *major, minor, diminished,* and *augmented.*

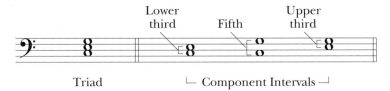

Triad   └─ Component Intervals ─┘

Major and Minor Triads. A root-position triad is MAJOR if the lower of the two thirds is a major third *and* if the interval between root and fifth is a perfect fifth. If those two conditions are met, the upper third will always be minor.[1]

---

[1]Later in this chapter, we will discuss triad construction and identification based on the key signature of the root. For the present, we will study triads through their component intervals.

Major Triad in Root Position

Triads are identified according to the pitch name of the root and the quality of the triad. The preceding example is an A♭ major triad. Notice the identification of other root-position major triads shown here.

Like the major triad, the root-position MINOR TRIAD has a perfect fifth between root and fifth. The lower third, however, is minor; the upper third, major.

Minor Triad in Root Position

Minor triads are identified through the pitch name of the root and the quality of the triad. Study the major and minor triads in the next example.

Notice that the root and the fifth of the pairs of major and minor triads above are the same. The third of the triad imparts the characteristic modal flavor just as the third scale degree does in major and minor scales.

RECORDED EXAMPLE 27
TRACK 44
Major and Minor Triads

Arpeggiation. The pitches in the previous example are sounded at the same time (harmonic or chordal performance). In a melody, triads and chords are often ARPEGGIATED—that is, sounded sequentially in the manner of a harp. Play Recorded Example 27, Track 44, and listen to the qualities of arpeggiated major and minor triads.

Play Track 45 and hear the same triads in a harmonic context.

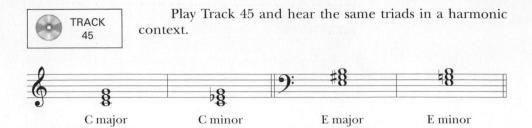

EXERCISE 9-1

Fundamental Skills

Major and Minor Triads

The following triads are either major or minor in quality. Identify the root by writing the correct pitch name in the first blank (B, A♭, F♯, or whatever). Use the second blank to identify the quality as major ("M") or minor ("m"). Begin your identification of quality with the lower third of each triad. If the third is major, the triad is major; if it is minor, the triad is minor. In this exercise, you may assume that the fifths will be perfect.

EXERCISE 9-2

Musicianship Skills

EAR TRAINING: Major and Minor Triads

(Not Recorded) Your instructor will play a number of triads. You will hear root-position major or minor triads first arpeggiated, then played simultaneously as chords. Cover the answer to the right of each blank, listen to the triad played, then write "M" or "m" as appropriate. Check your response by moving the mask to reveal the correct answer. There are six triads in each line.

1. ____ M   ____ m   ____ m   ____ M   ____ M   ____ m

2. ____ M   ____ m   ____ m   ____ M   ____ M   ____ M

3. ____ M   ____ m   ____ m   ____ M   ____ m   ____ m

4. ____ M   ____ m   ____ M   ____ m   ____ M   ____ M

5. ____ M   ____ m   ____ m   ____ M   ____ M   ____ m

Diminished and Augmented Triads. Whereas major and minor triads have in common a perfect fifth between root and fifth, diminished and augmented triads are alike in that their fifths are *not* perfect. In a DIMINISHED TRIAD, the lower third is minor; the fifth, diminished. When those two conditions are met, the upper third will be minor as well.

Diminished Triad in Root Position

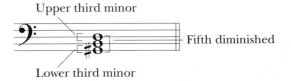

Upper third minor

Fifth diminished

Lower third minor

Four different root-position diminished triads are shown in the next example.

A diminished triad   C♯ diminished triad   F diminished triad   E♭ diminished triad

The AUGMENTED TRIAD incorporates a major third and an augmented fifth above the root; the upper third is major.

Augmented Triad in Root Position

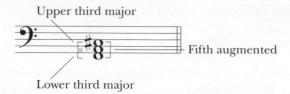

Upper third major

Fifth augmented

Lower third major

The triads in the following example are augmented in quality.

A augmented triad   C♯ augmented triad   F augmented triad   E♭ augmented triad

RECORDED EXAMPLE 28

TRACK 46

Triads of All Qualities

Now play Recorded Example 28, which includes triads of all four qualities. Listen first to the unique sounds of diminished and augmented triads that are arpeggiated (Track 46). Because the fifths are not perfect, you will probably hear these triads as somewhat unstable.

C diminished   C augmented   E diminished   E augmented

TRACK 47

On Track 47, the same triads are performed harmonically.

C diminished   C augmented   E diminished   E augmented

TRACK 48

Play Track 48 and compare all four qualities of triads as you study their notation, shown below. The triads are sounded harmonically, as notated.

Bb major   Bb minor   Bb diminished   Bb augmented

B major   B minor   B diminished   B augmented

EXERCISE 9-3 _____

Fundamental Skills

Diminished and Augmented Triads

The following root-position triads are either diminished or augmented. In the first blank, write the pitch name of the root; use the second blank to record the quality. Use "A" for an augmented triad and "d" for diminished. Look first at the lower third. If it is minor, the triad is diminished; if major, the quality is augmented.

1.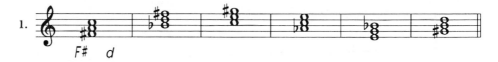

    F# d

2.

3.

4.

EXERCISE 9-4 _____

Musicianship Skills

EAR TRAINING: Triad Qualities

(Not Recorded) Your instructor will again play a number of triads—first melodically, then harmonically. In the first set of exercises, differentiate between major ("M") and augmented ("A"). In the second set, distinguish between minor ("m") and diminished ("d"). You will be asked to identify all triad qualities in a later exercise. Cover the answer to the right of each blank, listen to the triad played, then write the appropriate letter. Move the mask and check your answer.

Major or Augmented

1. _____ M   _____ A   _____ A   _____ M   _____ A   _____ A

2. _____ A   _____ M   _____ M   _____ A   _____ M   _____ M

3. _____ A   _____ M   _____ A   _____ M   _____ M   _____ M

4. _____ M   _____ A   _____ A   _____ A   _____ M   _____ A

5. _____ M   _____ A   _____ M   _____ M   _____ A   _____ M

Minor or Diminished

1. _____ m   _____ m   _____ m   _____ d   _____ m   _____ d

2. _____ d   _____ m   _____ d   _____ m   _____ m   _____ m

3. _____ m   _____ d   _____ d   _____ m   _____ d   _____ d

4. _____ m   _____ d   _____ m   _____ m   _____ m   _____ d

5. _____ d   _____ d   _____ m   _____ d   _____ d   _____ m

Triad Identification: All Qualities

Earlier, you differentiated between major and minor and between diminished and augmented triads by measuring the lower third. Now that you have studied all four traditional qualities, begin not with the third but with the fifth. If the fifth is perfect, the quality must be either major or minor (diminished and augmented triads have fifths of other qualities). If the fifth is *not* perfect, the triad is *neither* major *nor* minor. Analysis of the lower third (between root and third) differentiates between the two remaining possibilities (as in Skill Exercises 9-1 and 9-2). If the fifth is perfect and the lower third is major, the triad is major.[2] If the fifth is not perfect and the lower third is major, the triad is augmented. The following chart illustrates the identification process.

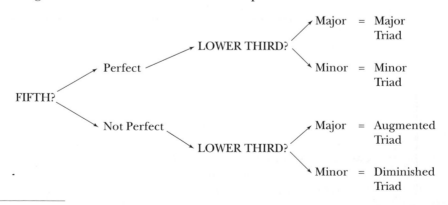

_____

[2]This statement assumes that only the four traditional qualities—major, minor, diminished, and augmented—will be encountered. In music before about 1600 and after about 1875, triads of other qualities exist.

Triads and Key Signatures

Although triads can be identified and constructed by calculating or duplicating intervals above the root, another method is simpler and more reliable. As we did in earlier chapters with scales and intervals, we may construct or identify triads quickly by comparing the upper pitches with the key signature represented by the root.

Major and Minor Triads. If the third and the fifth of a root-position triad are pitches in the major key signature of the root, *that triad is major in quality.* Given the first triad below, we know immediately that the quality is major because the third and the fifth, B and D, are pitches in the key of G (the root). Likewise, we can see at once that the second triad, C-E♭-G, is *not* major, since there is no E♭ in the key of C major.

Major triad   Not major

If the third of a major triad is lowered a half step, the resulting triad is minor in quality. Look again at the second example above. We have already determined that the pitches C, E♭, and G *do not* constitute a major triad. Now, if we compare the notated triad with one that we know to be major, we should see differences easily. Compared with a major triad with C as the root (C-E-G), the triad C-E♭-G has a lowered third; by definition, it is minor in quality.

C major triad   ?   Major with   C minor triad
                                          lowered third

We can use the same process to construct major triads. Given the root, write the third and the fifth as basic pitches, then apply the major key signature of the root to the third and the fifth.

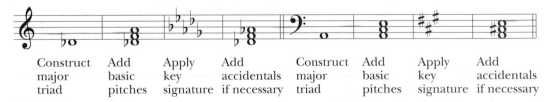

| Construct major triad | Add basic pitches | Apply key signature | Add accidentals if necessary | Construct major triad | Add basic pitches | Apply key signature | Add accidentals if necessary |

If we want to construct a minor triad, we can employ the same process, but we must lower the third a half step.

Construct major triad | Add basic pitches | Apply key signature | Add accidentals if necessary | Lower third

For those who know the minor key signatures as well as the major ones, triad construction and identification are even easier. If the third and the fifth of a triad correspond to the *minor* key signature represented by the root, *that triad is minor in quality*. To construct a minor triad on B, we might use the key signature of B *major* and then lower the third as discussed earlier. We can save a step, however, by applying the key signature of B *minor* to the third and the fifth.

| Construct
minor triad | Apply minor
key signature | Add accidentals
if necessary |

Diminished and Augmented Triads. If you are familiar with major key signatures, construct diminished and augmented triads beginning with one that is major (as described previously), then make alterations as follows:

- *For a minor triad,* lower the third (as discussed).
- *For a diminished triad,* lower the third *and* the fifth.
- *For an augmented triad,* raise the fifth.

Major	Minor	Diminished	Augmented
	Lowered third	Lowered third Lowered fifth	Raised fifth

Again, if you know minor key signatures, construct a diminished triad by beginning with one that is minor, then lowering the fifth.

Minor	Diminished
	Lowered fifth

EXERCISE 9-5

Fundamental Skills

Triad Construction

A. Construct root-position triads of the qualities specified on the given pitches. First, write the third and the fifth as basic pitches; next, add the major key signature of the root. Finally, add these accidentals to the third or the fifth (or both) *if necessary*.

Major Triads

3.

4.

5.

6.

Write minor triads using the process practiced above, but after applying the major key signature to the basic pitches, lower the third.

Minor Triads

	Root	Basic pitches	Key signature	Lower third	Minor triad
7.					
8.					
9.					
10.					

11.

12.

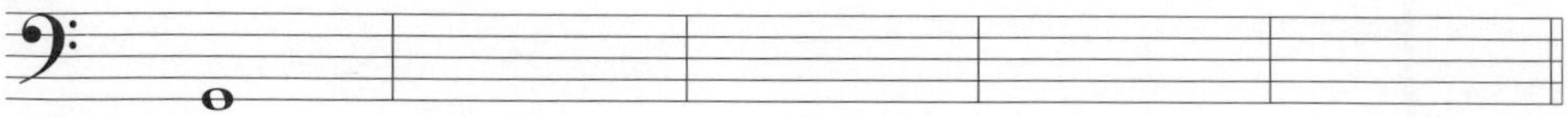

Augmented Triads

13.

Root	Basic pitches	Key signature	Raise fifth	Augmented triad

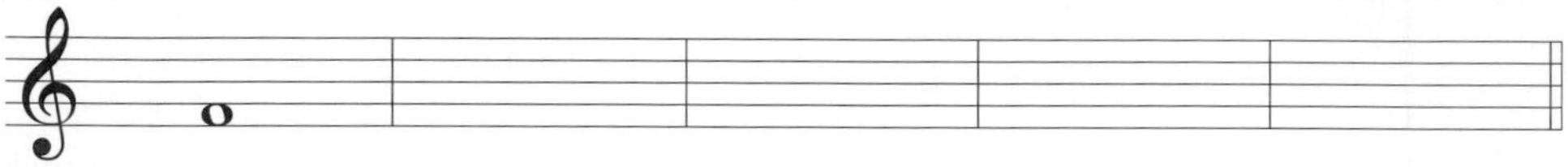

14.

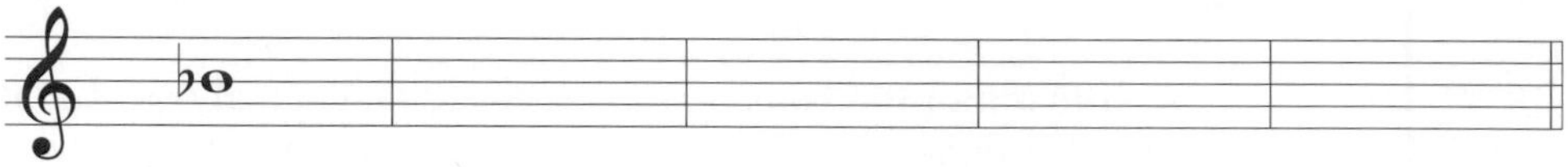

15.

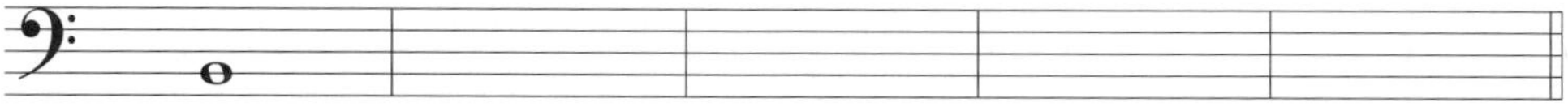

16.

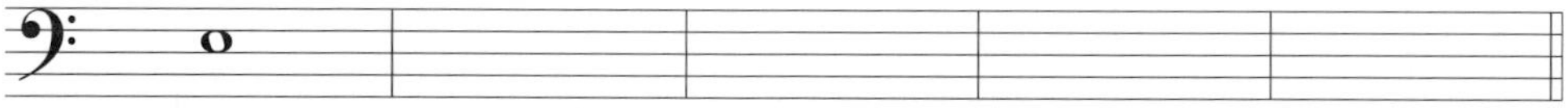

17.

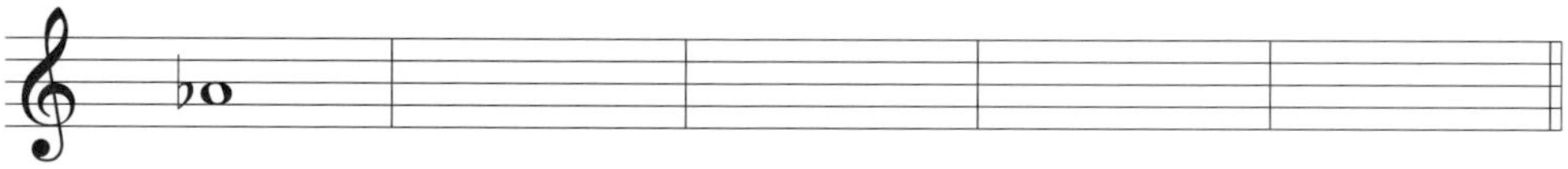

18.

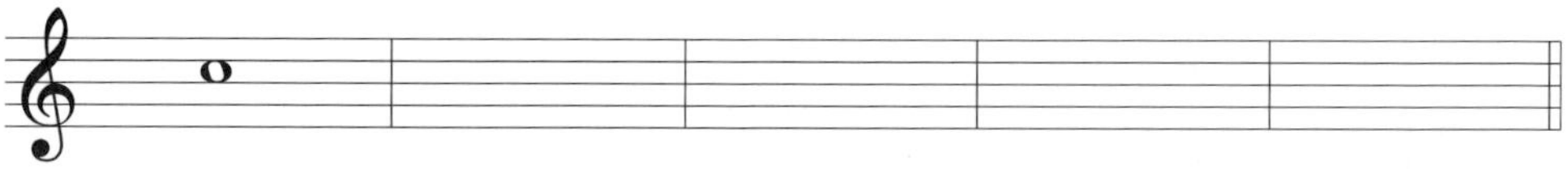

Diminished Triads

Root	Basic pitches	Key signature	Lower third and fifth	Diminished triad

19.

20.

21.

22.

23.

24.

B. Begin by writing the specified pitch in an appropriate clef. Next, use this pitch as the root for a root-position triad of the quality suggested. Employ the octave sign as necessary.

1. G_4 major	9. E_3 diminished
2. C_3 minor	10. B_5 major
3. $B\flat_2$ minor	11. F_2 minor
4. A_5 diminished	12. $G\flat_5$ major
5. C_6 augmented	13. $E\flat_2$ minor
6. $F\sharp_3$ major	14. $A\flat_3$ major
7. D_4 diminished	15. G_4 augmented
8. $E\flat_4$ augmented	16. $C\sharp_3$ diminished

1.   2.   3.   4.   5.   6.   7.   8.

9.   10.   11.   12.   13.   14.   15.   16.

EXERCISE 9-6

Fundamental Skills

Identifying Triad Quality

All four qualities of root-position triads are included in these exercises. Identify the root name in the first blank and the quality ("M," "m," "d," or "A") in the second blank.

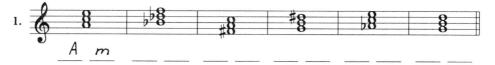

A m ___ ___ ___ ___ ___ ___ ___ ___ ___ ___

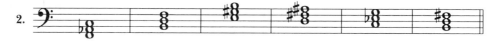

___ ___ ___ ___ ___ ___ ___ ___ ___ ___

___ ___ ___ ___ ___ ___ ___ ___ ___ ___

___ ___ ___ ___ ___ ___ ___ ___ ___ ___

EXERCISE 9-7

Musicianship Skills

KEYBOARD: Root-Position Triads

Return to the four lines of Skill Exercise 9-6 and play each triad at the keyboard. Use the thumb, third, and fifth fingers for the root, third, and fifth, respectively. First play the triad melodically (arpeggiated), then harmonically as a chord. Practice hands separately, then play the triads with left and right hands together. Listen carefully to the characteristic sound of each triad.

EXERCISE 9-8

Musicianship Skills

EAR TRAINING: Recognizing Triad Quality

RECORDED EXAMPLE 29
TRACK 49
Recognizing Triad Quality

You will hear root-position triads of all four qualities in Recorded Example 29. Listen first for the quality of the fifth. If it is *perfect,* the triad is major or minor; if it is *not perfect,* the triad is diminished or augmented. Concentrate next on the lower third. This will separate major from minor, or diminished from augmented. As before, use a mask to cover the answer, which appears to the right of each blank. Listen to the triad, respond instinctively, then check your answer. There are six triads in each line. In lines 1, 3, and 5, you will hear the triad arpeggiated, then played as a chord. In the even-numbered lines, the triads are chordal. You may want to repeat this exercise for additional practice. Consider using another sheet to record your answers, then check them against this page.

1. ___ M   ___ m   ___ M   ___ m   ___ M   ___ M

2. ___ m   ___ d   ___ d   ___ m   ___ M   ___ m

3. ___ M   ___ A   ___ M   ___ A   ___ M   ___ m

4. ___ d   ___ m   ___ M   ___ m   ___ d   ___ A

5. ___ m   ___ M   ___ A   ___ d   ___ d   ___ M

Ear-Training and Sight-Singing Studies: Judging Your Progress

Most students begin ear-training and sight-singing studies with a minimum of prior experience. In large part, your progress will depend upon (1) classroom instruction and experiences, (2) practice outside class, and (3) individual talent. For some students, a couple of hours in class each week are sufficient to develop existing aural skills. For most, however, individual practice *outside class* is mandatory both for basic understanding and for steady progress.

The sight-singing and ear-training exercises in this text are not intended to facilitate *mastery* of the aural skills materials presented. Much more class time and a considerably wider variety of exercises will be necessary for most students to reach their full potentials in these areas. Text exercises demonstrate the scope and variety of skills generally associated with professional music study.

Especially if aural skills materials are difficult for you, consider several points relating to your individual practice.

1. No two students have identical natural abilities; therefore, no two students should expect to progress at the same rates.
2. When you practice sight singing or ear training, you *must* have a keyboard available so that you can judge your work. Without reinforcement, practice may do more harm than good. Accordingly, two or more students working together will usually accomplish a great deal more than the same students working separately.
3. Limit your goals. In the next exercise, for example, you are asked to sing major and minor thirds. If this is difficult for you at first, concentrate on a more narrow facet of the process, such as simply matching pitches or singing scale degrees 1-2-3 accurately. Move on to singing the thirds themselves when other parts of the exercise are easier for you.

EXERCISE 9-9

Musicianship Skills

SIGHT SINGING: Major and Minor Thirds

A. Major and minor thirds are important in defining triad quality. This exercise involves singing intervals. First, sound the given pitch on the piano. Next, match this pitch, and, assuming it as the tonic, sing the first three scale degrees of a major or minor scale. Finally, sing a major or minor third from the first to the third scale degrees (omitting the second). Play the same interval on the piano to check your accuracy. The numbers 1, 2, and 3 on the score below stand for scale degrees. Your instructor, however, may ask you to sing using solfège syllables or another system.

Major Thirds

Example

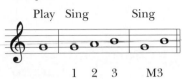

1.

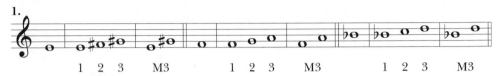

2.

3.

4.

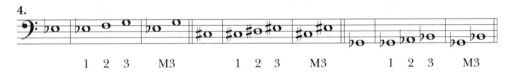

Minor Thirds

Example

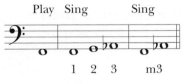

1.

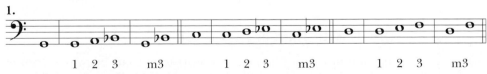

2.

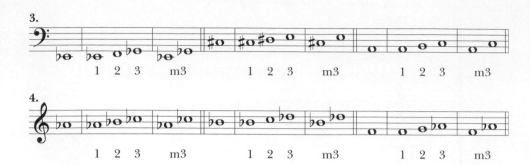

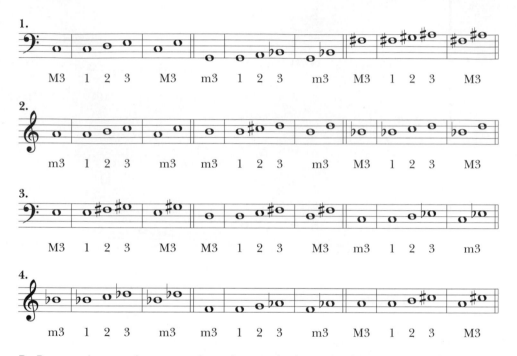

Mixture of Major and Minor Thirds

B. Repeat the previous exercises, but omit the stepwise segment. Sound the given pitch on the piano, match that pitch, then sing the major or minor third ascending and descending. Check your accuracy against the keyboard.

Triads with Third or Fifth Given

Sometimes you will need to construct a triad beginning not with the root but with a given third or fifth. If the pitch G is identified as the root, for example, a root-position major triad involves the pitches G, B, and D. When the pitch G is the *third*, however, the root-position triad is E♭, G, and B♭. Given the third of a triad, descend a major third to find the root.

| Given root | Root-position | Given third | Root-position |
| (major) | triad | (major) | triad |

When the fifth is the given pitch, construct a root-position triad by first descending a perfect fifth to find the root, then filling in the basic pitches and any necessary accidentals as you have done previously.

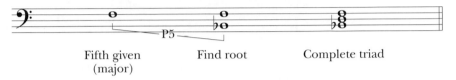

| Fifth given | Find root | Complete triad |
| (major) | | |

From a given third or fifth, construct minor, diminished, or augmented triads in the same manner.

Minor Triad

With given third:

- Descend a minor third to find the root.
- Add the root and a perfect fifth above the root to complete the triad.

With given fifth:

- Descend a perfect fifth to locate the root.
- Add the root and a minor third above the root to complete the triad.

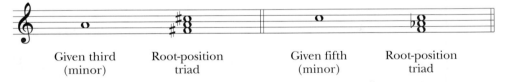

| Given third | Root-position | Given fifth | Root-position |
| (minor) | triad | (minor) | triad |

Diminished Triad

With given third:

- Descend a minor third to find the root.
- Add the root and a diminished fifth above the root to complete the triad.

With given fifth:

- Descend a diminished fifth to locate the root.
- Add the root and a minor third above the root to complete the triad.

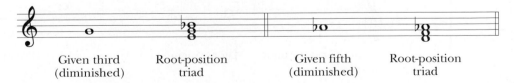

| Given third | Root-position | Given fifth | Root-position |
| (diminished) | triad | (diminished) | triad |

Augmented Triad

With given third:

- Descend a major third to find the root.
- Add the root and an augmented fifth above the root to complete the triad.

With given fifth:

- Descend an augmented fifth to locate the root.
- Add the root and a major third above the root to complete the triad.

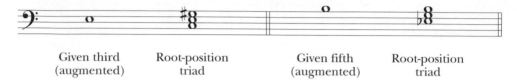

Given third   Root-position   Given fifth   Root-position
(augmented)   triad   (augmented)   triad

EXERCISE 9-10

Fundamental Skills

Triads with Given Third or Fifth

A. Beginning on the given third or fifth, construct root-position triads of the qualities indicated. Be sure to add any necessary accidentals (although, of course, you *may not* change the given pitch).

Given Third

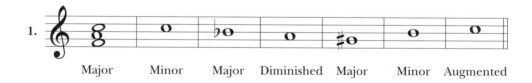

1. Major   Minor   Major   Diminished   Major   Minor   Augmented

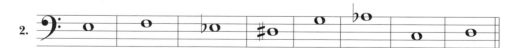

2. Minor   Diminished   Augmented   Major   Minor   Major   Augmented   Minor

3. Diminished   Minor   Major   Augmented   Minor   Major   Diminished   Major

Given Fifth

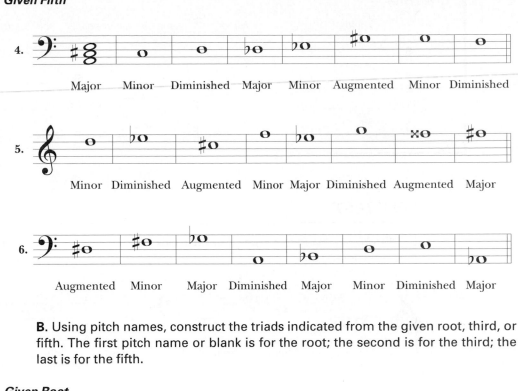

Major   Minor   Diminished   Major   Minor   Augmented   Minor   Diminished

Minor   Diminished   Augmented   Minor   Major   Diminished   Augmented   Major

Augmented   Minor   Major   Diminished   Major   Minor   Diminished   Major

B. Using pitch names, construct the triads indicated from the given root, third, or fifth. The first pitch name or blank is for the root; the second is for the third; the last is for the fifth.

Given Root

	Major	*Minor*	*Diminished*	*Augmented*
1.	F _A_ _C_	B♭ ____ ____	G ____ ____	C ____ ____
2.	A♭ ____ ____	B ____ ____	D ____ ____	F ____ ____
3.	C♯ ____ ____	E♭ ____ ____	F♯ ____ ____	B ____ ____
4.	D♭ ____ ____	A ____ ____	C♯ ____ ____	E♭ ____ ____

Given Third

	Major	*Minor*	*Diminished*	*Augmented*
5.	_Ab_ C _Eb_	____ E♭ ____	____ D ____	____ B ____
6.	____ F♯ ____	____ E ____	____ G ____	____ F♯ ____
7.	____ A♭ ____	____ B ____	____ C ____	____ E♭ ____
8.	____ D ____	____ F♯ ____	____ B♭ ____	____ G ____

Given Fifth

	Major			Minor		Diminished		Augmented	
9.	*Ab* *C*	Eb	_____ _____	D	_____ _____	C	_____ _____	F#
10.	_____ _____	G	_____ _____	Ab	_____ _____	B	_____ _____	E
11.	_____ _____	Db	_____ _____	E	_____ _____	F#	_____ _____	G#
12.	_____ _____	C#	_____ _____	F	_____ _____	B	_____ _____	D

SELF-TEST

1. (30 points) Construct root-position triads of the qualities indicated above the given roots.

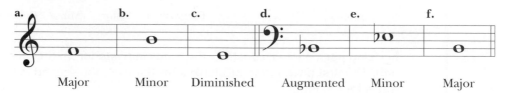

Major   Minor   Diminished   Augmented   Minor   Major

2. (40 points) Identify the root name and the quality of each triad.

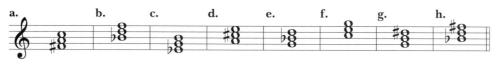

_____   _____   _____   _____   _____   _____   _____   _____

3. (30 points) Use the given third or fifth to construct root-position triads of the qualities specified.

Given Third   *Given Fifth*

Major   Diminished   Minor   Augmented   Minor   Major

SUPPLEMENTARY STUDIES

Drill Exercises

1. Analyze the following triads; then, compare your analysis with the given quality. If necessary, add an accidental to the third or the fifth, or both, to make the quality conform to that specified.

Minor   Major   Dimished   Augmented   Minor   Major   Minor   Diminished

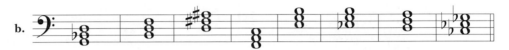

Diminished   Major   Augmented   Minor   Major   Augmented   Diminished   Major

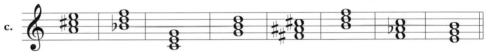

Major   Minor   Diminished   Augmented   Major   Minor   Minor   Diminished

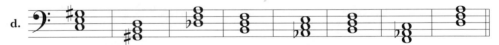

Augmented   Diminished   Major   Augmented   Major   Minor   Minor   Major

2. Write root-position triads of the qualities specified.

Major

Minor

Diminished

c.

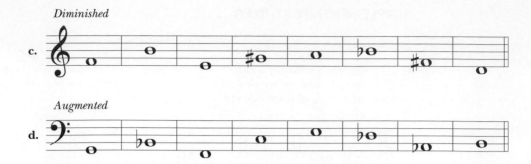

Augmented

d.

3. Use the given pitches as the *third* and construct root-position triads of the qualities indicated.

Minor   Major   Augmented   Minor   Diminished   Major   Minor   Augmented

4. Use the given pitches as the *fifth* and construct root-position triads as specified.

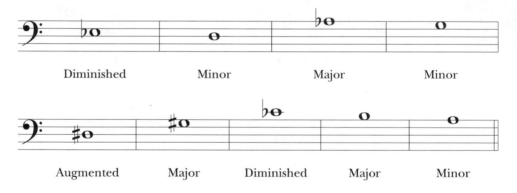

Diminished   Minor   Major   Minor

Augmented   Major   Diminished   Major   Minor

Fundamental Skills in Practice

5. The following melodies include outlines of root-position triads (bracketed). Use the blank staff to write the triads as superimposed thirds with accidentals as necessary. Identify the root and the quality of each triad.

J. S. Bach, Courante

a.

D MAJOR

NAME _____

L. van Beethoven, Sonata for Piano, Op. 53

Dolly Parton, "Nine to Five"

NAME _____

6. The following compositions have been reduced to their basic tertian structures: triads in root position. Identify the root and the quality of each triad, using the blanks provided. That done, analyze the harmony of each composition by counting the total number of triads and the number of times each different diatonic triad occurs (tonic, supertonic, mediant, and so on). How many different triad qualities do you find? How frequent are augmented and diminished triads? Try to draw conclusions regarding which triad or triads are most and least important. Are there some diatonic triads that do not occur at all in one or more of the compositions?

    You will notice that some pitches are not included in the harmonic reduction. These are called *nonharmonic tones*—dissonant pitches that fall into various categories and constitute an important element of a music theory course. Finally, pitches that constitute the seventh of a *seventh chord* have also been omitted from the reduction. Dominant seventh chords will be discussed in a later chapter.

Carl Maria von Weber, *Variation on an Original Theme*

a.

C major

Robert Schumann, "Chorale" from *Album for the Young*

b.

G major

NAME _____

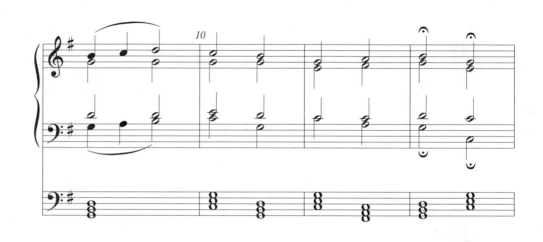

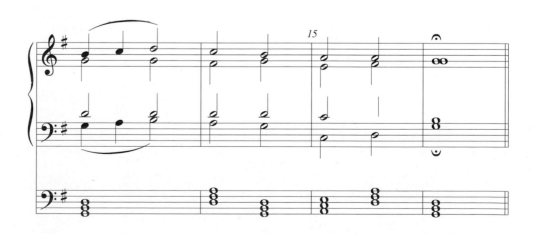

Inverted Triads

ESSENTIAL TERMS

- close position
- doubling
- figured bass
- first inversion
- music theory
- open position
- realization
- second inversion
- spacing

As early as the ninth century, scholars discussed the *theory* of Western music, posing rules for composition and guidelines for style. Today, we recognize music *fundamentals* as the basic elements of pitch and rhythm. Music theory, on the other hand, is a field more concerned with the way those materials are used in creating music. As we continue our studies of triads in this chapter with a discussion of inversions, we are approaching the field of music theory. Spelling and recognizing triads as abstract materials fall within fundamentals studies. Theoretical matters like relative stability, on the other hand, center on progressions (series) of triads within a given key.

INVERTED TRIADS

Just as an interval is sometimes inverted, the relationship between the root and the bass of a triad is flexible. As we discussed in the last chapter, a triad is in root position when the root is the lowest-sounding pitch. If the root appears *above* the bass, however, two new arrangements of the same triad are possible. These new versions—one with the third in the bass, the other with the fifth in the bass—are termed *first* and *second inversions*, respectively.

First Inversion

When the third of a triad is the lowest-sounding pitch, that triad is in FIRST INVERSION. In inverted triads, the root is always above the bass, but whether it is the highest or the middle pitch is not a factor in determining inversion. The basic first-inversion triad has component intervals different from those of a triad in root position. Instead of a third and a fifth above the bass (which is also the root), the first-inversion triad has a third and a *sixth* above the bass (which is *not* the root).

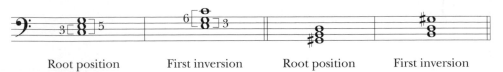

Root position   First inversion   Root position   First inversion

Second Inversion

If the fifth of a triad appears in the bass, the triad is in SECOND INVERSION. The component intervals in a second-inversion triad—a fourth and a sixth above the bass—differ from those in both root position and first inversion. Compare the root-position and inverted triads shown here.

Root position   First inversion   Second inversion

Quality. The inversion of a triad changes neither the root name nor the quality. The major triads above, for example, all have A♭ as the root. Because the bass is so important in traditional music, however, the relationship between root and bass (whether these are the same or different) is usually designated along with the root name and the quality. Inverted triads tend to be less stable than those in root position, and we typically take note of the root–bass relationship in any analysis.

RECORDED EXAMPLE 30

TRACK 50

Root-Position and Inverted Triads

Before going further, you might replay Recorded Example 28 (Track 48, page 254). Those passages offer a number of major and minor triads in root position. Now, follow the score below and listen to Recorded Example 30 (on this page) to experience the distinctive sounds of inverted triads.

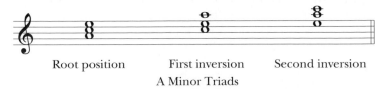

Root position   First inversion   Second inversion

A Minor Triads

Root position   First inversion   Second inversion

Bb Major Triads

Open and Close Position

When the root, the third, and the fifth of a triad are as close together as possible, the spatial position is termed CLOSE. If the spatial position is not close, then it is OPEN (there are only two possibilities). A root-position triad in open position has more than an octave between the bass (lowest pitch) and the soprano (highest pitch). In close position, this same distance is less than an octave.

C Major Triad in Root Position

Close position   Open positions

Construction of Inverted Triads

Building inverted triads is not a new process but, rather, an additional step in a process you already know. Begin as you did in the previous chapter by writing (preferably *visualizing*) a root-position triad of the quality needed. Next, rearrange the three pitches so that the *third* is in the bass. Inverted triads occur in both open and close positions; unless directed otherwise, however, use *close position* throughout the remaining chapters of this text.

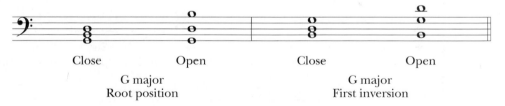

Close   Open   Close   Open

G major   G major
Root position   First inversion

To construct a second-inversion triad, first visualize or sketch an appropriate triad in root position, then arrange the pitches so that the *fifth* is in the bass. Although writing the root directly above the bass and making the third the highest pitch is the closest arrangement, many other possibilities exist.

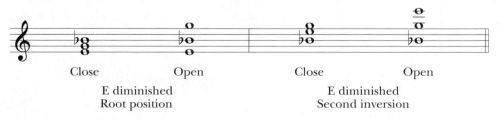

Close   Open   Close   Open

E diminished   E diminished
Root position   Second inversion

EXERCISE 10-1

Fundamental Skills

Constructing Root-Position and Inverted Triads

A. Study the following root-position triads. In the blank, identify the root and the quality as you did in Chapter 9. In the first blank measure, rewrite the triad in first inversion. Use the second blank measure for second inversion. Employ close position throughout.

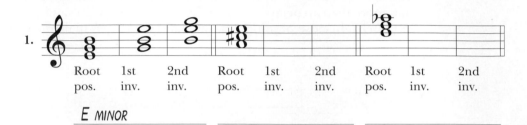

1.

| Root pos. | 1st inv. | 2nd inv. | Root pos. | 1st inv. | 2nd inv. | Root pos. | 1st inv. | 2nd inv. |

E MINOR

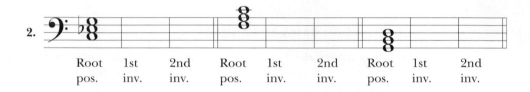

2.

| Root pos. | 1st inv. | 2nd inv. | Root pos. | 1st inv. | 2nd inv. | Root pos. | 1st inv. | 2nd inv. |

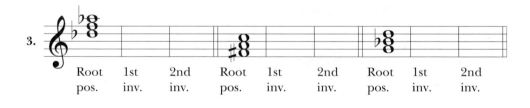

3.

| Root pos. | 1st inv. | 2nd inv. | Root pos. | 1st inv. | 2nd inv. | Root pos. | 1st inv. | 2nd inv. |

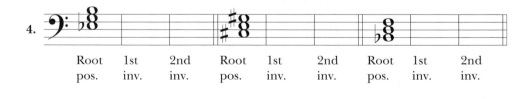

4.

| Root pos. | 1st inv. | 2nd inv. | Root pos. | 1st inv. | 2nd inv. | Root pos. | 1st inv. | 2nd inv. |

B. Construct root-position or inverted triads as directed. Try to think through the process at first; if that seems difficult, write out pitch names. As a temporary practice only, construct the root-position triad on scratch paper (as in section A of this exercise). Use close position.

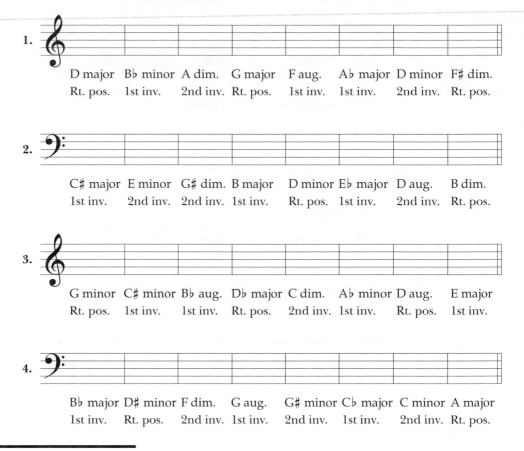

1.

D major	B♭ minor	A dim.	G major	F aug.	A♭ major	D minor	F♯ dim.
Rt. pos.	1st inv.	2nd inv.	Rt. pos.	1st inv.	1st inv.	2nd inv.	Rt. pos.

2.

C♯ major	E minor	G♯ dim.	B major	D minor	E♭ major	D aug.	B dim.
1st inv.	2nd inv.	2nd inv.	1st inv.	Rt. pos.	1st inv.	2nd inv.	Rt. pos.

3.

G minor	C♯ minor	B♭ aug.	D♭ major	C dim.	A♭ minor	D aug.	E major
Rt. pos.	1st inv.	1st inv.	Rt. pos.	2nd inv.	1st inv.	Rt. pos.	1st inv.

4.

B♭ major	D♯ minor	F dim.	G aug.	G♯ minor	C♭ major	C minor	A major
1st inv.	Rt. pos.	2nd inv.	1st inv.	2nd inv.	1st inv.	2nd inv.	Rt. pos.

Triad Construction: Given Bass

As we know, a given bass pitch is not always the root of a triad; it may also be the third or the fifth. Whereas your goal in Chapter 9 was to construct root-position triads of various qualities, you will now begin with a given bass pitch, then construct triads of any quality *and* in any root–bass relationship.

Given the pitch A as the root, the third, and the fifth, respectively, of root-position minor triads, we can reckon the pitches involved as discussed previously (see page 256 to review this process). Major, diminished, or augmented triads would be constructed similarly.

Construct Minor Triads

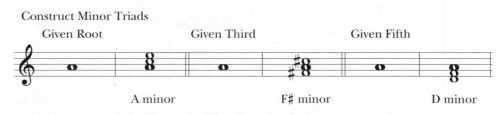

Given Root	Given Third	Given Fifth
A minor	F♯ minor	D minor

If the given bass is A, and if we want a minor triad in *first inversion,* then we know that the bass is also the third. The full triad is still F♯-A-C♯ (as above). But now, the pitches C♯ and F♯ will appear *above* the bass note, A. If the same bass and quality are given but *second inversion* is stipulated, then the full triad is D-F-A, with D and F sounding above the bass.

Minor	Minor	Minor
Root position	First inversion	Second inversion

Regardless of the quality desired, the process is the same. First, build the basic triad as you did in Chapter 9. Next, move the appropriate pitches above the bass and in either close or open position as needed. The following triads are in close position.

Major	Diminished	Augmented	Diminished
First inversion	First inversion	Second inversion	First inversion

EXERCISE 10-2

Fundamental Skills

Constructing Triads with Given Bass

A. Complete the triads specified *above* the given bass. Use open or close position as directed.

1. Use *close* position.

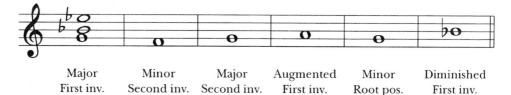

Major	Minor	Major	Augmented	Minor	Diminished
First inv.	Second inv.	Second inv.	First inv.	Root pos.	First inv.

2. Use *close* position.

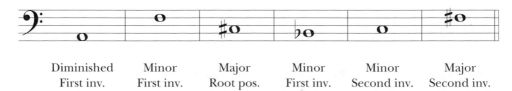

Diminished	Minor	Major	Minor	Minor	Major
First inv.	First inv.	Root pos.	First inv.	Second inv.	Second inv.

3. Use *open* position.

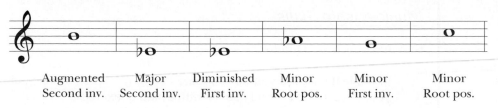

| Augmented | Major | Diminished | Minor | Minor | Minor |
| Second inv. | Second inv. | First inv. | Root pos. | First inv. | Root pos. |

4. Use *open* position.

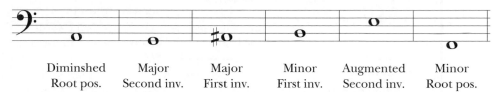

| Diminshed | Major | Major | Minor | Augmented | Minor |
| Root pos. | Second inv. | First inv. | First inv. | Second inv. | Root pos. |

B. For these exercises, first write the specified pitch in an appropriate clef. If necessary, employ the octave sign to avoid ledger lines. Next, use the pitch you wrote as the bass of a root-position, first-inversion, or second-inversion triad of the quality indicated. Use close position.

1. G_4
   Major, First inv.

2. $E\flat_3$
   Diminished, Second inv.

3. $B\flat_6$
   Major, Root pos.

4. D_2
   Minor, Second inv.

5. E_4
   Augmented, Second inv.

6. $F\sharp_4$
   Major, Second inv.

7. $A\flat_2$
   Minor, First inv.

8. $C\sharp_5$
   Augmented, root pos.

9. $G\sharp_4$
   Diminished, Root pos.

10. B_3
    Minor, Second inv.

1.   2.   3.   4.   5.

6.   7.   8.   9.   10.

EXERCISE 10-3

Musicianship Skills

Recognizing Triad Quality

In the last chapter, you differentiated among the four triad qualities. Strengthen your perception of triad quality with a similar exercise.

RECORDED EXAMPLE 31
TRACK 51
Root-Position and Inverted
Major and Minor Triads

Place your cover sheet at the end of the first blank (but be sure to cover the answer—the letter to the right of the blank). Play Recorded Example 31 (Track 51) and listen to each major or minor triad. Write "M" or "m" to identify the triad quality as appropriate. Some of the triads are inverted; however, you are asked to identify only quality in this exercise. Move your cover sheet to check the answer.

1. _____ M   _____ m   _____ M   _____ m   _____ m   _____ M

2. _____ m   _____ M   _____ m   _____ m   _____ M   _____ M

3. _____ m   _____ m   _____ m   _____ M   _____ M   _____ m

4. _____ M   _____ m   _____ m   _____ m   _____ M   _____ M

TRACK 52

Listen to the instructions on Track 52, then replay Track 51 in its entirety. As you listen a second time, use the first blank of each frame to identify triad quality as before ("M" or "m"). In addition, now determine whether the triad is in root position (write "R") or inverted (write "I"). Use the second blank of each frame for this information. You are not asked here to differentiate between first and second inversions.

1. __ __ M R   __ __ m R   __ __ M R   __ __ m R   __ __ m I   __ __ M R

2. __ __ m I   __ __ M R   __ __ m I   __ __ m R   __ __ M I   __ __ M I

3. __ __ m R   __ __ m I   __ __ m I   __ __ M R   __ __ m I   __ __ m R

4. __ __ M I   __ __ m R   __ __ m I   __ __ m R   __ __ M I   __ __ M R

TRIAD IDENTIFICATION

When a triad appears in root position and in a close spatial arrangement, the three pitches fall over consecutive lines or spaces. Inverted triads in close position *do not* have such an obvious visual arrangement and are therefore easily distinguished from triads in root position. The pitches of inverted triads in close position always involve lines *and* spaces.

Root position   Inverted

Before you can identify triad quality, root name, and root–bass relationship, you must rethink any inversions (rewrite at first, if necessary) to appear in root position and in close spatial arrangement. Because the pitches occur over consecutive spaces within an octave, the first triad below is obviously in root position; the root is A and the quality is major. The second triad, however, is clearly *not* in root position because the pitches, which, again, are in close position, involve lines *and* spaces. The triad is inverted, meaning that the lowest pitch, E♭, is *not* the root.

A major triad   Root ? Quality ?

Locate the root of an inverted triad by first arranging the pitches in close position so that they fall over consecutive lines or spaces. When you do this, however, take care to leave the bass *unchanged;* altering the bass will misrepresent the structure of the triad. If we consider the unidentified triad above, the pitch E♭ is clearly not the root. If G were the root of the triad, the pitches would fall over consecutive lines and would be G, B, and D. Since our triad includes neither B nor D, G is *not* the root. With C as the root, the pitches fall over consecutive thirds (C-E♭-G). Our triad is C minor and is in first inversion.

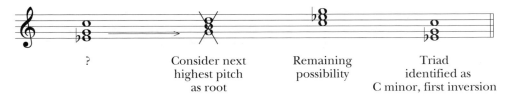

?   Consider next   Remaining   Triad
                  highest pitch   possibility   identified as
                    as root   C minor, first inversion

Doubling and Spacing

When triads appear as simple structures in close position, identification is not especially challenging. In the creative process, however, root-position and inverted triads appear in a variety of forms that make the identification of the basic material more complex.

Doubling.   Sometimes composers duplicate, or DOUBLE, one or more pitches of a triad to form a larger structure known as a CHORD.[1] Naturally, any doubling changes the sound of the triad, but the identification of the basic "raw material" is unaffected as long as all three pitches are present at least once. Notice that all the following chords are identified as diminished with A as the root.

---

[1]We can also correctly refer to a triad as a "chord," although the latter term is usually reserved for structures with four or more pitches.

A diminished triad   A diminished chords

Spacing. In addition to doubling, composers often use alternative *spacings* to affect the color of a simple triad. SPACING refers to the choice of octave for the pitches of a triad or chord. Each of the following triads has a different sound, but each is identified as B♭ augmented and is in root position.

B♭ augmented triads

RECORDED EXAMPLE 32
TRACK 53
Barbara Strozzi, Aria

Recorded Example 32 is from an aria (song) by the Venetian composer Barbara Strozzi (1619–1664?). This passage (Track 53) comprises only three different triads: C minor, G major, and A♭ major. These are used in various inversions, doublings, and spacings to form a complete musical phrase.[2]

Barbara Strozzi, Aria

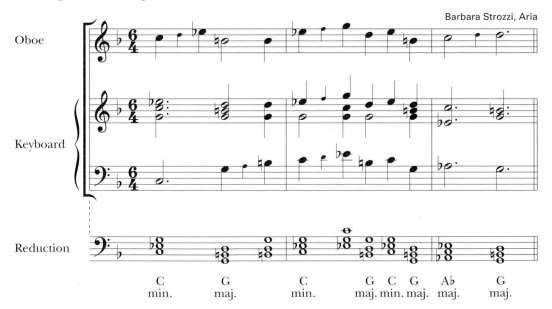

---

[2]The pitches with small noteheads are nonharmonic tones that lie outside the triadic harmony.

Listen to Track 54, which is a reduction of the chords in the preceding aria to their simplest, triadic material. Follow the chord diagram below as you listen. Finally, return to Track 53 and hear the fundamental materials as they are employed in a complete musical phrase.

Analysis with Alternative Doublings and Spacings. When alternative inversions, doublings, and spacings are combined, triads are more difficult to identify. Regardless of the complexity of the chord, however, the bass is always the lowest-sounding pitch. Begin by identifying the bass (use a work staff at first, but strive later to do this mentally). Second, move upward to the next different pitch name in the chord (discount any octave duplication of the bass), and write this new pitch immediately above the bass on your work staff. Progress upward through the chord (again, discounting octave duplications) until you encounter a third pitch name. Write this pitch immediately above the other two and in the same octave (the three pitches should be in close position).

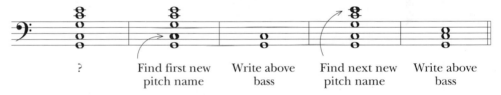

| ? | Find first new
pitch name | Write above
bass | Find next new
pitch name | Write above
bass |

Assuming that no chord has more than three different pitch names, the procedure just described results in a triad in its closest spatial position.[3] With this information, we can determine the quality of the triad and its root–bass relationship as before.

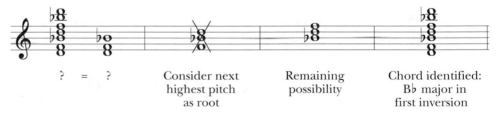

| ? = ? | Consider next
highest pitch
as root | Remaining
possibility | Chord identified:
B♭ major in
first inversion |

[3]Seventh chords, with four different pitches, will be discussed in Chapter 12.

EXERCISE 10-4

Fundamental Skills

Identifying Triads

A. The following triads appear in close position. In the upper blank, identify the root (pitch name) and the quality ("M," "m," "d," or "A"). Use the lower blank for the root–bass relationship (root position, first inversion, or second inversion).

Quality: <u>D M</u>

Root - bass: <u>2ND</u>

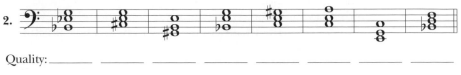

Quality: _____

Root - bass: _____

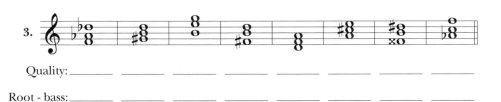

Quality: _____

Root - bass: _____

B. Use the lower staff to reduce the chords to a basic triad in close position; next, identify root, quality, and root–bass relationship as before.

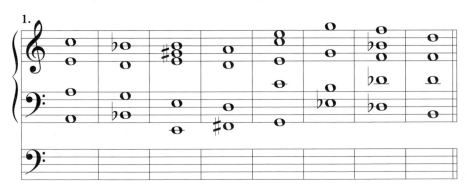

Quality: _____

Root - bass: _____

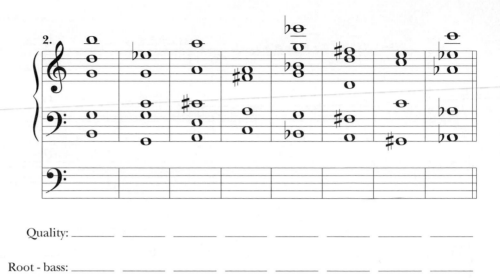

Quality: _____ _____ _____ _____ _____ _____ _____ _____

Root - bass: _____ _____ _____ _____ _____ _____ _____ _____

Figured Bass

In traditional harmony, the bass line plays a major role in establishing a feeling for key. In the early seventeenth century, in fact, composers did not write out chords in full, but merely notated the bass of each chord and added numerals and other symbols to indicate how desired pitches should be added. This system of shorthand notation is called FIGURED BASS, and although the practice had been abandoned by about 1750, some of the figures and symbols survived in contemporary musical analysis.

The following passage is a facsimile of a violin sonata published in 1700 by Arcangelo Corelli (1653–1713). The solo melody is given in the middle line; an alternative, ornamented version appears directly above it. The lowest line is the bass, which would have been played on a cello or a similar instrument. Notice that the numerals and other figures, which specify the precise structure and quality of each chord, were printed above the bass line. Later composers moved these figures below the bass.

Arcangelo Corelli, Sonata

Arabic-Numeral Designations.[4]   Figured-bass numerals are convenient abbreviations for the words we have used previously to describe the "root–bass
relationship." In root position, a third and a fifth occur above the bass. The figures $\frac{5}{3}$, therefore, may replace the words "root position." Note, however, that
octave placement is not normally specified by a figured-bass designation. The
numeral 5 directs the performer to play a particular pitch name above the bass.
In a REALIZATION (that is, the construction of a full texture from a figured bass),
octave choice is usually left to the performer's discretion. For our purposes,
however, we will continue to employ close position in all cases.

Figured bass	Realized triad	Figured bass	Realized triad	Figured bass	Realized triad
$\begin{matrix}5\\3\end{matrix}$ (Major)		$\begin{matrix}5\\3\end{matrix}$ (Minor)		$\begin{matrix}5\\3\end{matrix}$ (Diminished)	

---

[4]Roman numerals have another role in analysis and will be discussed in the next chapter.

Notice in the previous example that the numerals are the same regardless of the *quality* of the intervals they represent. The numeral 5, for example, stands for a diatonic fifth above the bass.

If the triad is in first inversion, the root is above the bass. Intervals sounding above the bass in close position will be a third and a *sixth*. The full designation for a first-inversion triad, therefore, is $\frac{6}{3}$.

Figured bass	Realized triad	Figured bass	Realized triad	Figured bass	Realized triad

$\frac{6}{3}$ (Major) $\frac{6}{3}$ (Minor) $\frac{6}{3}$ (Diminished)

In second inversion, the root is again above the bass and the intervals present are a sixth and a fourth. We designate a second-inversion triad with the numerals $\frac{6}{4}$.

Figured bass	Realized triad	Figured bass	Realized triad	Figured bass	Realized triad

$\frac{6}{4}$ (Major) $\frac{6}{4}$ (Minor) $\frac{6}{4}$ (Diminished)

EXERCISE 10-5

Fundamental Skills

Figured Bass

A. For each of the triads given, write the pitch name of the root in the first blank, the quality of the triad in the second blank, and numerals in the third blank to indicate the intervals sounding above the bass ($\frac{5}{3}$, $\frac{6}{3}$, or $\frac{6}{4}$).

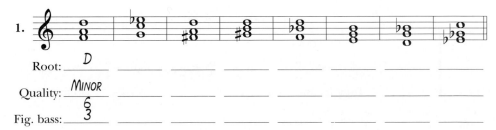

Root: ___D___ ___ ___ ___ ___ ___ ___ ___

Quality: ___MINOR___ ___ ___ ___ ___ ___ ___ ___

Fig. bass: ___$\frac{6}{3}$___ ___ ___ ___ ___ ___ ___ ___

Root: _____ _____ _____ _____ _____ _____ _____

Quality: _____ _____ _____ _____ _____ _____ _____

Fig. bass: _____ _____ _____ _____ _____ _____ _____

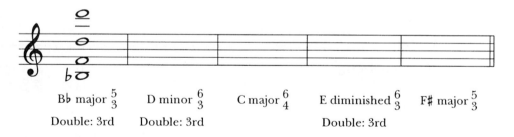

Root: _____ _____ _____ _____ _____ _____ _____

Quality: _____ _____ _____ _____ _____ _____ _____

Fig. bass: _____ _____ _____ _____ _____ _____ _____

B. Use open or close position (as specified) to write the triads indicated. Employ the octave(s) of your choice, but adhere to the doublings designated. If the triad is B♭ major ⁵₃, for example, and "double 3rd" is specified, your chord will have two pitches D as well as a B♭ and an F. If no doubling is indicated, write only the root, the third, and the fifth.

1. Use *open* position.

B♭ major ⁵₃	D minor ⁶₃	C major ⁶₄	E diminished ⁶₃	F♯ major ⁵₃
Double: 3rd	Double: 3rd		Double: 3rd	

2. Use *close* position.

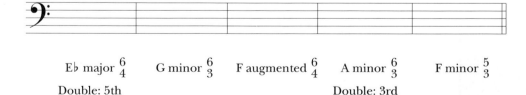

E♭ major ⁶₄	G minor ⁶₃	F augmented ⁶₄	A minor ⁶₃	F minor ⁵₃
Double: 5th			Double: 3rd	

3. Use *open* position.

Gb major $\frac{6}{3}$ C# minor $\frac{5}{3}$ Db major $\frac{6}{4}$ A diminished $\frac{6}{3}$ E augmented $\frac{6}{3}$

Double: Root   Double: Root   Double: 5th   Double: 3rd

4. Use *close* position.

G augmented $\frac{5}{3}$ Bb minor $\frac{6}{4}$ Ab major $\frac{6}{3}$ B diminished $\frac{6}{3}$ C minor $\frac{5}{3}$

Double: 5th   Double: 3rd

EXERCISE 10-6

Musicianship Skills

KEYBOARD: Root Position and Inverted Triads

Return to the three lines of Skill Exercise 10-5. Play each of the triads in section A on the piano. Use the left hand for triads written in the bass clef and the right hand if the triad is notated in the treble clef. First, arpeggiate the triad up and down using a comfortable fingering pattern. Next, play the three pitches of the triad as a chord. When you can play the triads hands separately, add the right or the left hand in another octave and play hands together.

EXERCISE 10-7

Musicianship Skills

SIGHT SINGING: Major and Minor Triads

A. Play the first pitch of each series on the piano. Next, using the syllable or number system recommended by your instructor, sing scale degrees 1–5 ascending and descending. Finally, omit scale degrees 2 and 4 to sing complete ascending or descending triads.

Major

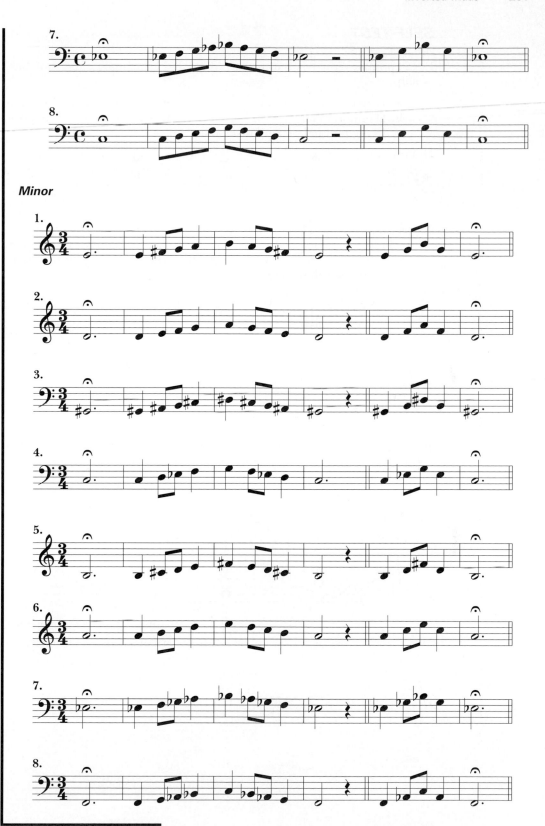

Minor

SELF-TEST

1. (20 points) Write triads using the designated root, quality, and root–bass relationship.

   a. B major, root position
   b. D minor, first inversion
   c. E♭ augmented, second inversion

   d. F minor, second inversion
   e. C♯ diminished, root position

   a.   b.   c.   d.   e.

2. (30 points) Identify the root name, the quality, and the root–bass relationship of the following triads and chords. Write the pitch name of the root in the first blank; use "M," "m," "d," or "A" to identify the quality in the second blank; and use figured-bass designations ($\frac{5}{3}$, $\frac{6}{3}$, or $\frac{6}{4}$) in the lowest blank.

   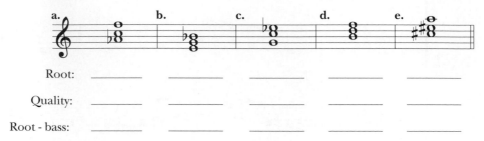

   Root: _____   _____   _____   _____   _____

   Quality: _____   _____   _____   _____   _____

   Root - bass: _____   _____   _____   _____   _____

3. (20 points) Use the given pitch as the bass to construct the triads specified. Employ the octaves of your choice, but place at least one pitch in each staff.

   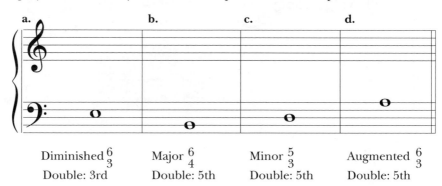

   Diminished $\frac{6}{3}$ Major $\frac{6}{4}$ Minor $\frac{5}{3}$ Augmented $\frac{6}{3}$
   Double: 3rd   Double: 5th   Double: 5th   Double: 5th

4. (30 points). Use the standard figured-bass numerals to identify the root–bass relationship of the following chords. First, reduce the chord to its simplest position. Next, identify the root and write that pitch name in the first blank. Identify the quality in the second blank and use the third blank for the figured-bass numerals.

Root: _____ _____ _____ _____ _____

Quality: _____ _____ _____ _____ _____

Root - bass: _____ _____ _____ _____ _____

SUPPLEMENTARY STUDIES

Drill Exercises

1. The given pitch is the bass. Use this pitch to construct root-position, first-inversion, and second-inversion triads of the qualities specified. Employ close position throughout.

a.

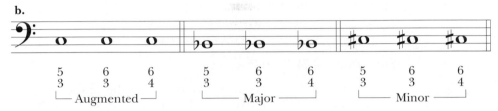

b.

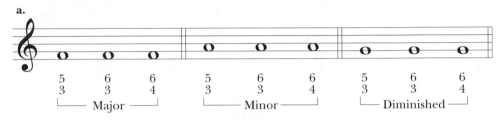

c.

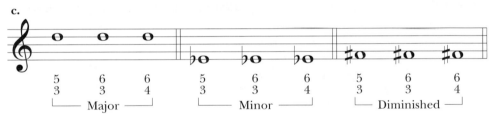

d.

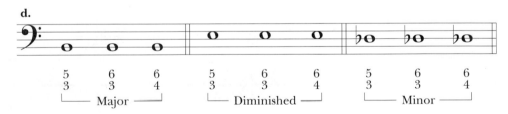

2. Identify the pitch name of the root, the quality, and, using figured-bass numerals, the root–bass relationship of the following triads and chords.

Root: _____ _____ _____ _____ _____ _____

Quality: _____ _____ _____ _____ _____ _____

Fig. bass: _____ _____ _____ _____ _____ _____

b.

Root: _____ _____ _____ _____ _____ _____

Quality: _____ _____ _____ _____ _____ _____

Fig. bass: _____ _____ _____ _____ _____ _____

c.

Root: _____ _____ _____ _____ _____ _____

Quality: _____ _____ _____ _____ _____ _____

Fig. bass: _____ _____ _____ _____ _____ _____

Fundamental Skills in Practice

3. As you did in the previous chapter, study the bracketed triad outlines in the melodic line, then rewrite the triad on the lower staff. Finally, identify quality and root–bass relationship. Consider the lowest pitch of each triad outline to be the bass.

Fanny Mendelssohn Hensel, *For Piano*

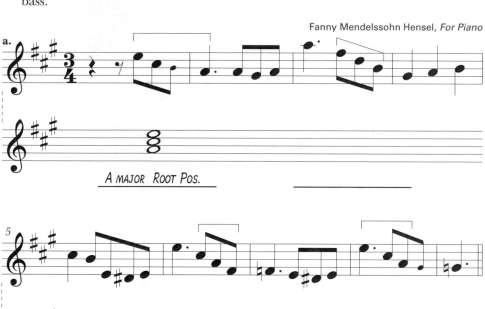

a.

A MAJOR ROOT POS. _____

5

NAME _____

Norman Gimbel/ Charles Fox, "Happy Days"

b.

4. Reduce the chords in the following compositions to simple, root-position, or inverted triads. Identify the basic tertian material of each chord with pitch name, quality, and figured-bass symbol. Nonharmonic tones and pitches that form the seventh of a seventh chord have been omitted. Stems mark the positions of these omitted pitches in the original compositions.

a.

Friedrich Kuhlau, Sonatina for Piano

B♭ major

Root: _____   _____   _____   _____

Quality: _____   _____   _____   _____

Fig. bass: _____   _____   _____   _____

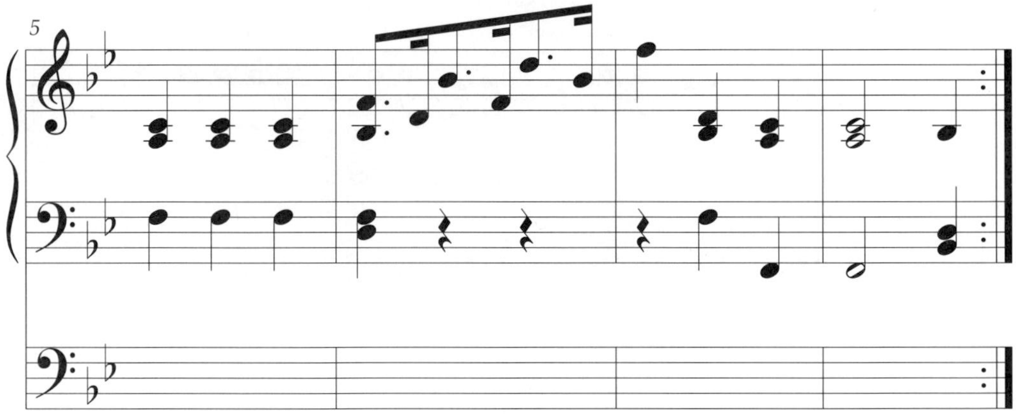

Root: _____   _____   _____ _____ _____

Quality: _____   _____   _____ _____ _____

Fig. bass: _____   _____   _____ _____ _____

NAME _____

J. S. Bach, Chorale Harmonization

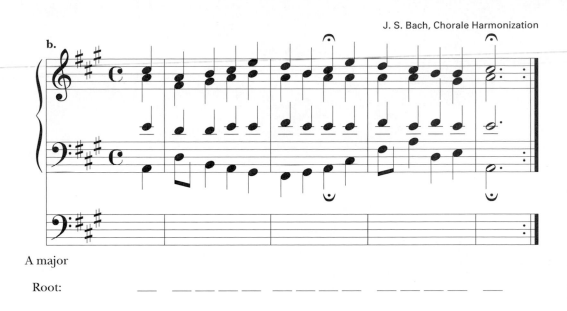

A major

Root: ___ ___ ___ ___ ___ ___ ___ ___ ___ ___ ___ ___ ___ ___ ___ ___ ___ ___

Quality: ___ ___ ___ ___ ___ ___ ___ ___ ___ ___ ___ ___ ___ ___ ___ ___ ___ ___

Fig bass: ___ ___ ___ ___ ___ ___ ___ ___ ___ ___ ___ ___ ___ ___ ___ ___ ___ ___

Johann Crüger, Chorale Harmonization

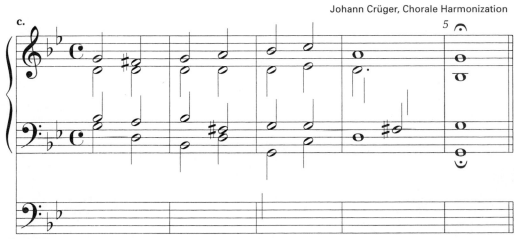

G minor

Root: __ __ __ __ __ __ __ __ __ __

Quality: __ __ __ __ __ __ __ __ __ __

Fig bass: __ __ __ __ __ __ __ __ __ __

CHAPTER 11

Diatonic Relationships

ESSENTIAL TERMS

- *progression*
- *roman-numeral analysis*
- *subtonic triad*

Scales, intervals, and triads are all *fundamental* in that they can be understood in the abstract. At the same time, however, they are *musical* elements with the power to govern the growth of a composition over a span of time. We can look at individual triads as being of a certain quality or structure, but when triads are used in an organized *series,* they are termed PROGRESSIONS. Traditional Western harmony is based upon progressions that define a key. As we have discussed, the triad built upon the first scale degree is known as the tonic. The tonic is the *goal* of a harmonic progression; other triads play clearly defined roles to reinforce the tonic. The names for diatonic triads built on scale degrees 2–7 are those that you learned earlier.

Tonic Supertonic Medicant Subdominant Dominant Submediant Leading tone

Bb Major

Diatonic Triads. Triad names refer to the relationship between a given triad and the tonic. The SUPERTONIC TRIAD, for example, has its root one whole

307

step above (super) the tonic. The term "mediant" designates a third relation. The MEDIANT TRIAD, therefore, is built upon the third degree of the scale.

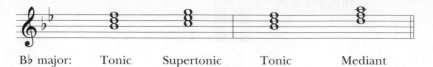

Bb major: Tonic   Supertonic   Tonic   Mediant

The SUBMEDIANT TRIAD is not "below the mediant" but, rather, the *lower* mediant. In Bb major, for example, the triad on the third scale degree (the mediant) is D minor; the submediant is a third *below* the tonic (G minor in the case of Bb major).

Bb major: Submediant   Tonic   Mediant   Tonic

A fifth-related relationship is one of the most powerful in establishing a feeling for key. The DOMINANT is the triad built upon the fifth scale degree—a perfect fifth above the tonic. The triad with the same perfect-fifth root relationship, but one *below* the tonic, is the SUBDOMINANT—the triad built on the fourth scale degree (which lies a perfect fifth below the tonic).

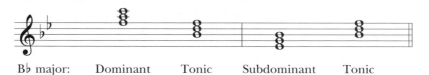

Bb major: Dominant   Tonic   Subdominant   Tonic

The Leading-Tone Triad.   By definition, the leading tone is a pitch a diatonic half step below the tonic; the diatonic triad built on this pitch is always diminished in quality and is termed the LEADING-TONE TRIAD.

Bb: Leading tone   Tonic

Quality in Diatonic Triads. The qualities of triads in major keys are inflexible. The tonic, subdominant, and dominant triads are major in quality; the supertonic, mediant, and submediant triads are minor; and the leading-tone triad is diminished.

D Major: Diatonic Triads in Scale Degree Order

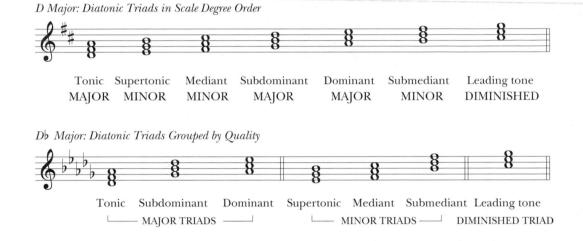

Tonic	Supertonic	Mediant	Subdominant	Dominant	Submediant	Leading tone
MAJOR	MINOR	MINOR	MAJOR	MAJOR	MINOR	DIMINISHED

Db Major: Diatonic Triads Grouped by Quality

Tonic	Subdominant	Dominant	Supertonic	Mediant	Submediant	Leading tone
└─ MAJOR TRIADS ─┘			└─ MINOR TRIADS ─┘			DIMINISHED TRIAD

Constructing Diatonic Triads

Construct individual diatonic triads by determining the key signature, reckoning the scale degree specified, and then adding accidentals as necessary. If you begin by writing the key signature, of course, the accidentals are unnecessary. Asked to construct the dominant triad in G major, for example, begin with the appropriate key signature: one sharp. The pitch D (the fifth scale degree in G) is the root of the dominant triad. Above D, the third and the fifth will be diatonic pitches within the key of G major.

Construct	Key signature	Appropriate scale degree	Basic pitches

G major: Dominant

If you used accidentals rather than a key signature in the preceding example, the F♯ would still be necessary to reflect the key of G major. If we wanted the subdominant triad in A♭ major, we would first note the key signature (four flats), next locate the fourth scale degree (D♭), and finally add the third and the fifth *within the key of A♭ major.*

Construct	Key signature	Appropriate scale degree	Basic pitches

A♭ major: Subdominant

Key Identification in Analysis. Identify major keys in analysis with an uppercase letter (and an accidental if necessary, of course). A colon following the letter indicates that succeeding chords conform to that key. Minor keys are identified with a lowercase letter. The keys of C major and E♭ minor, for instance, would be specified as **C:** and **e♭:**, respectively.[1] In E major, the designation **E: submediant** connotes a specific set of pitches.

E: Submediant

Likewise, the reference **G♭: submediant** cites a triad built upon the sixth degree of the G♭ major scale (with other pitches conforming to that key).

G♭: Submediant

EXERCISE 11-1

Fundamental Skills

Constructing Diatonic Triads in Major

A. Following the procedure described earlier, construct diatonic triads in the keys suggested.

	Key signature	Scale degree	Basic pitches			Key signature	Scale degree	Basic pitches
1.				**2.**				

F: Mediant   B♭: Supertonic

	Key signature	Scale degree	Basic pitches			Key signature	Scale degree	Basic pitches
3.				**4.**				

E: Subdominant   A: Leading Tone

---

[1]Diatonic triads in minor keys will be discussed beginning on page 315.

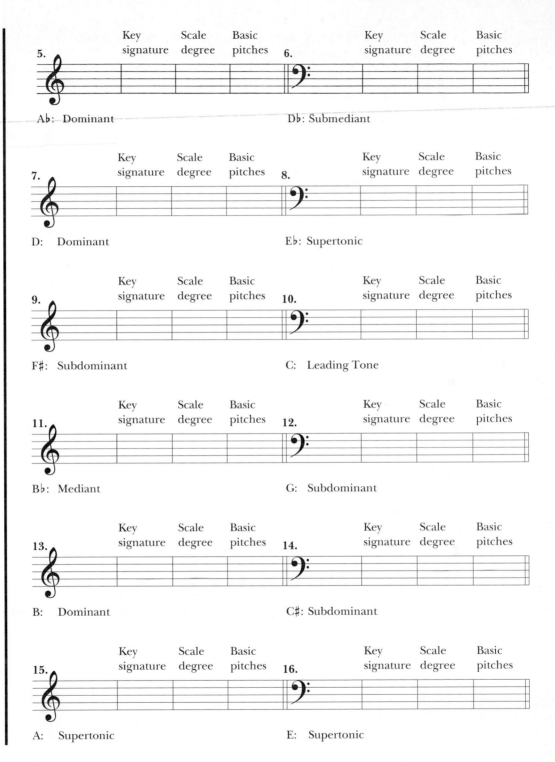

5.
	Key signature	Scale degree	Basic pitches

A♭: Dominant

6.
	Key signature	Scale degree	Basic pitches

D♭: Submediant

7.
	Key signature	Scale degree	Basic pitches

D: Dominant

8.
	Key signature	Scale degree	Basic pitches

E♭: Supertonic

9.
	Key signature	Scale degree	Basic pitches

F♯: Subdominant

10.
	Key signature	Scale degree	Basic pitches

C: Leading Tone

11.
	Key signature	Scale degree	Basic pitches

B♭: Mediant

12.
	Key signature	Scale degree	Basic pitches

G: Subdominant

13.
	Key signature	Scale degree	Basic pitches

B: Dominant

14.
	Key signature	Scale degree	Basic pitches

C♯: Subdominant

15.
	Key signature	Scale degree	Basic pitches

A: Supertonic

16.
	Key signature	Scale degree	Basic pitches

E: Supertonic

B. Continue as before, but perform the same steps mentally. Do not enter a key signature; use accidentals as necessary.

1.

B♭: Supertonic   E: Dominant   E♭: Dominant   C: Mediant   A: Leading tone

2.

D: Subdominant   D♭: Tonic   G: Leading tone   F♯: Submediant   C♭: Subdominant

3.

G♭: Supertonic   A: Tonic   E: Subdominant   D♭: Mediant   B: Dominant

4.

F: Submediant   C: Subdominant   B♭: Subdominant   A: Dominant   C♭: Leading tone

5.

B: Supertonic   D♭: Mediant   F: Submediant   B♭: Mediant   A: Subdominant

6.

F♯: Subdominant   C♭: Dominant   A♭: Subdominant   E: Leading tone   E♭: Mediant

EXERCISE 11-2

Fundamental Skills

Diatonic Triad Names in Major

All the following triads are in root position, and only *major* keys are included in the present exercise. First, write the name of the major key in the first blank. Next, study the given chord and determine its identity in that key (tonic, mediant, sub-dominant, and so on).

1.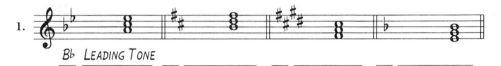

    B♭ LEADING TONE   _____   _____   _____

2.

_____   _____   _____   _____

3.

_____   _____   _____   _____

4.

_____   _____   _____   _____

5.

_____   _____   _____   _____

6.

_____   _____   _____   _____

Roman-Numeral Designations

In analysis, we use roman numerals as abbreviations for triad names (supertonic, subdominant, and so on). The numerals I through VII stand for the triads built upon the first through the seventh scale degrees, respectively. In addition to identifying the root (V = dominant, IV = subdominant, and the like), the numerals are usually altered to show the *quality* of the triad as well. Uppercase (capital) roman numerals indicate a *major* triad; *minor* triads are represented by lowercase numerals. A raised circle symbol (°) appears with a lowercase roman numeral to accentuate the unstable nature of a diminished triad.

F: I   ii   iii   IV   V   vi   vii°   (I)

Using a key designation and a roman-numeral reference, we can represent a complete triad with a single symbol. View, for example, the triads represented by the symbols shown here. The letter followed by a colon, of course, identifies the key.

D: iii   B♭: vii°   C♯: ii   F: vi   A: V   D♭: V

EXERCISE 11-3

Fundamental Skills

Roman-Numeral Analysis: Major Keys

In the given key, write roman numerals to designate the chords. Remember to use uppercase numerals for major triads and lowercase for minor. The circle (°) must be added to the leading-tone triad for a correct analysis.

1. G: ___   ___   ___   ___   ___   ___   ___   ___

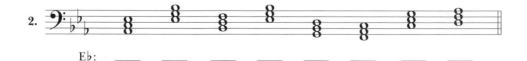

2. E♭: ___   ___   ___   ___   ___   ___   ___   ___

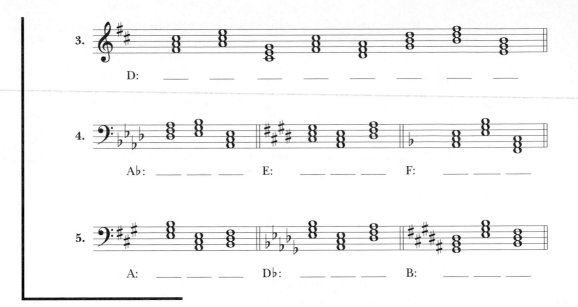

3. D: ___ ___ ___ ___ ___ ___ ___

4. Ab: ___ ___ ___   E: ___ ___ ___   F: ___ ___ ___

5. A: ___ ___ ___   Db: ___ ___ ___   B: ___ ___ ___

Triad Quality in Minor

In major keys, triads appear in three qualities: The tonic, subdominant, and dominant are always major; the supertonic, mediant, and submediant are minor. The leading-tone triad is diminished. In minor, however, some triads have varying qualities, depending upon the composer's choice of the natural or raised sixth and seventh. In C minor, for example, the qualities shown below result from diatonic triads built upon each degree of a natural minor scale.

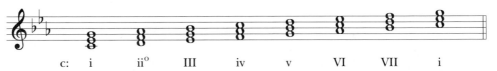

c: i   ii°   III   iv   v   VI   VII   i

Without the raised sixth or seventh, diatonic triads in minor keys are minor, major or diminished in quality (as shown in the preceding example). If the raised seventh is applied (changing B♭ to B♮ in this case), three triads are affected. The mediant is now augmented; the dominant is major; and the leading tone is diminished.[2] If a triad is augmented, a plus sign (+) accompanies an uppercase roman numeral in analysis.

c: i   ii°   III⁺   iv   V   VI   vii°   i

---

[2]Without the raised seventh, of course, there can be no "leading-tone" triad. The triad built upon the seventh degree of a natural minor scale (the subtonic) is the SUBTONIC TRIAD.

If the raised sixth *and* the raised seventh are used (A♮ and B♮ in the next example), diatonic triad qualities are again changed.

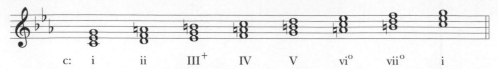

Although any of the chords shown in the three previous examples is *possible*, the most common choices made by traditional composers are shown in the following example.

The Dominant and Leading-Tone Triads in Minor. As we discussed in Chapter 8, the raised sixth and seventh in minor are created with accidentals. If a major triad on the dominant is specified, the seventh degree (which serves as the third of the dominant triad) must be raised a half step. Otherwise, the triad is minor—not major. You may find it helpful to remember that, with the addition of the raised seventh, V and vii° are *identical* in major and minor. Check your construction of these triads in minor against the same triads in the parallel major.

EXERCISE 11-4

Fundamental Skills

Roman-Numeral Analysis: Minor Keys

Supply roman numerals to designate the given chords. Use uppercase for major and lowercase for minor. In addition, the circle symbol (°) accompanies a diminished leading-tone or supertonic triad. An augmented triad is emphasized with the plus sign.

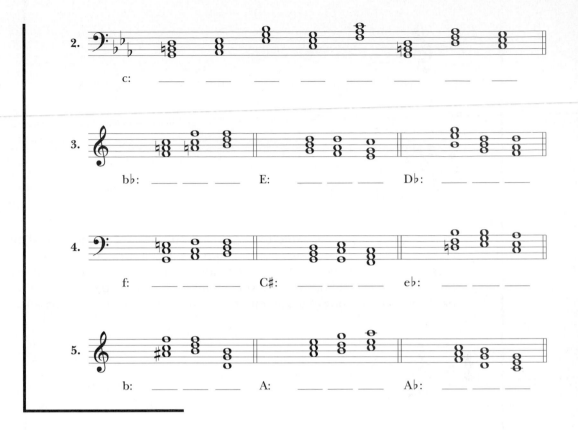

2.

c: _____ _____ _____ _____ _____ _____ _____

3.

bb: _____ _____ _____   E: _____ _____ _____   Db: _____ _____ _____

4.

f: _____ _____ _____   C#: _____ _____ _____   eb: _____ _____ _____

5.

b: _____ _____ _____   A: _____ _____ _____   Ab: _____ _____ _____

EXERCISE 11-5

Fundamental Skills

Triad Construction

A. Major Keys. Build root-position triads that conform to the given analytical symbols. Begin with a key signature. Next, write the root of the triad represented by the roman numeral. Finally, add the third and the fifth (no accidentals will be necessary).

1.

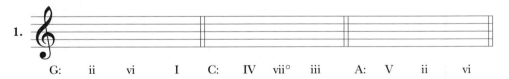

G: ii   vi   I   C: IV   vii°   iii   A: V   ii   vi

2.

Eb: I   vii°   IV   Gb: vi   iii   V   D: IV   V   I

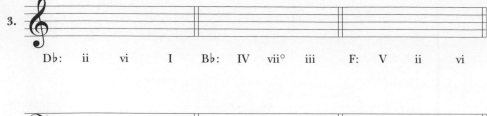

3.

Db: ii   vi   I   Bb: IV   vii°   iii   F: V   ii   vi

4.

Ab: I   vii°   IV   F#:   vi   iii   V   B: IV   V   I

B. Minor Keys. Use the same process that you followed in the preceding exercises: Enter the appropriate key signature, write the root on the staff, then provide the third and the fifth. For some triads (principally V and vii°), you will need to add an accidental outside the key. Verify your answer by checking the dominant and leading-tone triads in minor against their spellings in the parallel major.

1.

g: ii°   VI   i   f#:   iv   vii°   III+   d: V   ii   VI

2.

d: i   vii°   IV   ab: VI   III   V   e: iv   V   i

3.

g#:   V   ii°   IV   bb: IV   V   VI   a: III+   V   i

4.

g#:   iv   V   i   c#:   iv   V   VI   d: V   ii   iv

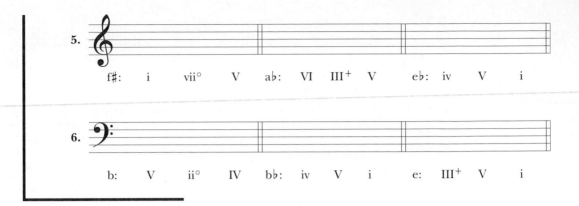

5. f#:   i   vii°   V   ab: VI   III⁺   V   eb: iv   V   i

6. b: V   ii°   IV   bb: iv   V   i   e: III⁺   V   i

Inversions

Although roman numerals indicate the quality of the triad and define its relationship with the tonic, they do not reflect the important relationship between the root and the bass. Arabic numerals, introduced in the last chapter, are employed along with a roman numeral to show whether a triad is in root position or inverted. Remember that the abbreviated arabic numerals always refer to *diatonic* intervals sounding above the bass (not necessarily the root).

Abbreviated Arabic-Numeral Analysis. As we discussed in Chapter 10, the arabic numerals $\frac{5}{3}$, $\frac{6}{3}$, and $\frac{6}{4}$ identify triads in root position, first inversion, and second inversion, respectively. Used with roman numerals in analysis, however, two of these designations are simplified. If a triad is in root position, for example, we use the roman numeral alone. The arabic numerals are omitted. Likewise, in first inversion, the numeral 3 is omitted from the complete $\frac{6}{3}$ designation. On the other hand, the full arabic-numeral identification $\frac{6}{4}$ identifies a triad in second inversion.

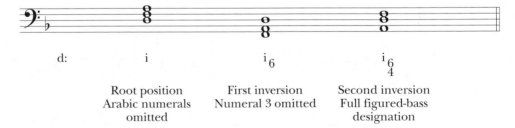

d: i   i₆   i $\frac{6}{4}$

Root position   First inversion   Second inversion
Arabic numerals   Numeral 3 omitted   Full figured-bass
omitted   designation

Individual diatonic triads in major or minor can be identified precisely through roman and arabic numerals, together with any additional symbol such as the circle or the plus sign. Experienced musicians, viewing only the series of symbols, can "hear" the progressions mentally. Before you listen to Recorded Example 33, review common analytical symbols in the following examples.

E: I   I₆   vii°₆   c#: V   V₆₄   III⁺

RECORDED EXAMPLE 33
TRACK 55
Sounds and Symbols: Major

Follow the score below as you play Recorded Example 33, an edited version of the Lutheran melody "In God's Dear Name, I Close My Weary Eyes," harmonized by J. S. Bach (1685–1750). This passage is in G major and includes a variety of diatonic chords. Listen to the phrase at least three times. First, study the entire score as you listen. Next, repeat Track 55 but with the music covered; view only the analytical symbols. Concentrate on differences in triad quality and root–bass relationships. Finally, play Track 55 a third time as you again follow the score.

J. S. Bach, "In God's Dear Name, I Close My Weary Eyes" (edited)

G: I   I₆ V I₆ vii°₆ I   I₆ IV I₆ ii V   I

TRACK 56

Track 56 is a minor-mode variation of the preceding chorale. Listen to the passage three times as you did earlier.

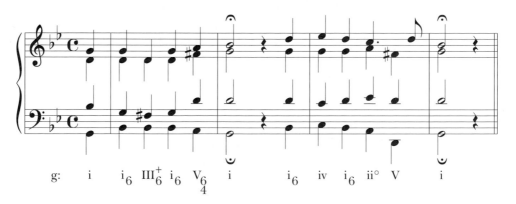

g: i   i₆ III⁺₆ i₆ V₆₄ i   i₆ iv i₆ ii° V   i

EXERCISE 11-6

Fundamental Skills

Roman-Numeral Analysis

A. Use roman and arabic numerals, along with any other symbols, to identify the triads in the keys indicated. Please note that although many different possibilities exist in minor, those included in these exercises conform to the *most common* qualities discussed on page 316.

1.

a: $\quad \underline{i_6} \quad \underline{ii^o} \quad \underline{i} \quad$ G: $\quad \underline{\quad} \quad \underline{\quad} \quad \underline{\quad} \quad$ f#: $\quad \underline{\quad} \quad \underline{\quad} \quad \underline{\quad}$

2.
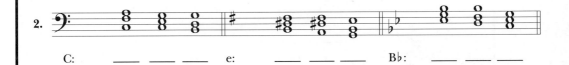

C: $\quad \underline{\quad} \quad \underline{\quad} \quad \underline{\quad} \quad$ e: $\quad \underline{\quad} \quad \underline{\quad} \quad \underline{\quad} \quad$ B♭: $\quad \underline{\quad} \quad \underline{\quad} \quad \underline{\quad}$

3.

b♭: $\quad \underline{\quad} \quad \underline{\quad} \quad \underline{\quad} \quad$ E: $\quad \underline{\quad} \quad \underline{\quad} \quad \underline{\quad} \quad$ D♭: $\quad \underline{\quad} \quad \underline{\quad} \quad \underline{\quad}$

4.

f: $\quad \underline{\quad} \quad \underline{\quad} \quad \underline{\quad} \quad$ C#: $\quad \underline{\quad} \quad \underline{\quad} \quad \underline{\quad} \quad$ e♭: $\quad \underline{\quad} \quad \underline{\quad} \quad \underline{\quad}$

5.

b: $\quad \underline{\quad} \quad \underline{\quad} \quad \underline{\quad} \quad$ A: $\quad \underline{\quad} \quad \underline{\quad} \quad \underline{\quad} \quad$ A♭: $\quad \underline{\quad} \quad \underline{\quad} \quad \underline{\quad}$

6.
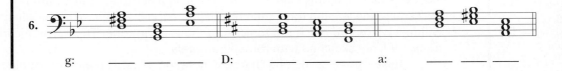

g: $\quad \underline{\quad} \quad \underline{\quad} \quad \underline{\quad} \quad$ D: $\quad \underline{\quad} \quad \underline{\quad} \quad \underline{\quad} \quad$ a: $\quad \underline{\quad} \quad \underline{\quad} \quad \underline{\quad}$

B. Reverse the process from the previous exercise and construct triads that correspond to the given analytical symbols. Begin with the key signature, but remember that accidentals must be added to the dominant and leading-tone triads in minor. You will also need an accidental (raised sixth scale degree) to build IV (a major subdominant) in minor keys.

EXERCISE 11-7

Musicianship Skills

SIGHT SINGING: Tonic and Dominant

The tonic triad and the leading-tone pitch combine to establish tonality with considerable clarity. In this exercise, you will sing a complete tonic outline (1-3-5-8), descend to the leading tone, then return to the tonic. Be aware of the security you will feel when you reach the tonic from the leading tone. The harmonic implications, I-V-I, are sketched with roman numerals.

These exercises include rhythmic notation. Establish a comfortable tempo, then sing the passage without hesitation. Find your first pitch on the piano (you may need to sing in a different octave, of course), then sing the pattern. Check your pitch after you sing.

Major Keys

The following exercises are minor-mode versions of the preceding ones. Notice that leading tones are provided as accidentals. Observe also that a *lower-case* roman numeral identifies the (minor) tonic.

Minor Keys

7.

C#: i   V   i   g: i   V   i   a: i   V   i

8.

d#: i   V   i   f: i   V   i   g#: i   V   i

EXERCISE 11-8

Musicianship Skills

KEYBOARD: Tonic and Dominant

Return to Skill Exercise 11-7 and perform the tonic-dominant segments at the piano. Play first with the right hand alone, then with the left hand. More experienced students may want to try hands together in two different octaves. You will probably find the following fingering schemes convenient and comfortable, although others are possible. Rotate your hand in the direction of the arpeggio (melodic triad outline) as you ascend.

    5   3   2   1   2   1   1   2   3   5   4   5
            Left Hand   Right Hand

SELF-TEST

1. (40 points) The following composition includes many chords that we have studied thus far (although pitches outside the harmony and other more advanced materials have been removed or edited). As you did in the last chapter, reduce the chords to their raw, triadic material, then provide an appropriate analytical symbol where blanks appear.

J. S. Bach, Chorale Harmonization ("Be Not Dismayed")

a: ___ i ___ ___ ___ i V i₆ i ___ i i₆ ___ i ___

2. (30 points) Identify the following triads with roman and arabic numerals as well as any other necessary symbol.

b: _____ _____ _____   E: _____ _____ _____

3. (30 points) Write triads as indicated. Use a key signature and add any necessary accidentals.

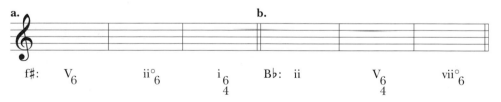

f#: V₆   ii°₆   i 6/4   Bb: ii   V 6/4   vii°₆

SUPPLEMENTARY STUDIES

Drill Exercises

1. Begin by supplying the appropriate key signature. Next, use the upper blank to write a diatonic triad name for the given root-position or inverted triad (tonic, supertonic, mediant, and so on). In the lower blank, provide an appropriate analytical symbol for the given chord in the specified key.

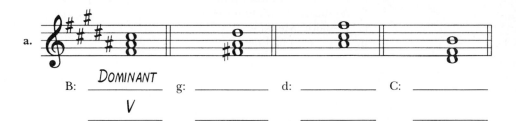

B: _DOMINANT_   g: _____   d: _____   C: _____

    _V_   _____   _____   _____

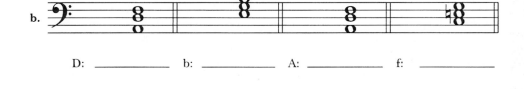

D: _____   b: _____   A: _____   f: _____

_____   _____   _____   _____

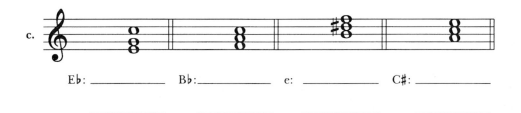

E♭: _____   B♭: _____   e: _____   C♯: _____

_____   _____   _____   _____

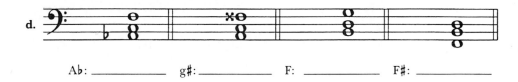

A♭: _____   g♯: _____   F: _____   F♯: _____

2. Construct the root-position triads indicated. First, provide the key signature; next, write the appropriate triad root. Finally, add the third and the fifth. Remember: You will need to add an accidental to the dominant and leading-tone triads in minor.

    a. F major: Supertonic
    b. D♭ major: Dominant
    c. E minor: Dominant
    d. G major: Submediant
    e. C minor: Subdominant
    f. A♭ major: Leading tone
    g. B major: Mediant
    h. C minor: Leading tone

3. Write the root-position and inverted triads indicated. Begin with the appropriate key signature. Since some of the triads are inverted, you may want to construct one in root position on scratch paper before entering the inverted form on the staff provided. As always in minor, add accidentals to V and vii°.

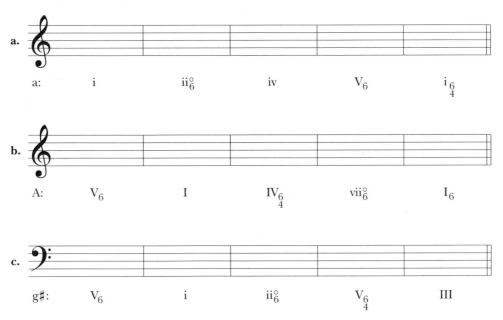

NAME _____

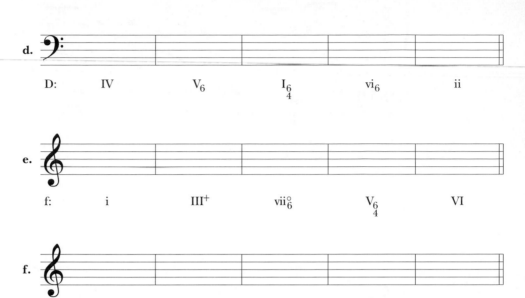

d.

D: IV V_6 I_6^4 vi_6 ii

e.

f: i III^+ vii°_6 V_6^4 VI

f.

A♭: ii_6 I_6 vii°_6 I IV_6

Fundamental Skills in Practice

4. Several harmonized phrases follow for reduction and analysis. As before, some elements of the original composition have been omitted or edited. Use the lowest staff to reduce the chord to its essential, triadic material. Provide an analytical symbol in the blank. Ignore small notes.

J. S. Bach, Chorale Harmonization ("The Star Proclaims the King Is Here")

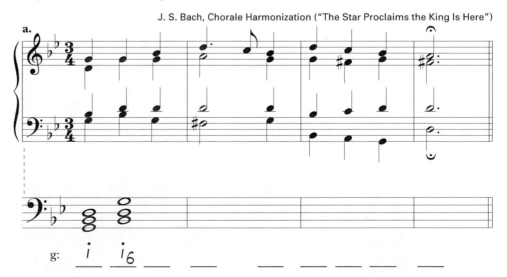

a.

g: i i_6 ___ ___ ___ ___ ___ ___

Louise Reichardt, *A Poem by Tieck*

b.

G: ___ ___ ___ ___ ___ ___ ___

Dimitri Bortniansky, *St. Petersburg*

c.

C: ___ ___ ___ ___ ___ ___ ___ ___

___ ___ ___ ___ ___

CHAPTER 12

Basic Concepts of Tonal Harmony

ESSENTIAL TERMS

- *authentic cadence*
- *cadence*
- *consonance*
- *deceptive cadence*
- *dissonance*

- *half cadence*
- *plagal cadence*
- *seventh chord*
- *voice leading*

Many contemporary theorists use the terms "tonality" and "key" synonymously, in reference to the establishment of a pitch center (the tonic) and the choice between the major and the minor *mode*. The tonality or key of D major, for example, refers to the establishment of D as the central pitch and indicates that the mode is major. Likewise, the key of G minor signifies that the most important pitch in a given composition is G and that the mode is minor. Many of the means by which we establish tonality lie outside the scope of a music fundamentals text. In this final chapter, however, we will approach two of these topics: dissonance and cadences.

CONSONANCE AND DISSONANCE

The concepts of consonance and dissonance are relative, but in general they refer respectively to sounds that are stable (CONSONANCE) and sounds that are less stable (dissonance). Although the term "dissonance" has had varied meanings historically, for our purposes a DISSONANCE is a pitch, an interval, a triad, or a chord that has a strong tendency to *resolve*—that is, to move or progress toward a more stable sonority.

Tendency Tones. We can see the interplay of stable and unstable elements in the structure of traditional melody itself. The first, third, and fifth scale degrees are stable; the other pitches tend to gravitate toward one of these. The fourth scale degree, for example, often falls to the third. This melodic motion, which reinforces the mode as major or minor, is particularly important following a leap.

RECORDED EXAMPLE 34
TRACK 57
Tendency Tones

Listen to Recorded Example 34, which includes several illustrations of tendency tones (Tracks 57–60). The first phrase of the melody notated below is in D major. In addition to leaps from dominant to tonic pitches, the phrase gathers momentum through a leap up to the unstable fourth scale degree. As we expect, the fourth scale degree falls to the third.

TRACK 58

The pull of the leading tone to the tonic is even stronger than the motion of the fourth scale degree down to the third. In the second phrase of the melody (below), the leap is to the leading tone; the subsequent resolution to the tonic strengthens the tonality of D major.

TRACK 59

Listen now to the third and fourth phrases of the melody. In the third phrase, the tendencies of the fourth and seventh scale degrees are *combined*. The melodic interval between them is a diminished fifth; the resolution is stepwise as the fourth scale degree falls again to the third. The fourth phrase brings the complete melody to a close with an outline of the tonic triad (measure 13), an augmented fourth, and the strong leading tone/tonic melodic motion (measures 15–16).

Follow the score below and listen to the structure of the entire sixteen-measure melody as heard on Track 60 of Recorded Example 34.

The "Devil in Music." Especially in harmonic contexts, the augmented fourth was considered so dissonant by Medieval composers that they referred to it in their writings as "the Devil in Music." Also known as a TRITONE, the augmented fourth (and in modern use, its inversion, the diminished fifth) has always been carefully resolved by traditional Western composers.[1] As a harmonic dissonance, typical resolutions of both the augmented fourth and the diminished fifth are shown here.

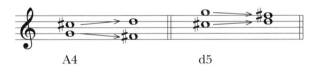

Play Recorded Example 35 and listen to the dissonant effect of the melodic tritone. In the second line, study the traditional resolutions of harmonic tritones and note the psychological effect of "arrival" when the dissonance is resolved.

RECORDED EXAMPLE 35
TRACK 61
The Tritone

---

[1]The term "tritone" refers to the three whole steps between the two pitches.

Dissonances such as the tritone are inherently unstable and have strong tendencies to resolve. Traditional composers use dissonance to create a stronger feeling for key than could be accomplished with consonance alone. The dissonance creates tension; the tension is relaxed as a resolution to a consonant pitch or interval occurs. The greater the dissonance, the greater the tension (and, therefore, the stronger the feeling for key when the dissonance is resolved).

EXERCISE 12-1

Fundamental Skills

Tritones

A. As we have discussed, the tritone is an important organizing element in traditional music. Formed from the fourth and seventh scale degrees, the augmented fourth *expands* to a sixth (major or minor, depending upon the mode); the diminished fifth *contracts* to a third—again, either major or minor in quality. A number of tritones are given below. Analyze each as either A4 or d5 and write that designation in the blank. Next, resolve the tritone by step in the key indicated.

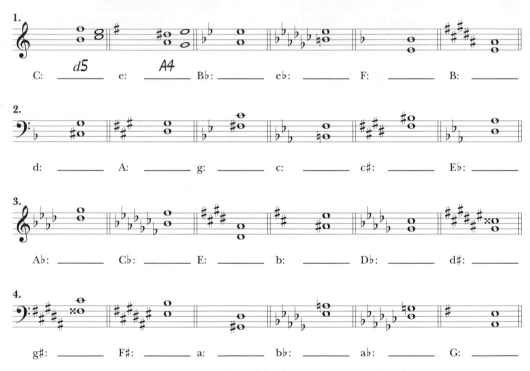

B. Construct and resolve augmented fourths or diminished fifths by writing the fourth and seventh scale degrees in the keys indicated. In minor, you will need to raise the seventh scale degree. In the blank, identify the interval to which you resolve the tritone (M3, m3, M6, or m6).

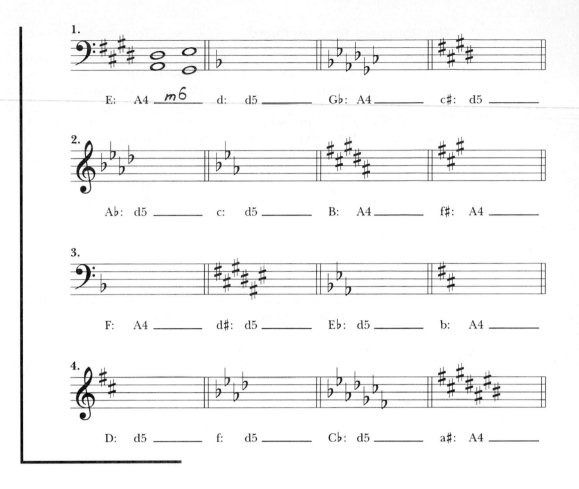

1.

E: A4 _m6_   d: d5 _____   G♭: A4 _____   c♯: d5 _____

2.

A♭: d5 _____   c: d5 _____   B: A4 _____   f♯: A4 _____

3.

F: A4 _____   d♯: d5 _____   E♭: d5 _____   b: A4 _____

4.

D: d5 _____   f: d5 _____   C♭: d5 _____   a♯: A4 _____

EXERCISE 12-2

Musicianship Skills

KEYBOARD: Tritones and Resolutions

Return to Section A of Skill Exercise 12-1 and perform each tritone and its resolution at the keyboard. Use both hands; play the lower pitch with the left hand, the upper with the right hand. Follow the fingering guidelines from earlier keyboard drills: Do not use the thumb on a black key, do not use the same finger for both pitches, and so on. Listen carefully to the dissonance and its resolution.

The Dominant Seventh Chord

Although major, minor, and diminished triads form the core of traditional Western harmony, composers use several other chords both for color and as a means of clarifying the tonality. SEVENTH CHORDS, for example, contain not only a third and a fifth above the root, but the interval of a seventh as well. The seventh chord built on the dominant pitch is the most common in traditional music. The DOMINANT SEVENTH CHORD is also known as a "major-minor" seventh because it is formed from a major triad with a superimposed minor seventh.[2]

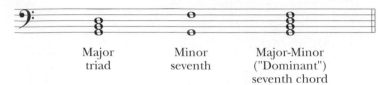

Major
triad

Minor
seventh

Major-Minor
("Dominant")
seventh chord

Roman-Numeral Designations. In analysis, we identify root-position seventh chords with the appropriate roman numeral plus the arabic numeral 7 to designate the dissonant seventh.

G: V^7 g: V^7 B♭: V^7 b♭: V^7

The dominant seventh chord is a relatively unstable sonority and, accordingly, is classified as a HARMONIC DISSONANCE. In traditional music, the dominant seventh usually progresses *(resolves)* to the tonic. The seventh itself (the fourth scale degree) descends by step to the third of the tonic triad. By definition, a dominant seventh chord is a major triad with minor seventh above the root. In minor keys, you must remember to raise the third of the dominant triad (as shown below).

RECORDED EXAMPLE 36
TRACK 62
Dominant Seventh Chords

Play Track 62 of the CD (Recorded Example 36) and study the score as you listen to examples of the component intervals of dominant seventh chords in the keys of C major and F minor.

C: V   +   m7 V^7 f: V   +   m7 V^7

TRACK
63

As you study the following score, listen to Track 63 and experience the dominant seventh chord and its resolution in a harmonic context. Observe that the dissonant seventh (the fourth scale degree) descends by step.

---

[2]Although many additional qualities and three inversions of seventh chords exist, the present discussion will include only dominant sevenths in root position.

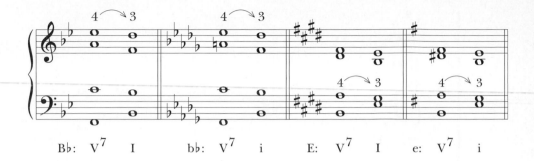

Bb: V⁷   I   bb: V⁷   i   E: V⁷   I   e: V⁷   i

EXERCISE 12-3

Fundamental Skills

Constructing and Recognizing
Dominant Seventh Chords

A. Construct root-position dominant seventh chords in the major and minor keys indicated. First, enter the appropriate key signature. Next, construct the dominant triad; then, add a diatonic seventh above the root. In minor, another step is always necessary: *Raise the third of the triad.*

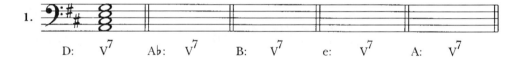

1.   D: V⁷   Ab: V⁷   B: V⁷   e: V⁷   A: V⁷

2.   c: V⁷   F: V⁷   g#: V⁷   E: V⁷   g: V⁷

B. Some of the following chords are simple, root-position triads with root, third, or fifth doubled; others are dominant seventh chords with four distinct pitches. Use roman and arabic numerals to identify the chords in the keys indicated.

1.

F: ___ V⁷ ___ vi   D: ___ ___   g: ___ ___   f#: ___ ___

f: _____ _____   e: _____ _____   c: _____ _____   a: _____ _____

CADENCES

A CADENCE is a musical point of conclusion. Harmonically, cadences involve two different chords: subdominant and dominant, for example, or dominant and tonic. As a comma creates a pause in a sentence, so some cadences create a musical pause. Other cadences are more final (similar to the role of a period).

The Authentic Cadence.   A progression of the dominant triad to the tonic creates a strong feeling for key. When these two chords (V–I) *end* a musical phrase, the cadence is termed AUTHENTIC.[3]

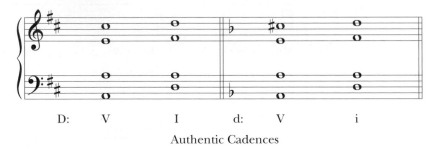

D: V   I   d: V   i

Authentic Cadences

When a seventh is added to the dominant triad in an authentic cadence, the resolution to tonic and the tonal effect are enhanced. In traditional compositions, the seventh of a seventh chord almost always descends *by step* to the third of the tonic triad.

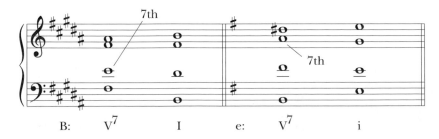

B: V^7 I   e: V^7 i

---

[3]Authentic cadences are further classified as "perfect" or "imperfect." Such distinctions, however, exceed the scope of this text.

The Half Cadence.   The HALF CADENCE is a musical comma—a temporary pause. Half cadences conclude with the dominant chord; the dominant is preceded by the tonic (I–V), the subdominant (IV–V), or the supertonic (ii–V).

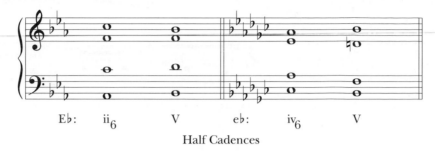

Half Cadences

The Plagal Cadence.   A third type of traditional cadence, known as PLAGAL, consists of the progression subdominant to tonic (IV–I).

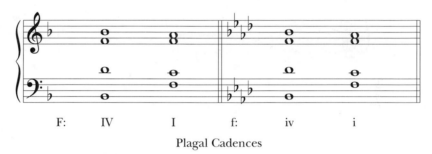

Plagal Cadences

The Deceptive Cadence.   Composers sometimes delay an arrival at the tonic by using a substitute—usually the submediant—in place of the tonic itself. When it occurs at the end of a phrase, the progression V–vi is known as a DECEPTIVE CADENCE.

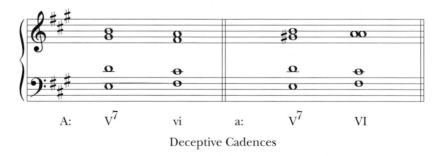

Deceptive Cadences

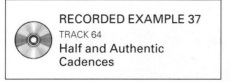

RECORDED EXAMPLE 37
TRACK 64
Half and Authentic
Cadences

Listen to Recorded Example 37, which illustrates two different cadences. The first phrase of Mozart's Sonata in D Major ends with a half cadence (ii–V); the second phrase, which modulates (changes) to A major, concludes with a stronger, authentic cadence. When two successive phrases are contrasted with weaker and stronger cadences (as we see in this example), the listener perceives a single, definitive passage called a PERIOD.

W. A. Mozart, Sonata in D Major, K. 284

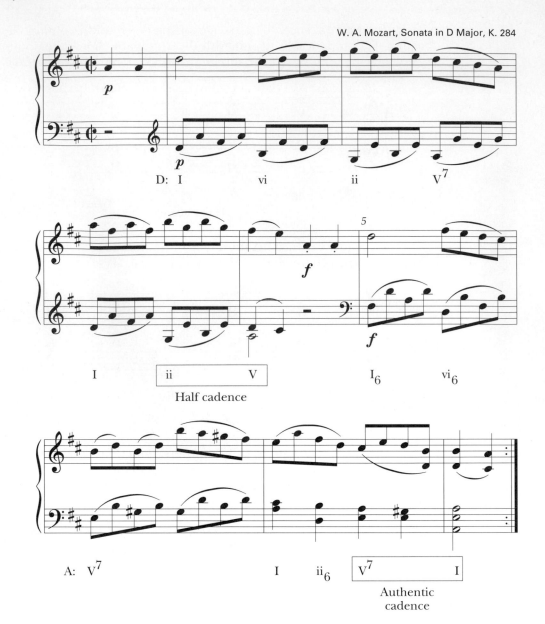

Track 65 of Recorded Example 37 includes a deceptive cadence in A major (measure 4). The passage ends with an authentic cadence (measure 7).

W. A. Mozart, Quintet for Clarinet, K. 581

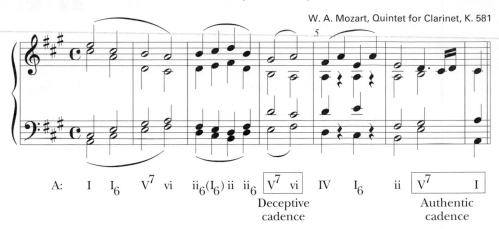

$$\text{A:} \quad \text{I} \quad \text{I}_6 \quad \text{V}^7 \quad \text{vi} \quad \text{ii}_6(\text{I}_6) \text{ ii} \quad \text{ii}_6 \quad \boxed{\text{V}^7 \quad \text{vi}} \quad \text{IV} \quad \text{I}_6 \quad \text{ii} \quad \boxed{\text{V}^7 \qquad \text{I}}$$

Deceptive cadence   Authentic cadence

The plagal cadence, heard on Track 66, is often associated with sacred music. Over the years, this cadence has been stylized into the familiar "A-men" formula in hymns.

Otto Nicolai, Chorale Harmonization ("Wake, Awake")

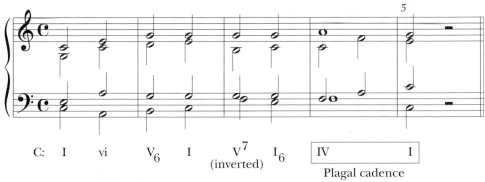

$$\text{C:} \quad \text{I} \quad \text{vi} \quad \text{V}_6 \quad \text{I} \quad \text{V}^7 \quad \text{I}_6 \quad \boxed{\text{IV} \qquad \text{I}}$$

(inverted)   Plagal cadence

EXERCISE 12-4

Fundamental Skills

Identifying Cadences

> **A.** Consider these two-chord progressions to be cadences. In the two upper blanks, use roman numerals to identify the chords in the given key. In the lower blank, classify the cadence as "authentic," "half," and so on.

e: _____ _____   E♭: _____ _____   d♯: _____ _____

_____   _____   _____

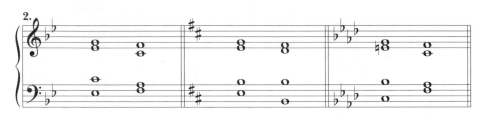

B♭: _____ _____   b: _____ _____   f: _____ _____

_____   _____   _____

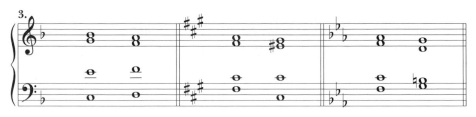

F: _____ _____   f♯: _____ _____   c: _____ _____

_____   _____   _____

D: _____ _____   b♭: _____ _____   E: _____ _____

_____   _____   _____

B. The following phrases conclude with one of the cadence types just discussed. Analyze the final two chords in the key indicated. Write the appropriate roman numerals in the upper blanks and identify the cadence in the blank below.

P. I. Tchaikovsky, *Old French Song*

g: _____ _____

_____

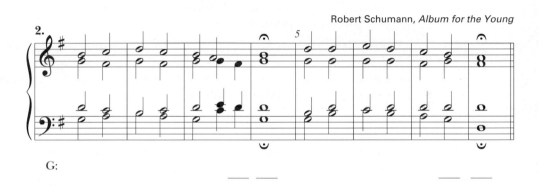

Robert Schumann, *Album for the Young*

G: _____ _____

_____

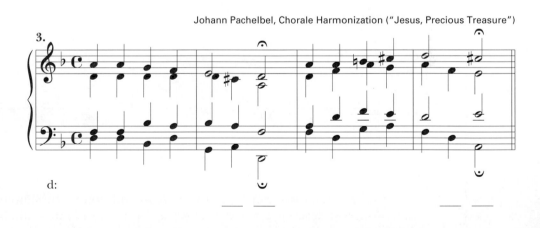

Johann Pachelbel, Chorale Harmonization ("Jesus, Precious Treasure")

d: _____ _____

_____

Constructing Cadences: Two-Voice Texture

Before you can create traditional multivoice compositions, you need instruction and experience in two important fields of music study: *harmony* and *counterpoint*. HARMONY is the study of chords and their various roles in establishing a key center. The second field, COUNTERPOINT ("note-against-note"), concerns the simultaneous linear movement of two or more melodies (voices). In most music schools, both harmony and counterpoint are covered in several different courses and, of course, lie outside the scope of this fundamentals text. As an introduction, however, we will look at the linear movement involved in writing cadences in two voices.

Guidelines for Voice Leading. VOICE LEADING is the movement of individual voices as they flow from one chord to another. Although voice-leading choices are often relative (and even based on personal preferences), the guidelines given here will help you to write effective two-voice cadences. Inversions and alternative choices make smooth voice leading easier, but we will employ only root position for the present.

Authentic Cadences. Use the fifth and first scale degrees, respectively, in the bass to form an authentic cadence. In the soprano, among other possibilities, use scale degrees 2–1 descending or 7–8 ascending. The first two principles of voice leading govern authentic cadences in two voices:

Voice-Leading Principles

1. Move the soprano from its position in the first chord to the *closest* pitch in the next chord. In other words, avoid leaps.

2. Move the two voices in contrary (opposite) motion whenever possible. *Never* move in parallel (same direction) perfect fifths or perfect octaves.

Authentic Cadences

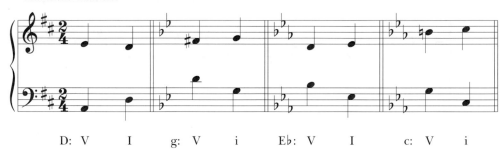

D: V   I   g: V   i   E♭: V   I   c: V   i

Authentic Cadences with Implied Seventh. In addition to the simple two-voice framework just described, you may also use the seventh of a dominant seventh chord in the soprano. This pitch, however (which is the fourth scale degree), must resolve by descending step to the third of the tonic triad in the next chord (voice-leading principle 3). Contrary motion between soprano and bass is again preferable.

3. The seventh of a seventh chord should descend by step.

Authentic Cadences with Implied Dominant Seventh

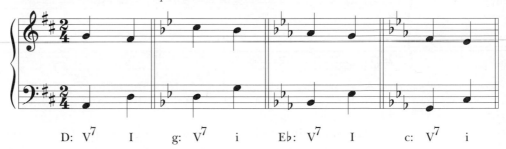

D: V⁷   I   g: V⁷   i   E♭: V⁷   I   c: V⁷   i

Deceptive Cadences. As with authentic cadences, the 2–1 or 7–8 soprano motion is most common in a deceptive cadence. The soprano may also function as the seventh of a dominant seventh assuming the proper resolution (down by step).

Deceptive Cadences

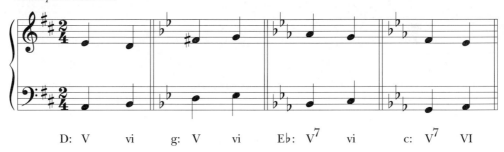

D: V   vi   g: V   vi   E♭: V⁷   vi   c: V⁷   VI

Half Cadences. As in authentic cadences, the soprano voice in half cadences usually moves by step. Use the tonic pitch followed by the leading tone for a IV–V or I–V half cadence. As shown here, other possibilities exist for the soprano.

Half Cadences

F: IV   V   D♭: I   V   A: ii   V   d: iv   V

Plagal Cadences. Since the tonic pitch is common to both subdominant and tonic triads, composers often employ this pitch in the soprano through both chords in a plagal cadence. Other possibilities include a descending 6–5 or a descending 4–3 melodic motion in the soprano.

Plagal Cadences

| a: | iv | i | E: | IV | I | B: | IV | I | g: | iv | i |

Although the pitches in the following cadences are correct (except for missing leading tones as noted), several errors exist that should be avoided.

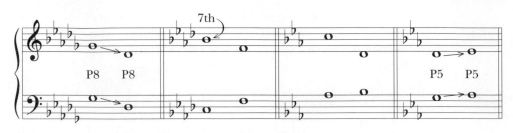

| Db: | IV | I | f: | V⁷ | I | Eb: | IV | V | c: | V | VI |

| | Plagal | | | Authentic | | | Half | | | Deceptive | |

Error: Parallel perfect intervals — Seventh unresolved — Unnecessary leap in soprano — Parallel perfect intervals

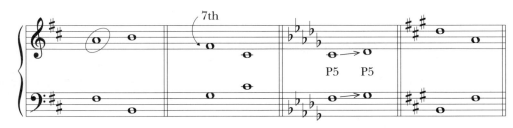

| b: | V | i | C: | V⁷ | I | bb: | V | VI | f#: | iv | I |

| | Authentic | | | Authentic | | | Deceptive | | | Plagal | |

Error: Missing leading tone — Seventh unresolved — Parallel perfect intervals — Unnecessary leap in soprano

EXERCISE 12-5 _____

Fundamental Skills

Cadences in Two Parts

A. Observe the given key, cadence type, roman numerals, and bass pitch. Add a soprano that forms good voice leading with the bass. If a dominant seventh (V^7) is specified, the seventh must be in the soprano and it must resolve down by step. If you employ the leading tone in minor, remember to add the necessary accidental (and resolve the leading tone to the tonic in the next chord).

1.

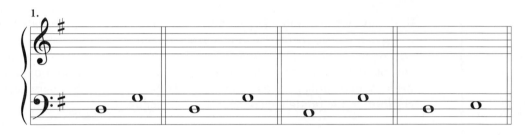

G:	V	I	V^7	I	IV	I	V	vi
	Authentic		Authentic		Plagal		Deceptive	

2.

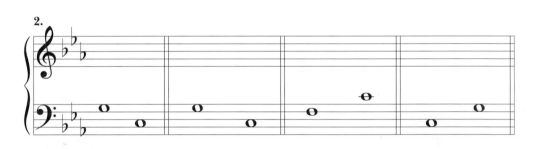

c:	V	i	V^7	i	iv	i	i	V
	Authentic		Authentic		Plagal		Half	

3.

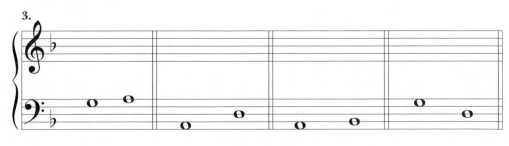

d:	iv	V	V^7	i	V^7	VI	iv	i
	Half		Authentic		Deceptive		Plagal	

4.

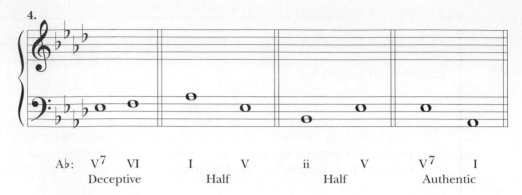

Ab:	V⁷	VI		I	V		ii	V		V⁷	I
	Deceptive			Half			Half			Authentic	

Ab: V^7 VI   I V   ii V V^7 I
Deceptive   Half   Half   Authentic

B. Begin by providing a key signature, then add roman numerals to conform to the specified cadences. (In some cases, you will have only one choice; in others, two or more possibilities will exist.) Finally, write the soprano and the bass to complete the cadences in two voices. All chords should be in root position; where there is an asterisk, use a dominant seventh. Add any necessary accidentals and conform to the guidelines of smooth voice leading.

1.

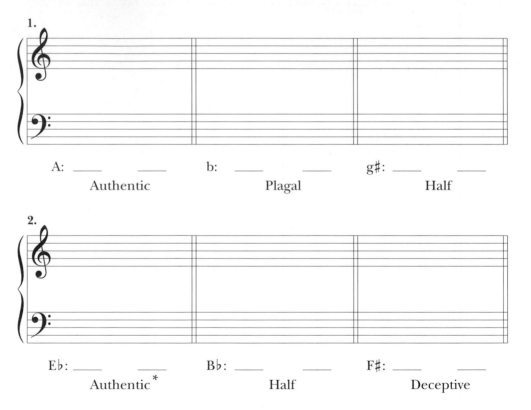

A: ____   ____   b: ____   ____   g#: ____   ____
   Authentic   Plagal   Half

2.

Eb: ____   ____   Bb: ____   ____   F#: ____   ____
   Authentic*   Half   Deceptive

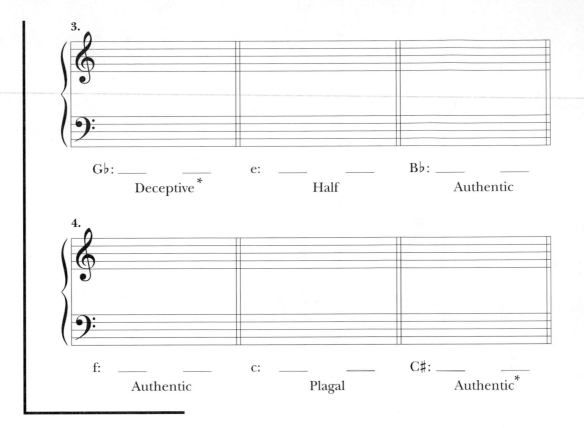

3.

Gb: ____ ____   e: ____ ____   Bb: ____ ____
Deceptive*   Half   Authentic

4.

f: ____ ____   c: ____ ____   C#: ____ ____
Authentic   Plagal   Authentic*

EXERCISE 12-6

Fundamental Skills

Analysis Including Dominant Seventh Chords

The following passages include all the harmonic materials covered in this text: triads in root position and inversion, cadences, and dominant seventh chords. In the key specified, provide all roman and arabic numerals plus any other symbols necessary. Identify cadences. As before, passages from music literature have been edited to remove more advanced materials. Ignore the smaller notes; these pitches are outside the harmony.

Joseph Haydn, Sonata in C Major

1.

C: ____ ____   ____ ____   ____ ____

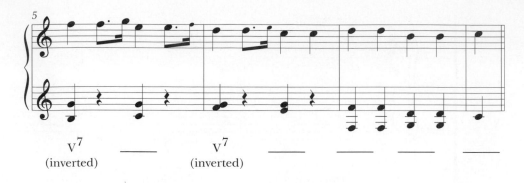

V^7 _____ V^7 _____ _____ _____ _____

(inverted)   (inverted)

Franz Schubert, Dance (edited)

D: _____ _____ _____ _____

_____ _____ _____ _____

_____ _____ _____ _____

L. van Beethoven, Sonata in D Major, Op. 28

D:

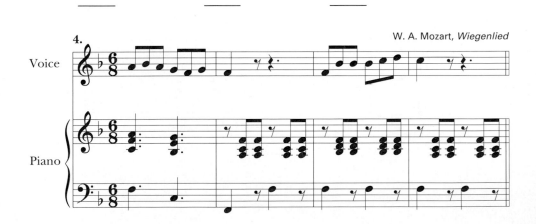

W. A. Mozart, *Wiegenlied*

Voice

Piano

F:

SELF-TEST

1. (30 points) Use roman and arabic numerals (as well as additional symbols if necessary) to identify the following chords in the keys indicated. Write the name of the cadence in the lower blank.

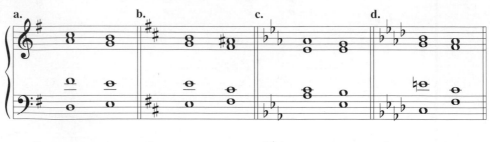

G: _____ _____   b: _____ _____   E♭: _____ _____   f: _____ _____

_____ _____   _____ _____   _____ _____   _____ _____

2. (20 points) Write the chords indicated by the given analytical symbols. Begin by providing the key signature, and remember to add accidentals as necessary in minor keys.

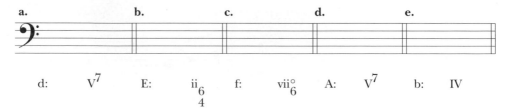

d: V⁷   E: ii₆₄   f: vii°₆   A: V⁷   b: IV

3. (30 points) Use proper voice leading to write the following cadences with soprano and bass. Chords should be in root position. Use the blank to identify the cadence.

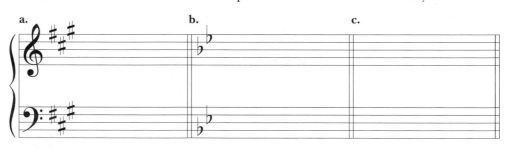

A: V   I   g: iv   V   C: IV   I

_____ _____   _____ _____   _____ _____

4. (20 points) Locate one voice-leading or chord-spelling error in each of the following progressions. Circle the note concerned, then briefly describe the error below. Consider the roman numerals to be correct; any deviation constitutes an error.

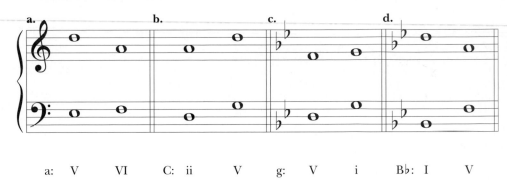

a: V   VI   C: ii   V   g: V   i   Bb: I   V

SUPPLEMENTARY STUDIES

Drill Exercises

1. Begin with a key signature and write root-position dominant seventh chords in the keys indicated. Add an accidental to chords in minor.

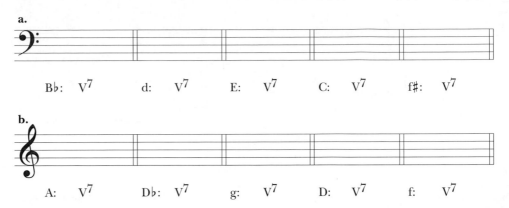

a.

$\text{B}\flat\text{:} \quad \text{V}^7 \qquad \text{d:} \quad \text{V}^7 \qquad \text{E:} \quad \text{V}^7 \qquad \text{C:} \quad \text{V}^7 \qquad \text{f}\sharp\text{:} \quad \text{V}^7$

b.

$\text{A:} \quad \text{V}^7 \qquad \text{D}\flat\text{:} \quad \text{V}^7 \qquad \text{g:} \quad \text{V}^7 \qquad \text{D:} \quad \text{V}^7 \qquad \text{f:} \quad \text{V}^7$

2. Use block chords plus roman and arabic numerals to sketch cadences requested. Write the roman numerals in the blanks. Provide the key signature.

G: _____   _____   d♯: _____   _____   E: _____   _____
        Half   Plagal   Authentic

A: _____   _____   e: _____   _____   A♭: _____   _____
    Authentic   Deceptive   Authentic

Fundamental Skills in Practice

3. Analyze the cadences that end the following phrases. The points of cadence are indicated with blanks. Write the appropriate roman and arabic numerals and identify the cadence type.

J. S. Bach, Chorale Harmonization ("Now Thank We All Our God")

A: _____   _____

_____

L. van Beethoven, Sonatina in G Major

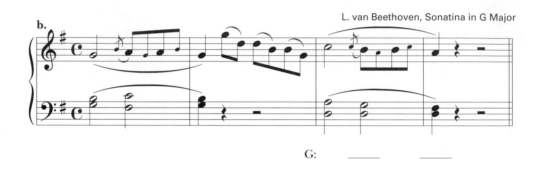

G: _____   _____

_____

Joseph Haydn, Sonata in D Major

D: _____   _____

_____

D: _____   _____

_____

NAME _____

d.   Giacomo Carissimi, *Non Posso Vivere*

F: _____   _____

_____

Robert Schumann, *Album for the Young*

e.

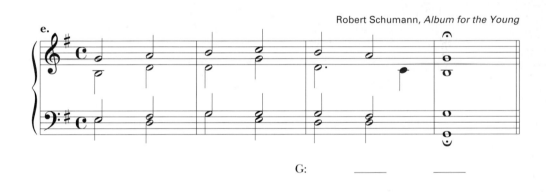

G: _____   _____

_____

f.   Joseph Haydn, Sonata in A Major

A: _____ _____

_____

4. Provide roman- and arabic-numeral analysis for the following passages. Identify all cadences (these are marked with longer blanks).

W. A. Mozart, Sonata in B♭ Major, K. 333

B♭: ___ ___ ___ ___ ___ ___

_____

b. Andante

Carl Maria von Weber, Variations

C: ___   ___   ___

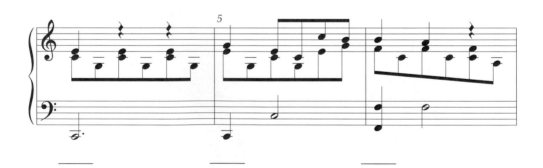

___   ___   ___

NAME _____

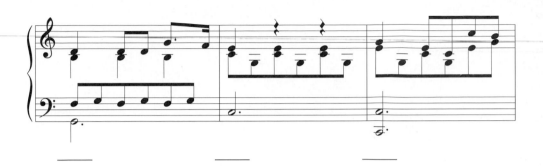

APPENDIX A

The Nature of Sound

ESSENTIAL TERMS

- *acoustics*
- *amplitude*
- *frequency*
- *fundamental*
- *harmonic*
- *harmonic series*
- *hertz*
- *partial*
- *psychoacoustics*
- *sound waves*
- *timbre*

ACOUSTICS AND PSYCHOACOUSTICS

In addition to possessing measurable *physical* properties, sounds, such as those of a clarinet or an automobile horn, make an impression on us *psychologically*. Since duration can be measured with precision, it is a physical property; the duration of a sound might be exactly seven seconds, for example. Hearing the sound as loud, soft, or somewhere in between, on the other hand, is a relative psychological sensation. Exposed to the same sound, one listener might think it loud; another might consider it relatively soft. ACOUSTICS is the branch of science that deals with the physical properties of sound; PSYCHOACOUSTICS is a relatively new field through which the psychological responses to sound are explored.

Sound Waves

Before sound can be transmitted, the air surrounding the sound source must be set in motion. On the violin, the vibrations of a string disturb the air molecules; in the flute and other wind instruments, the air inside the instrument itself

361

vibrates. The vibrating string or column of air causes the surrounding air parti-cles to be set in motion in regular patterns of vibration. These patterns of mole-cular motion are known as SOUND WAVES. Like waves in the water, sound waves travel spherically from the source, growing more and more faint until they die out completely. If the sound is a musical tone (as opposed to noise), the pat-terns or waves are regular and controlled. Counting the number of these vibra-tions within a given time span measures the *frequency* of the sound.

Frequency.   FREQUENCY is determined by the number of sound waves (pat-terns of molecular vibration) created by the vibrating string or air column. The frequency of a sound wave is measured in cycles or vibrations per second (c.p.s.). A more modern term for this measurement is *hertz* (Hz). Most musical sounds lie between about 50 Hz and 2000 Hz. A tone in the upper register of a flute, for example, produces about 1,600 sound waves per second (1600 Hz). The lowest note on the double bass, on the other hand, produces only about 40 sound waves per second (40 Hz). The limits of human audition fall between approximately 20 Hz and 20,000 Hz.

Pitch.   The frequency of a sound produces the psychological response we call PITCH. The greater the frequency of a sound, the higher the pitch; sounds with lesser frequencies produce tones of lower pitch. An electronic instrument known as an oscilloscope is used to measure the frequency of sound waves. The first representation below is of a relatively high pitch as it might appear on an oscilloscope; the second is lower; the third, lower still.

Amplitude and Intensity

Sounds differ not only in pitch but in other aspects as well. The acoustical prop-erty known as *amplitude,* for example, plays a role in most musical works. AMPLI-TUDE is the degree of disturbance in air molecules caused by the sound. We translate differences in amplitude into perceptions of a sound's being loud or soft. If a sound has relatively greater amplitude (that is, if it creates a relatively great disturbance of the air particles), we perceive the sound as loud. Lesser amplitude creates the sensation of a softer tone. Notice that the two sounds rep-resented below are of the same frequency; they differ in amplitude. The first would be the louder; the second, the softer.

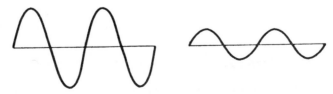

Timbre and Quality

Almost any musical sound is made up of many different frequencies—some relatively strong, others weaker. The various frequencies present in a tone are known as HARMONICS. A flute can be distinguished from a trumpet even if the sounds are of identical frequency and amplitude. This is primarily because the harmonics present in the tone of the trumpet are greater in number and relatively stronger than those of the flute. Differences in harmonics largely determine the acoustical property known as TIMBRE. We perceive differences in timbre as differences in the QUALITY of a tone—the corresponding psychological response. Even if we cannot see the performers, we can identify most orchestral instruments by the qualities of their tones. The same phenomenon allows us to recognize a familiar voice over the telephone.

The Harmonic Series

One of the most important factors affecting tone quality is the natural *harmonic series*. When a tone is sounded on an acoustic musical instrument such as the flute or the trumpet, in addition to the FUNDAMENTAL (the lowest frequency heard), there are other, weaker frequencies that are audible as well. The frequencies sounding above the fundamental are termed PARTIALS; the strength and quantity of these partials determine the quality or timbre of a musical tone. The higher frequencies above a fundamental are called OVERTONES. The fundamental is included in the counting of partials but excluded in the counting of overtones.

The HARMONIC SERIES is a natural phenomenon that occurs when a sound source is set into motion. The relationship of the partials and the overtones to the fundamental is invariable. Each fundamental produces exactly the same range of partials and overtones. The harmonic series for the fundamentals C and A♭ are shown in the next example. Harmonic series for other fundamentals are merely transpositions of these series.

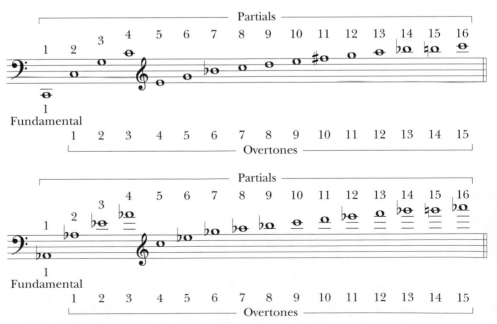

Duration and Length

Whereas the frequency, amplitude, and timbre of a tone cannot be measured without the use of electronic equipment, the fourth acoustical property—DURATION—can be calculated easily in minutes or seconds. The duration of a tone determines its LENGTH.

Other Modes and Scales

ESSENTIAL TERMS

- Aeolian mode
- chromatic scale
- Dorian mode
- Ionian mode

- Lydian mode
- Mixolydian mode
- Phrygian mode
- whole-tone scale

In addition to major and minor scales, past and present composers have used other scale series as the basis of a composition. Although composers of the Common Practice Period limited themselves to two modes (major and minor), other melodic series were employed before 1675 and after about 1875.

CHURCH MODES

The earliest patterns used to organize Western music were the CHURCH MODES— series of whole steps and half steps beginning on the basic pitches, C through A. Three of the original modes are classified as minor; three are classified as major. Major modes have two whole steps between the first and third degrees; minor modes have a whole step plus a diatonic half step between those same pitches.

Major Modes.   The basic pitch series beginning on C, F, and G are major modes known as IONIAN, LYDIAN, and MIXOLYDIAN, respectively. Ionian mode is the equivalent of the major scale.

Ionian   Lydian   Mixolydian

Minor Modes.   Minor modes occur on the basic pitch series beginning on D, E, and A. The DORIAN MODE has a tonic on D, the PHRYGIAN MODE begins on E, and the tonic of the AEOLIAN MODE is A. The Aeolian mode corresponds to the natural minor scale.

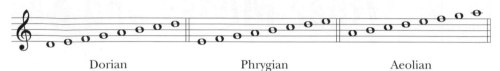

Dorian   Phrygian   Aeolian

RECORDED EXAMPLE 38
TRACK 67
Major Modes

Listen to Recorded Example 38 and the several different modes. First, you will hear Ionian (our major scale), then Lydian, and finally, Mixolydian. The following scores show all three modes transposed to begin on the pitch G.

Ionian Mode (Major)

Lydian Mode

Mixolydian Mode

Now hear the minor modes, beginning with Aeolian (natural minor). Again, all three modes have been transposed to G.

Aeolian Mode (Natural Minor)

Dorian Mode

Phrygian Mode

Transposition of Modes. Transpose modes by noting the difference between the given mode and a major or natural minor scale. Except for the Locrian (not discussed here), other modes differ by one flat or sharp from the corresponding major or minor key signature.

Major Modes

IONIAN	Major scale
LYDIAN	Major scale with raised fourth degree (with sharp added to key signature)
MIXOLYDIAN	Major scale with lowered seventh degree (with flat added to key signature)

Minor Modes

AEOLIAN	Natural minor scale
DORIAN	Natural minor scale with raised sixth (with sharp added to key signature)
PHRYGIAN	Natural minor scale with lowered second (with flat added to key signature)

OTHER SCALES

The Pentatonic Scale

Whereas major and minor scales as well as the modes have seven different pitches, the PENTATONIC SCALE has only five. The pitches of a pentatonic scale are derived from a series of perfect fifths reduced to a single octave.

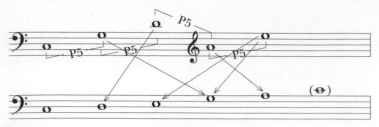

Pentatonic Scale

Various forms of the pentatonic scale are possible, but the most common form can be written as a major scale with fourth and seventh scale degrees omitted.

D Major Scale

D Pentatonic

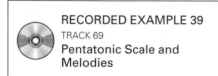

RECORDED EXAMPLE 39
TRACK 69
Pentatonic Scale and Melodies

The pentatonic scale occurs in the folk music of virtually all regions of the world. Play Track 69 of Recorded Example 39 to hear a pentatonic scale (beginning on G). Following the scale, you will hear an American folk song ("She's Gone Away") and an old melody from Korea ("Arilang"). Both melodies are pentatonic.

Pentatonic Scale

American, "She's Gone Away"

Korean, "Arilang"

The Whole-Tone Scale

In the late nineteenth century, some composers began using a scale with only one type of interval: the whole step. The WHOLE-TONE SCALE consists of six whole steps. The seventh pitch is an enharmonic octave duplication of the first pitch. Double flats and double sharps are not used in constructing whole-tone scales.

Whole-Tone Scales

RECORDED EXAMPLE 40

TRACK 70

Whole-Tone Scale and Melody

Melodies based on the whole-tone scale have a distinctive sound. Listen to Recorded Example 40, which includes a whole-tone scale and a whole-tone melody by the French composer Claude Debussy. Debussy (1862–1918) was especially fond of this scale, which has an exotic flavor.

Whole-Tone Scale

Claude Debussy, Preludes for Piano

The Chromatic Scale

A scale consisting entirely of half steps is the CHROMATIC SCALE. Tradition dictates that the scale be written with sharps ascending and flats descending.

Chromatic Scale on C

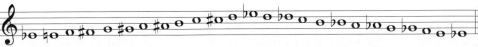

Chromatic Scale on E♭

Terms and Symbols of Tempo and Expression

ESSENTIAL TERMS

- *dynamics*
- *expression*
- *metronome*
- *tempo*

One of the most complex aspects of notating music concerns nuance. Although the composer can designate a certain group of specific pitches and even indicate the precise length of each of those pitches, the performer ultimately decides on certain less exact parameters, such as loudness, articulation (the manner in which the note is begun), and general effect. Over the centuries, composers developed a vocabulary of terms and symbols to aid the performer in understanding how to approach musical nuance. Many of these terms are Italian—reflecting an almost total domination by Italian musicians during the seventeenth and early eighteenth centuries.

Tempo

Although many twentieth-century composers have used their native languages to indicate the tempo—the general *speed* of the beat—Italian terms for this purpose are still predominant. Terms for tempo are relative. The word *Andante* (It.: "going"), for example, is usually interpreted as a "walking speed," giving the performer a good, but general, idea of the composer's intentions. The word *Lento* (It.: "slow") indicates a relatively slow tempo, and *Presto* (It.: "quick") suggests a fast beat.

The Metronome. In the early part of the nineteenth century, the METRO-NOME was invented—a device that permits the composer to indicate a specific number of beats per minute. Rather than relying on the performer's interpretation of general tempo indications, composers simply write the letters *M.M.* (for Maelzel Metronome) followed by a note and the number of those notes to be played in one minute. Sometimes the letters *M.M.* are omitted.

M.M. ♩ = 132   M.M. ♩ = 72   ♪ = 100   ♩. = 60

Dynamics

Like terms for tempo, indications of dynamic level are relative. In addition to abbreviations of Italian terms, composers employ symbols to indicate a gradual increase or decrease in volume.

*pianissimo (**pp**)*: very soft	*mezzo forte (**mf**)*: medium loud
*piano (**p**)*: soft	*forte (**f**)*: loud
*mezzo piano (**mp**)*: medium soft	*fortissimo (**ff**)*: very loud
Gradually louder	Gradually softer

Expression

Composers often indicate a specific effect they want the performer to achieve, such as "tender" or "detached." Again, such commonly used terms are primarily Italian.

Composers also often add symbols to notes to indicate the manner of performance.

short   long   unbroken   accented   heavy

APPENDIX D

The C-Clefs

---

z

ESSENTIAL TERMS

• alto clef   • tenor clef

In addition to the treble and bass clefs, another clef is often encountered in traditional music. The MOVABLE C-CLEF (𝄡) locates the pitch C on the line that runs through the center of the symbol. Especially in older music, a variety of C-clefs is found. The SOPRANO CLEF identifies the first line as C.

C   D   E   F   G   A   B   C   D   E

Soprano Clef

The MEZZO-SOPRANO CLEF places the pitch C on the second line.

A   B   C   D   E   F   G   A   B   C

Mezzo-Soprano Clef

The alto and tenor clefs are used in a similar manner.

F   G   A   B   C   D   E   F   G   A

Alto Clef

D   E   F   G   A   B   C   D   E   F

Tenor Clef

Alto Clef. When the C-clef points to the *third* line, it is termed the ALTO CLEF. The alto clef identifies the pitch C_4; other pitches on the staff fall in sequence above or below C.

Alto Clef

The viola reads its part in the alto clef. Identify the pitches below by letter name.

L. van Beethoven, Sonata, Op. 27, No. 2

Franz Schubert, Symphony No. 5

Tenor Clef. If the C-clef identifies the *fourth* line as C_4, it is known as the TENOR CLEF. Pitches on the staff are named as usual above and below C.

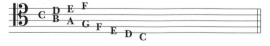

Tenor Clef

The trombone and the bassoon, among other instruments, read their parts in the tenor clef. Identify the pitches below by letter name.

Antonin Dvořák, *Scherzo Capriccioso*

J. S. Bach, *English Suite No. 3*

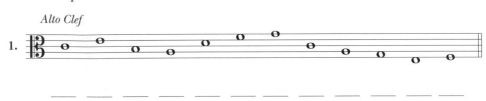

Write pitch names for the notes shown.

Alto Clef

1.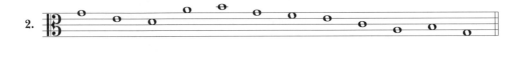

2.

Identify pitches in the following compositions.

Edouard Lalo, *Concerto Russe*

3.

Johannes Brahms, Sonata in A Major

4.

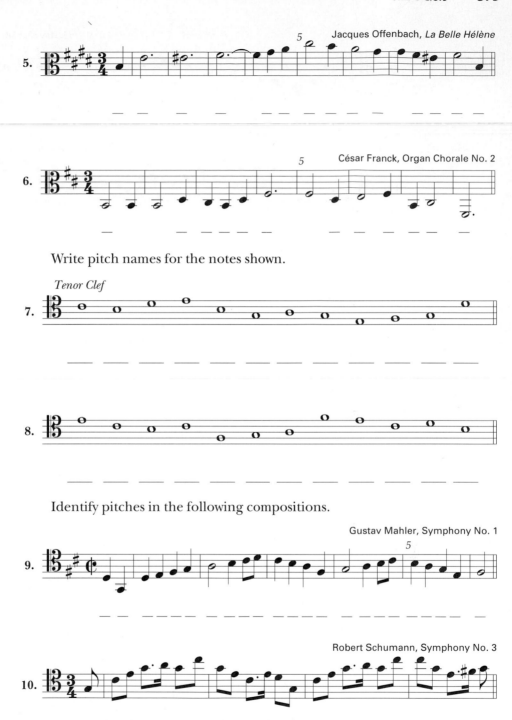

Write pitch names for the notes shown.

Tenor Clef

Identify pitches in the following compositions.

Gustav Mahler, Symphony No. 1

Robert Schumann, Symphony No. 3

Answers to Self-Tests

CHAPTER 1

1. **a.** barline **b.** beam **c.** quarter note (stem) **d.** half rest
   e. whole note **f.** half note

2. ½ 2 1½ 2 ¼

3.

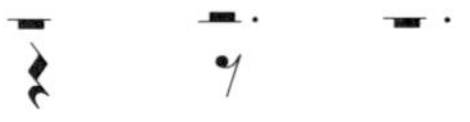

4. **a.** 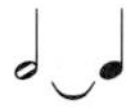 **b.**

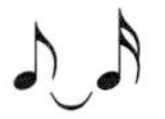

5. **a.**

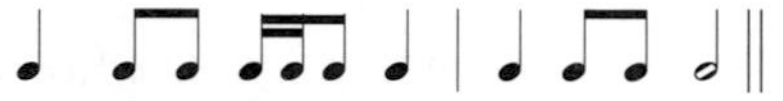

   b. 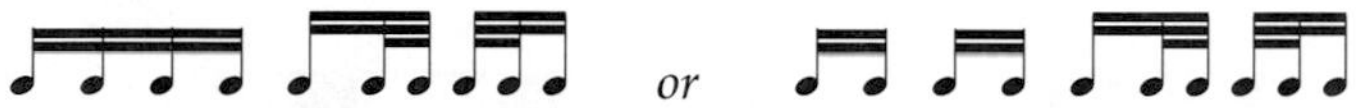 *or*

CHAPTER 2

1. **a.** treble clef **b.** C; tie (or half/quarter notes) **c.** G; dotted quarter note
   d. sharp sign **e.** half rest **f.** E; half note

2. **a.** **b.**

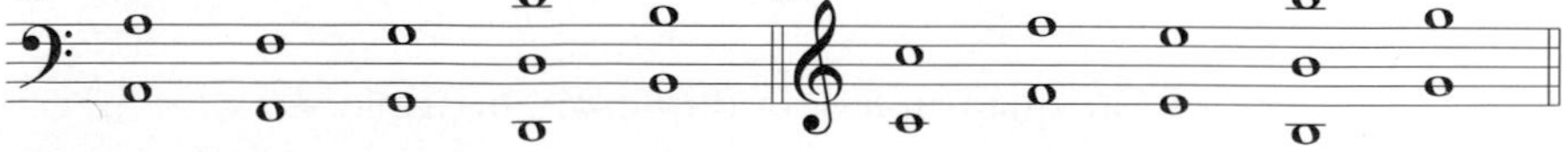

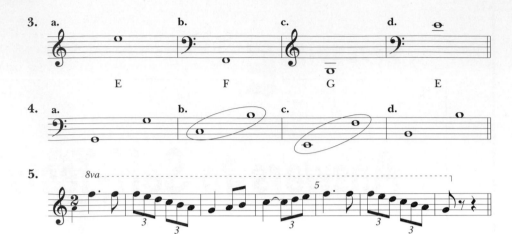

CHAPTER 3

1. Notation in other clefs may be correct.

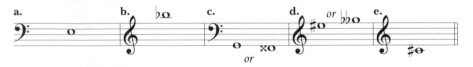

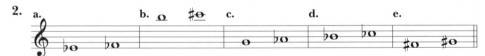

4. a. half step   **b.** whole step   **c.** half step   **d.** whole step

5.

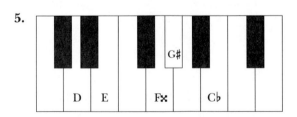

CHAPTER 4

1. a. quadruple, ♩ or duple, ♩   **b.** triple, ♩

2. a. 𝄴   **b.** ¾

3.

4. a.

b.

CHAPTER 5

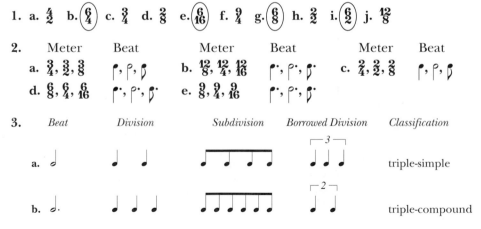

1. a. $\frac{4}{2}$ **b.** $\frac{6}{4}$ **c.** $\frac{3}{4}$ **d.** $\frac{2}{8}$ **e.** $\frac{6}{16}$ **f.** $\frac{9}{4}$ **g.** $\frac{6}{8}$ **h.** $\frac{2}{2}$ **i.** $\frac{6}{2}$ **j.** $\frac{12}{8}$

2.

	Meter	Beat		Meter	Beat		Meter	Beat
a.	$\frac{3}{4}, \frac{3}{2}, \frac{3}{8}$	♩, ♩, ♪	**b.**	$\frac{12}{8}, \frac{12}{4}, \frac{12}{16}$	♩·, ♩·, ♪·	**c.**	$\frac{2}{4}, \frac{2}{2}, \frac{2}{8}$	♩, ♩, ♪
d.	$\frac{6}{8}, \frac{6}{4}, \frac{6}{16}$	♩·, ♩·, ♪·	**e.**	$\frac{9}{8}, \frac{9}{4}, \frac{9}{16}$	♩·, ♩·, ♪·			

3.

Beat	Division	Subdivision	Borrowed Division	Classification

4. a. ⅓ 1 1 ½
b. 1 ¾ 1
c. 1 1 2

5. **a.**

b.

CHAPTER 6

1. a. A♯ E♯ B♯   **b.** B♭ E♭ A♭   **c.** F♯ C♯ G♯   **d.** G♭ C♭ F♭   **e.** G♯ D♯ A♯

2. a.   **b.**

c.   **d.**

3. a. minor   **b.** minor   **c.** major   **d.** major   **e.** major

4. a. 3, mediant   **b.** 5, dominant   **c.** 6, submediant   **d.** 7, leading tone

5. a. E   **b.** B♭   **c.** E♯   **d.** C♯   **e.** D♭

6. a. W   **b.** N   **c.** D   **d.** C   **e.** N

CHAPTER 7

1. a. P4   **b.** M2   **c.** P5   **d.** m3   **e.** P4

2. a.   **b.**   **c.**   **d.**   **e.**

3. a.   **b.**   **c.**   **d.**   **e.**

4. a. d5, P5   **b.** (m3, dd4)   **c.** P4; d6   **d.** (M6; M6)

5. a.   **b.**   **c.**   **d.**

CHAPTER 8

1.

Db   bb   Bb   g   F#   d#   Gb   eb

2. **a.** A, C, D   **b.** C   **c.** A   **d.** E   **e.** A, B, C   **f.** A, D   **g.** D   **h.** D   **i.** E   **j.** B

3. **a.** harmonic minor   **b.** major   **c.** major   **d.** harmonic minor
     e. natural minor

4. **a.**   **b.**   **c.**

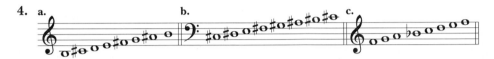

CHAPTER 9

1. **a.**   **b.**   **c.**   **d.**   **e.**   **f.**

2. **a.** F# diminished   **b.** Bb major   **c.** Eb augmented   **d.** A major
     e. G minor   **f.** C major   **g.** G augmented   **h.** Bb augmented

3. **a.**   **b.**   **c.**   **d.**   **e.**   **f.**

CHAPTER 10

1. **a.**   **b.**   **c.**   **d.**   **e.**

2. **a.** F, minor, $\frac{6}{3}$ **b.** E, diminished $\frac{5}{3}$ **c.** C, minor, $\frac{6}{4}$ **d.** B, diminished, $\frac{5}{3}$
     e. A, augmented, $\frac{6}{3}$

3. (There are other possibilities for correct answers.)

     a.   **b.**   **c.**   **d.**

4. **a.** C, augmented, $\frac{6}{3}$ **b.** G, minor, $\frac{6}{3}$ **c.** E, major, $\frac{5}{3}$ **d.** Bb, major, $\frac{6}{3}$
     e. A, minor, $\frac{6}{3}$

CHAPTER 11

1. **a.** $\underline{i}$ | i $\underline{iv_6}$ $\underline{i_6}$ iv | $\underline{V_6}$ i $\widehat{V}$ i_6 | i $\underline{V}$ i i_6 | $\underline{V_6}$ i $\underline{V}$ ‖

2. **a.** b: ii°_6 V_6 VI   **b.** E: vi I^6_4 vii°_6

3. **a.**

CHAPTER 12

1. **a.** G: V^7 vi   **b.** b: iv V   **c.** E♭: IV I   **d.** f: V^7 i
   deceptive   half   plagal   authentic

2. **a.**

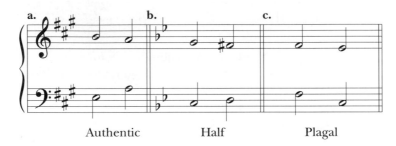

3. (There are many different possibilities for each cadence.)

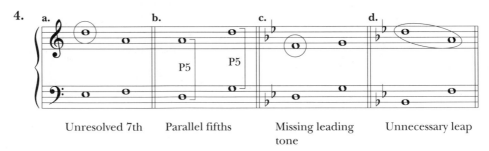

   Authentic   Half   Plagal

4.

Unresolved 7th   Parallel fifths   Missing leading   Unnecessary leap
                                      tone

Glossary

NOTE: Terms in *italics* are defined elsewhere in the glossary.

accent   A stress or emphasis given to a *note*. See also *metric accent*.

accidental   A symbol, such as the *sharp,* the *flat,* or the *natural sign,* that raises or lowers a *basic pitch* one or more *half steps.*

acoustics   A branch of science that deals with the physical properties of sound.

Aeolian mode   The octave series of *half steps* and *whole steps* beginning on A: A B C D E F G and A.

alla breve   An old term for $\frac{2}{2}$ *meter,* still used today and indicated by the symbol ₵. Also known as "cut time."

alto   The second-highest voice category in traditional four-part writing.

alto clef ( )   A *movable C-clef* that identifies the position of the pitch C on the *staff.*

amplitude   The degree of molecular disturbance caused by a sound source that produces the psychological sensation of loudness.

anacrusis   An incomplete *measure* that begins a composition or a section.

analysis   The systematic study of one or more aspects of a musical composition.

arabic-numeral identification   The use of arabic numerals to represent *intervals* sounding above a given *bass* note.

augmented interval   A *major interval* or a *perfect interval* that has been increased in size by one half step.

augmented second   An interval formed by a *whole step* plus a *chromatic half step.*

augmented triad   A type of *triad* that is constructed of a major *third* and an augmented *fifth* above the *root.*

authentic cadence   A concluding harmonic formula consisting of the *dominant* or the *leading tone* to *tonic* (V–I).

bar   See *measure.*

barline   A vertical line used to separate *measures.*

basic pitch   A pitch without an *accidental,* such as A B C D E F or G.

bass   (1) The lowest-sounding pitch in a *triad* or *chord.* (2) The lowest voice in traditional *four-part harmony.*

bassa   A term often used with the *octave sign* to indicate notes to be performed an *octave* lower than written.

bass clef ( )   A symbol that identifies the fourth line on the *staff* as the position of the pitch F.

beam   A thick horizontal line that connects two or more stemmed notes and indicates lesser rhythmic values. Beams are equivalent to *flags*.

beat   A monotonous pulse that underlies the rhythmic structure of a traditional composition.

beat division   The use of rhythmic values of less than one *beat*. Beat division is either *simple* or *compound*.

beat subdivision   The use of rhythmic values smaller than the *beat division*.

borrowed division   A division of the *beat* into three parts (a *triplet*) in a *simple meter* or into two parts (a *duplet*) in a *compound meter*.

breve (◻)   An older note value, little used in modern music, having twice the value of the *whole note*.

cadence   A musical point of conclusion. See *authentic cadence, deceptive cadence, half cadence,* and *plagal cadence*.

calligraphy   The process of notating music by hand.

chord   A group of three or more pitches. See also *tertian triad* and *seventh chord*.

chromatic   A term usually associated with music in which the *half step* predominates.

chromatic half step   A *half step* formed between pitches with the same letter name (G and G♯, for example).

chromatic scale   An *octave* series of half steps written typically with *sharps* ascending and *flats* descending.

church modes   The half-step and whole-step patterns through which early Western music was organized and the predecessors of our modern *major scale* and *minor scale*. See also *Dorian, Lydian, Mixolydian,* and *Phrygian modes*.

circle of fifths   A sequence of major and minor *keys* whose *tonics* lie a *perfect fifth* (seven half steps) from their closest neighbor above and below. Adjacent keys on the circle of fifths have all but one pitch in common.

clef   A symbol that designates the precise position of one note on the *staff*.

close position   The spatial arrangement of a *triad* or a *chord* so that the highest and lowest pitches are as close together as possible. See also *open position*.

common time   An alternative term for $\frac{4}{4}$ meter, represented by the symbol **C.**

compound beat division   A division of the *beat* into three smaller parts.

compound interval   An *interval* that is larger than an *octave*.

compound meter   A meter that employs *compound beat division*.

conductor   The leader of a musical *ensemble*.

consonance   A *pitch*, an *interval*, or a *chord* that is relatively stable. See also *perfect consonance* and *imperfect consonance*.

contrary motion   The linear movement of voices in opposite directions.

counting   The mental or audible assignment of rhythms to various *beats, divisions,* or *subdivisions* for accuracy in performance.

deceptive cadence   A harmonic concluding formula consisting of a progression of the *dominant triad* to the *submediant* (V–vi).

diatonic   A *pitch*, an *interval*, or a *triad* that conforms to the notes found in a given *scale*. In C major, for example, the pitches C D E F G A and B are diatonic; all other pitches are *nondiatonic*.

diatonic half step   A *half step* formed between two pitches with different letter names (F♯ and G, for example).

diminished interval   A *perfect interval* or a minor interval that has been decreased in size by one half step.

diminished triad   A *triad* that is constructed of a minor *third* and a diminished *fifth* above the *root*.

dissonance   (1) A *pitch*, an *interval*, or a *chord* that is relatively unstable. (2) A traditional category of interval that includes the *second,* the *seventh,* and the *tritone*.

division   See *beat division.*

dominant   The fifth scale degree or the *triad* with the fifth *scale degree* as its *root.*

dominant seventh chord   A type of *seventh chord,* consisting of a major *triad* with the addition of a minor *seventh* above the *root* of that triad.

Dorian mode   The series of basic pitches beginning on D: D E F G A B C and D.

dot (·)   A symbol added to a *note* or a *rest* to increase its value by one half.

double barline   Two vertical lines that indicate the end of a composition or a section.

double flat (♭♭)   An *accidental* symbol used to indicate a note one *whole step* lower than the corresponding *basic pitch.*

double sharp (×)   An *accidental* symbol used to indicate a note one *whole step* higher than the corresponding *basic pitch.*

doubling   The octave duplication of one or more pitches in *triads* and *chords.*

duple meter   A recurring metric pattern that is strong–weak.

duplet   A *borrowed division* in *compound meter* wherein the beat is divided into two equal parts.

duration   The length of a sound.

eighth note (♪)   A relative rhythmic value that is one-eighth the duration of the *whole note.*

enharmonics   Pitches notated differently but having the same *frequency.*

ensemble   A composition intended for two or more performers.

fifth   (1) A type of *interval* that usually consists of six or seven *half steps.* (2) A *triad* member that lies a *fifth* above the *root.*

figured bass   An eighteenth-century system of abbreviated *chord* notation using arabic numerals. Figured bass is employed today in musical *analysis.*

first inversion   The arrangement of a *tertian triad* with the *third* in the *bass.*

flag (♩)   A curved line added to the *stem* of a *note* to indicate a reduced rhythmic value. Flags are equivalent to *beams.*

flat (♭)   An *accidental* symbol that lowers pitch one *half step.*

form   The term for the organized growth of musical elements over a given time span.

fourth   A type of *interval* that usually consists of five or six *half steps.*

frequency   The number of molecular vibrations per second produced by a sound source to create a musical tone. Greater and lesser frequency produces the psychological sensation of higher and lower *pitch.*

grand staff   A combination, usually of one treble and one bass *staff,* used for the notation of piano and other *keyboard* music.

half cadence   A harmonic concluding formula that consists usually of a progression of *supertonic, subdominant,* or *tonic* to the *dominant* chord (IV–V or I–V, for example).

half note (♩)   A relative rhythmic value that is one-half the duration of the *whole note.*

half step   The smallest *interval* in Western music. On the *keyboard,* a half step is found between any two adjacent keys. See also *diatonic half step* and *chromatic half step.*

harmonic dissonance   A relatively unstable *chord* containing a dissonant *interval* such as a *seventh.*

harmonic function   The arrangement of *triads* and *chords* into *progressions* that establish a feeling for *key.*

harmonic interval   Two pitches heard simultaneously.

harmonic minor scale   A form of *minor scale* in which the seventh degree has been raised a half step to provide a *leading tone.*

harmony   The vertical arrangement of pitches into *intervals, triads,* and *chords.*

hertz   A measurement of *frequency* (abbreviated Hz) equivalent to the number of molecular vibrations per second.

imperfect consonance   A category of *interval* comprising the major and minor *third* and the major and minor *sixth.*

interval   The distance between two pitches.

interval inversion   An alternative version of an original *interval* in which the relative positions of the two notes are reversed (the higher pitch is now the lower, for example).

interval quality   A precise measurement of interval size dependent on the number of *half steps* between pitches.

interval type   A general measurement of interval size dependent on the number of lines and spaces between pitches.

Ionian mode   The octave series of *half steps* and *whole steps* beginning on C: C D E F G A and B.

key   An effect produced when the *tonic* of a *scale* is heard as the most important pitch.

keyboard   The black- and white-key manual arrangement found on the piano, the organ, and other instruments.

key signature   A listing of the *accidentals* necessary to produce the effect of a given *key*.

leading tone   The pitch or the *triad* built on the seventh *scale degree* that lies a *half step* below the *tonic*.

ledger line   A temporary extension of the *staff* beyond the customary five lines and four spaces.

loco   A term that indicates a return to standard notation after an *ottava* passage.

Lydian mode   The octave series of half steps and whole steps beginning on F: F G A B C D E and F.

major interval   A category of *interval* consisting of *seconds, thirds, sixths,* and *sevenths*.

major scale   An organized series of pitches in which the arrangement of *whole steps* and *half steps is* Whole, Whole, Half, Whole, Whole, Whole, Half.

major triad   A type of *triad* consisting of a major *third* and a perfect *fifth* above the *root*.

measure   One complete metric pattern (also called a "bar"). In traditional music, measures are delineated by *barlines*.

mediant   The third *scale degree* or the *triad* with the third scale degree as its *root*.

melodic interval   Two pitches heard consecutively.

melodic minor scale   A *minor scale* in which both the sixth and the seventh degrees have been raised a *half step* in the ascending form. Descending melodic minor is identical to descending *natural minor*.

melody   An organized series of pitches in a single voice.

meter   A recurring pattern of strong and weak beats. See also *duple meter* and *triple meter*.

meter signature   Two numbers placed at the beginning of a composition to indicate the note receiving one *beat,* the manner of *beat division,* and the number of beats in a *measure*. Also called a "time signature."

metric accent   The regular strong and weak patterns of beats that create *meter*.

metronome   A device for producing a steady pulse at a given *tempo*.

minor scale   An organized series of pitches in which the *whole-step* and *half-step* pattern is Whole, Half, Whole, Whole, Half, Whole, Whole. See also *harmonic minor scale, melodic minor scale,* and *natural minor scale*.

minor triad   A type of *triad* consisting of a minor *third* and a perfect *fifth* above the *root*.

Mixolydian mode   The octave series of half steps and whole steps beginning on G: G A B C D E F and G.

mode   (1) The establishment of either the major or the minor effect within a given *key*. (2) One of eight specific arrangements of the seven basic pitches. See also *church modes*.

movable C-clef   A symbol that identifies the pitch C on the *staff*. See also *alto clef* and *tenor clef*.

music   Organized sound in time.

natural division   A division of the *beat* according to the metric plan: a two-part division in a *simple meter* and a three-part division in a *compound meter*.

natural minor scale   A minor scale that conforms to the *interval* pattern Whole, Half, Whole, Whole, Half, Whole, Whole. See also *harmonic minor scale* and *melodic minor scale*.

natural sign (♮)   An *accidental* symbol that cancels the effect of a *sharp* or a *flat*.

noise   Uncontrolled sound produced by irregular *sound waves*.

nondiatonic   Pitches that lie outside a given *scale*. In C major, for example, all pitches except C D E F G A and B are nondiatonic.

notation   A system through which sounds are represented by symbols.

note   The symbol for sound. Notes vary in appearance according to their rhythmic value.

notehead   The oval portion of a *note*.

octave   The purest and most stable *interval*, which forms the basis of practically all musical systems. Pitches that appear in different places on the *staff* but have exactly the same letter names (F–F or E♭–E♭, for example) are one or more octaves apart.

octave designation   A system of identifying *pitches* within a specific *octave* range.

octave sign (*8va*)   A symbol that indicates that a note or notes are to be played an *octave* higher or lower than written.

open position   The spatial arrangement of a *triad* or a *chord* so that the highest and lowest pitches lie an *octave* or more apart. See also *close position*.

ottava   An indication that notation is to be performed an *octave* higher or lower than written. See also *octave sign*.

parallel fifths   In *four-part harmony,* the movement from one chord of any two voices forming a *perfect fifth* to a perfect fifth in the same voices in the next chord.

parallel octaves   In *four-part harmony,* the movement of any two voices forming a perfect *octave* in one chord and moving to a perfect octave in the same voices in the next chord.

parallel relationship   Major and minor *keys* having the same *tonic* (G major and G minor, for example).

pentatonic scale   An ancient scale form that includes no half steps and that can be played over five consecutive black keys on the piano.

perfect consonance   A category of *interval* comprising the perfect octave, perfect fifth, perfect fourth, and perfect unison. See also *imperfect consonance*.

perfect fifth   An *interval* that is a fifth in type and comprising seven *half steps* between pitches.

perfect interval   An *interval* category consisting of *octaves, unisons, fourths,* and *fifths*.

Phrygian mode   The octave series of half steps and whole steps beginning on E: E F G A B C D and E.

pitch   The psychological sensation of perceiving a note as relatively higher or lower as determined by the *frequency*.

plagal cadence   A concluding harmonic formula consisting of a progression of the *subdominant triad* to the *tonic* (IV–I).

primary triad   In traditional *harmony,* the three most important *triads* in establishing a *key:* the *tonic,* the *subdominant,* and the *dominant.* See also *secondary triad.*

progression   A series of *chords* that establishes a feeling for key.

psychoacoustics   A study of the psychological properties of sound.

pure minor   See *natural minor scale*.

quadruple meter   A metric pattern that is a strong–weak–semistrong–weak accent scheme.

quarter note (♩)   A relative rhythmic value that is one-quarter the duration of the *whole note*.

realization   The construction of a full musical texture from a *figured base*.

relative relationship   Major and minor *keys* having the same *key signature* but different *tonics* (C major and A minor, for example). See also *parallel relationship*.

rests   The symbols employed to notate periods of silence. Like notes, rest symbols vary according to the length of silence they represent.

rhythm   The element of time in music.

roman-numeral identification   A system of musical *analysis* in which roman numerals and other symbols stand for various *diatonic triads* and *chords*.

root   The lowest member of a *triad* when the three pitches are arranged over consecutive lines or spaces. See also *root position*.

root position   The arrangement of a *tertian triad* with the *root* as the *bass*.

scale   A series of pitches arranged in a fixed order. See also *major scale* and *minor scale*.

scale degree   A number assigned to each pitch in a *scale* to define its relationship to the *tonic* pitch.

second   A type of *interval* usually comprising one or two *half steps*.

secondary triad   In traditional *harmony*, any *triad* other than those considered *primary*. The *supertonic, mediant, submediant,* and *leading tone* are secondary triads. See also *primary triads*.

second inversion   The arrangement of a *tertian triad* so that the *fifth* is in the *bass*.

seventh   A type of *interval* that usually consists of ten or eleven *half steps*.

seventh chord   A *chord* that is constructed of four different pitches: a *root*, a *third* and a *fifth* above the root, and also a *seventh* above the root. See also *dominant seventh chord*.

sharp (♯)   An *accidental* symbol that raises pitch one *half step*.

simple beat division   A division of the *beat* into two smaller parts.

simple meter   A meter with a *duple*, or strong–weak, accent pattern.

sixteenth note (♪)   A relative rhythmic symbol that is one-sixteenth the duration of the *whole note*.

sixth   A type of *interval* that usually consists of eight or nine *half steps*.

solfège   A system of teaching sight singing through syllables.

soprano   The highest of the four traditional voice categories. See also *alto, tenor,* and *bass*.

sound waves   Regular patterns of molecular motion created by a sound source.

spacing   In *triad* and *chord* construction, the arrangement of the pitches over one or several octaves. See also *open position* and *close position*.

staff   A grid of five lines and four spaces used for the precise *notation* of music. The plural of staff is "staves."

stem   A vertical line added to a *note* to indicate a decrease in rhythmic value.

subdivision   See *beat subdivision*.

subdominant   The fourth *scale degree* or the *triad* with the fourth scale degree as its *root*.

submediant   The sixth *scale degree* or the *triad* with the sixth scale degree as its *root*.

subtonic   The seventh *scale degree* that lies a *whole step* below the *tonic* or the *triad* with this pitch as its *root*.

supertonic   The second *scale degree* or the *triad* with the second scale degree as its *root*.

syncopation   The intentional misplacement of natural metric *accents*.

system   A set of two or more staves. See also *grand staff*.

tempo   The speed of the *beat*.

tenor   The next-to-lowest voice in traditional *four-part harmony*.

tenor clef (𝄡)   A *movable C-clef* that identifies the position of the pitch C on the *staff*.

tertian triad   A group of three pitches that can be arranged to fall over consecutive lines or consecutive spaces.

third   (1) A type of *interval* usually consisting of three or four *half steps*. (2) A *triad* member that lies a third above the root.

tie (⌒)   A symbol that combines the rhythmic values of two or more notes of the same pitch.

timbre   The term used to describe the quality of a musical tone.

time signature   See *meter signature*.

tonality   The establishment of *key* and *mode* (the key of E♭ major, for example).

tonic   The first pitch of a *scale* or the *triad* built on the first *scale degree*.

transcription   The process of revising the notation of music so that although the sound is the same, the visual appearance is different. The term "transcription" is also applied to music written for one medium that has been rewritten to be performed in a different medium (an orchestral work transcribed for piano, for example).

transposition The process of moving a series of pitches to a different *tonic* (and therefore a different *key*) without changing the original pattern of *intervals*.

treble clef (𝄞) The symbol that identifies the second line on the *staff* as the position of the pitch G.

triad A group of three pitches. See also *tertian triad*.

triad inversion A *tertian triad* arranged so that the *root* is above the *bass*. See also *first inversion* and *second inversion*.

triple meter A recurring metric pattern that is strong–weak–weak.

triplet A *borrowed division* in a *simple meter* wherein the beat is divided into three equal parts.

tritone An augmented fourth or a diminished fifth consisting of six *half steps*.

unison The *interval* between two or more pitches of the same *frequency*.

voice leading The horizontal movement of individual voices in traditional *four-part harmony*.

whole note (o) The greatest rhythmic value commonly used in traditional music.

whole step An *interval* consisting of two *half steps*.

whole-tone scale A series of six consecutive whole steps and ending with an octave duplication of the first pitch.

Index